Communication and Cybernetics 17

Editors: K.S.Fu W.D.Keidel W.J.M.Levelt H.Wolter

Communication and Cybernetics

Editors: K. S. Fu, W. D. Keidel, W. J. M. Levelt, H. Wolter

Vol. 1   W. Meyer-Eppler
Grundlagen und Anwendungen der Informationstheorie

Vol. 2   B. Malmberg
Structural Linguistics and Human Communication

Vol. 3   J. L. Flanagan
Speech Analysis/Synthesis and Perception

Vol. 4   G. Herdan
The Advanced Theory of Language as Choice and Chance

Vol. 5   G. Hammarström
Linguistische Einheiten im Rahmen der modernen Sprachwissenschaft

Vol. 6   J. Peters
Einführung in die allgemeine Informationstheorie

Vol. 7   K. Weltner
The Measurement of Verbal Information in Psychology and Education

Vol. 8   **Facts and Models in Hearing**
Edited by E. Zwicker, E. Terhardt

Vol. 9   G. Hammarström
Linguistic Units and Items

Vol. 10   **Digital Pattern Recognition**
Edited by K. S. Fu

Vol. 11   **Structure and Process in Speech Perception**
Edited by A. Cohen, S. G. Nooteboom

Vol. 12   J. D. Markel, A. H. Gray, Jr.
Linear Prediction of Speech

Vol. 13   R. G. Busnel, A. Classe
Whistled Languages

Vol. 14   **Applications of Syntactic Pattern Recognition, Applications**
Edited by K. S. Fu

Vol. 15   P. Kümmel
Formalization of Natural Languages

Vol. 16   K. Steinbuch
Kommunikationstechnik

Vol. 17   T. Kohonen
Associative Memory
A System-Theoretical Approach

Teuvo Kohonen

Associative Memory
A System-Theoretical Approach

Corrected Printing of the First Edition

With 54 Figures

Springer-Verlag
Berlin Heidelberg New York 1978

Professor Dr. Teuvo Kohonen
Helsinki University of Technology, Dept. of Technical Physics
SF-02150 Otaniemi/Finland

Professor King Sun Fu, PhD
Purdue University, School of Electrical Engineering
West Lafayette, IN 47907, USA

Professor Dr. Wolf Dieter Keidel
I. Physiologisches Institut der Universität Erlangen-Nürnberg
D-8520 Erlangen, Fed. Rep. of Germany

Professor Dr. Willem J. M. Levelt
Katholieke Universiteit, Faculteit der Sociale Wetenschappen
Nijmegen, Holland

Professor Dr. Hans Wolter
Institut für Angewandte Physik der Universität
D-3550 Marburg/Lahn, Fed. Rep. of Germany

ISBN 3-540-08017-1 Springer Verlag Berlin Heidelberg New York
ISBN 0-387-08017-1 Springer-Verlag New York Heidelberg Berlin

Library of Congress Cataloging in Publication Data. Kohonen, Teuvo. Associative memory. (Communication and cybernetics; v. 17). Bibliography: p. Includes index. 1. Memory. 2. Association storage. I. Title. Q360.K65. 001.53'92. 76-53787

This work is subject to copyright. All rights are reserved, whether the whole or part of the material is concerned, specifically those of translation, reprinting, re-use of illustrations, broadcasting, reproduction by photocopying machine or similar means, and storage in data banks. Under § 54 of the German Copyright Law where copies are made for other than private use, a fee is payable to the publisher, the amount of the fee to be determined by agreement with the publisher.

© by Springer-Verlag Berlin Heidelberg 1977
Printed in Germany

The use of registered names, trademarks, etc. in this publication does not imply, even in the absence of a specific statement, that such names are exempt from the relevant protective laws and regulations and therefore free for general use.

Offset printing, and book binding: Brühlsche Universitätsdruckerei Giessen

Preface

About the Scope of This Text

This book contains two types of material; first, the many divergent and often diffuse meanings given to the concepts of *association, associative memory,* and *associative recall* are expounded. A review of this kind was felt necessary because there apparently does not exist any single monograph which could serve as a reference to these topics. But the presentation of the main body of this text is motivated by quite other reasons: in recent years, plenty of interesting mathematical and system-theoretical material has been published which makes it possible to gain a view of associative memory which is different from the conventional abstract and computationally oriented approaches. It seems that the basic operation of associative memory, the storage of information together with the relations or links between the data items, and the selective recall of stored information relative to a piece of key or cue information presented, is not restricted to certain computer-technological implementations but can also be reflected in more general mathematically describable processes in certain physical or other systems, especially in their adaptive state changes. It further seems that some generally known forms of associative memory, namely, certain computer technological artifacts, or abstract systems of concepts or data, are in fact special representations of a class of processes characterized as associative memory.

The text in presentation is thus a new system-theoretically motivated approach to the phenomenon of associative memory, and it is hoped that the formalisms and some applications presented here might interest scientists working in the fields of cybernetics, computer science, mathematical psychology, physiology, and physics.

Various Aspects of Memory. The subject of memory has been approached by many branches of science. The rather incoherent views thereby gained may be consequent of emphasis laid on different aspects. For instance, in a similar way as the concept of computing involves the machine, the program code, and the information process that is realized when a program is run, so the concept of memory in a cybernetic system may mean 1) the material facilities, for instance, a computer memory, a physical system, or a set of organic elements which serve as a substrate for the representation of information, 2) the entirety of stored representations per se (in life sciences, sometimes named "memories"), 3) the abstract structure of knowledge that is implicit in the stored representations and their semantic relations, or 4) the recollections which, especially in the mental sense, may be sequences of events that are reconstructed in a process of reminiscence.

Acknowledgements

Many core ideas presented here have evolved in numerous discussions with my many collaborators. Especially during the writing of this book, I have got much valuable help from Messrs. Pekka Lehtiö and Erkki Oja. Many members of the staff of our laboratory have contributed to the computer simulations and other material contained in this book. I am indebted to the following persons who have been of great help in many ways: K.Bry, L. Hippeläinen, J. Hyvärinen, L. Häll, T. Junkkari, J. Karhunen, H. Laine, H. Pohjanpalo, J. Rekula, E. Riihimäki, J. Rovamo, P. Teittinen, J. Tuominen, and L. Vainio. Some remarks made on the contents by Academician Erkki Laurila, Professor James A. Anderson and Professor Michael A. Arbib, have been very useful. I am also grateful to my wife for her support.

This work has been made under the auspices of the Academy of Finland.

Otaniemi, Finland
January, 1977

T. Kohonen

Contents

Chapter 1. Introduction

1.1 On the Physical Embodiment of Associative Information Structures.......... 1
    1.1.1 A System-Model Approach to the Associative Memory................. 2
    1.1.2 Relational Structures of Knowledge............................... 3
    1.1.3 Acquisition and Retrieval of Knowledge as Structured Sequences..... 6
1.2 Implementations of Associative Recall....................................... 10
    1.2.1 Basic Characteristics of Associative Memories...................... 10
    1.2.2 The Content-Addressable Memory (CAM).............................. 12
    1.2.3 Hash-Coding... 13
    1.2.4 Holographic Associative Memories.................................. 15
    1.2.5 Nonholographic, Distributed Associative Memories.................. 17
1.3 Mathematical Notations and Methods... 22
    1.3.1 Vector Space Concepts... 22
    1.3.2 Matrix Notations.. 33
    1.3.3 Further Properties of Matrices.................................... 36
    1.3.4 Matrix Equations.. 39
    1.3.5 Projection Operators.. 45
    1.3.6 Matrix Differential Calculus...................................... 48

Chapter 2. Associative Search Methods

2.1 Addressing by the Contents... 51
    2.1.1 Hash-Coding Principles.. 52
    2.1.2 An Example of Hash-Coding: Multiple-Keyword Search................ 57
    2.1.3 A Processing Language for Associative Data Structures............. 60
2.2 Content-Addressable Memories.. 61
    2.2.1 Associative Recall by the Partial Match Operation................. 62
    2.2.2 Hardware Implementation of the CAM Structure 65
    2.2.3 Parallel Comparison of Magnitudes................................. 67

2.3 Optimal Associative Mappings... 69
    2.3.1 System Model for an Analog Associative Memory..................... 70
    2.3.2 Autoassociative Recall as an Orthogonal Projection................ 71
    2.3.3 The Novelty Filter.. 74
    2.3.4 Autoassociative Encoding.. 76
    2.3.5 Optimal Linear Associative Mappings............................... 78
    2.3.6 Optimal Nonlinear Associative Mappings............................ 83
    2.3.7 The Problem of Invariant Recognition.............................. 86
    2.3.8 Relationship Between Associative Mapping, Linear
          Regression, and Linear Estimation................................. 92
2.4 Relationship of Associative Mappings to Pattern Classification........... 94
    2.4.1 Discriminant Functions.. 94
    2.4.2 Comparison Methods.. 96
    2.4.3 Statistical Formulation of Pattern Classification................. 98

Chapter 3. Adaptive Formation of Optimal Associative Mappings

3.1 On the Implementation of Conditioned Responses in Simple
    Physical Systems.. 102
    3.1.1 A Simple Adaptive Linear System................................... 102
    3.1.2 On the Physical Realizability of Adaptive Elements................ 105
3.2 Adaptive Filters Which Compute Orthogonal Projections................... 108
    3.2.1 The Novelty Detector Paradigm..................................... 108
    3.2.2 Analysis of the Adaptive Linear Unit by Means of Matrix
          Products.. 112
    3.2.3 An Extremely Fast Adaptive Process Which Generates the
          Novelty Filter.. 114
    3.2.4 Adaptation With Forgetting.. 120
3.3 Recursive Generation of the Optimal Associative Mapping................. 122
    3.3.1 Linear Corrective Algorithms...................................... 122
    3.3.2 The General Setting for the Computation of $M = YX^+$............. 123
    3.3.3 Recursive Evaluation of the Best Exact Solution
          (Gradient Projection Method)...................................... 123
    3.3.4 Recursive Evaluation of the Best Approximate Solution
          (Regression Solution)... 125
    3.3.5 Recursive Solution in the General Case............................ 126

Chapter 4. On Biological Associative Memory

4.1 Physiological Foundations of Memory.................................... 128
    4.1.1 On the Mechanisms of Memory in Biological Systems................. 128
    4.1.2 Structural Features of Some Neural Networks....................... 131
    4.1.3 Functional Features of Neurons.................................... 135
    4.1.4 Modelling of the Synaptic Plasticity............................... 139
    4.1.5 Can the Memory Capacity Ensue from Synaptic Changes?............... 144

4.2 Computerized Models of Associative Memory in Neural Networks............. 147
    4.2.1 The Associative Network Paradigm.................................. 148
    4.2.2 The Novelty Filter Paradigm....................................... 154
    4.2.3 Review of Related Approaches...................................... 158

References 160

Author Index 165

Subject Index 167

Chapter 1
Introduction

1.1 On the Physical Embodiment of Associative Information Structures

In an attempt to approach the "intelligent" cybernetic functions as physical processes, one of the first tasks is to assign state variables to the conceptual items to be processed, as well as to the connections that obviously exist between them. The principles of the symbolic representation of information in computers may be well-known; it is much less obvious how the connections should be described. One possibility, especially in the representation and analysis of linguistic expressions, is to introduce elementary relations which consist of a pair of items and a symbolic attribute that links the items together (cf. Subsec. 1.1.2). It is possible to create rather complicated structures of concepts from elementary relations, and a widely held view is that knowledge in general might be representable by such relational structures.

Although linguistic constructs of the above type may readily be amenable to processing by the digital computers, it is not clear, however, how they could be implemented in biological organisms which do not have a computation-oriented organization. Nonetheless, structured knowledge or "memory" apparently has a prominent role in biological information systems, and it is there connected with many cybernetic functions. The fact that biological memory closely interacts with mental processes, too, is an old notion:

"Thus memory belongs to the faculty of the soul to which imagination belongs; all objects which are imaginable are essentially objects of memory; all those that necessarily involve images are objects of memory incidentally." (Aristotle, 384-322 B.C.)

The principles of biological information systems have remained almost a mystery although plenty of evidence has been collected which assigns basic physical and chemical properties to them. System theory thus faces a challenge to reveal at least the fundamentals of these principles. Not only is this approach interesting from the point of view of providing physical explanations to some mental effects, but such a theory has interest in its own right, possibly making it feasible to apply these principles to inorganic systems, too.

It is a generally held view that the organization and retrieval of information in biological memory is made by associations. What is exactly meant by that has seldom been defined. Sometimes associations may simply be understood as patterns formed of several distinct items and their attributes which are conditioned by their simultaneous or successive occurrence. Other, more exact meanings for associations will be given below.

1.1.1 A System-Model Approach to the Associative Memory

Even the most complex information processing operations must be based on some fundamental principles. In the operation of memory, the elementary process is the selective storage and recall of pieces of information. One of the simplest system models which can be characterized as a memory is depicted in Fig. 1.1; it consists of a memory medium somehow connected to the input and output channels. A characteristic

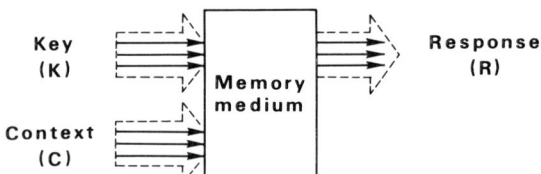

Fig. 1.1 System model of a memory with associative recall

of this kind of memory is an ability to hold in its internal state copies of signal patterns that have occurred in the input channel. In computer memories, the retrieval of a particular item is normally made by a specification of the location where it is stored. But a principle of retrieval which seems to be characteristic of biological memories is the *associative recall* of information; when a patterned *key* stimulus (K) is applied at the input, a specific *response* pattern (R) which is associated with the key is obtained at the output. Additional information which represents the *context* (C) in which the stimulus occurred may be applied at the input. Using a different context it is possible to specify an item to be recalled more closely.

Although this view is extremely simplified, it may give a first hint of how a system-theoretical approach to the physical memory, especially associative memory, can be made. But many questions, some of which are listed below, must thereby be answered:

1) What is the simplest type of physical system, possibly a network, in which selective responses between a great number of pairs of input-output-patterns can be implemented?

2) How can the associations be formed adaptively, i.e. by the influence of the occurring signals, without exterior control for their storage?

3) How can structured sequences of memorized events be represented and recalled?

4) How can structured knowledge be represented?

5) How can the retrieving process be recycled so that a piece of recalled information may act as new key information?

6) How can information be retrieved on the basis of defective or marred versions of key patterns or their fragments?

7) How can the system produce an invariant response to a class of patterns? (The problem of stimulus-equivalence).

It is now believed that the theoretical models discussed in this book yield answers to most of these problems, and computer simulations of such a system behaviour have been performed. It may be mentioned that several realizations of physical associative memory structures are already feasible, in principle at least; the main difficulty in the implementation of large-scale associative information processes is that a huge memory capacity is needed before the more interesting phenomena are demonstrable.

1.1.2 Relational Structures of Knowledge

In order to find out what are the requirements for the representation of knowledge in a system, the simplest formalism for the representation of abstract structures of semantic information is first reviewed. It is then pointed out that such structures are easily amenable to representation and processing by physical associative memories.

Relations. A semantic relation between two expressions x and y is defined, for instance, by uttering a statement of the type "the attribute R of object x is y". In this case x and R can be regarded as arguments of a *function* which attains the value y. Usually the domains of x and R consist of finite sets of discrete values (words or clauses) so that if the format of this statement is fixed, symbolically it is defined by an ordered triple (R,x,y). It may be obvious that there also exist more complex forms of linguistic statements for which different kinds of relations must be defined.

Sometimes a notation $x \xrightarrow{R} y$ is used for the simplest type of relation which is then read "x is related to y by R"; this kind of qualified expression, however, does not clearly have the form of a function. Variables in the ordered triple are often given the particular meanings A = "attribute", O = "object", and V = "value". An expression (A,O,V) is then read "the A of O is V".

Examples of relations are given below. Consider the following variables:
$A \in$ {pronunciation, colour}, $O \in$ {one, apple}, and $V \in$ {wən, red}. Then "one" is related to "wən" by the fact that "the pronunciation of one is wən", and an "apple"

is related to "red" by the fact that "the colour of apple is red". Formally these statements can be represented as (pronunciation, one, wən) and (colour, apple, red).

Relations can be represented in any physical memory as arrays of stored symbolic tokens corresponding to the variables. The role of A, O, and V is clear from the positions in the array. If there were an access to this memory on the basis of the pair (A, O), then the connected value V could be retrieved. It must now be mentioned that certain computational tasks have required, however, that when such linguistic relations are represented in usual computer memories, then the triples (A, O, V) are made accessible by programming methods on the basis of any of their elements. This will become more clear from the following:

Structures of Relations. The formation of abstract structures of relations is illustrated next. The ordered triple notation (A, O, V) is used in the declaration of the relations. The notation $O \xrightarrow{A} V$, on the other hand, is useful for the representation of connections in abstract graphs that result. Consider the following facts (Table 1.1):

Table 1.1 Stored triples

Fact	Formal representation
Brother of Ann is Steve	(brother, Ann, Steve)
Father of Ann is Pete	(father, Ann, Pete)
Father of Pete is Sam	(father, Pete, Sam)
Sex of Ann is female	(sex, Ann, female)
Sex of Pete is male	(sex, Pete, male)
Residence of Pete is London	(residence, Pete, London)
Residence of Ann is London	(residence, Ann, London)

An abstract structure of cross-references, depicted in Fig. 1.2, then follows. Note that the individual elements may occur in many declarations, although in the abstract

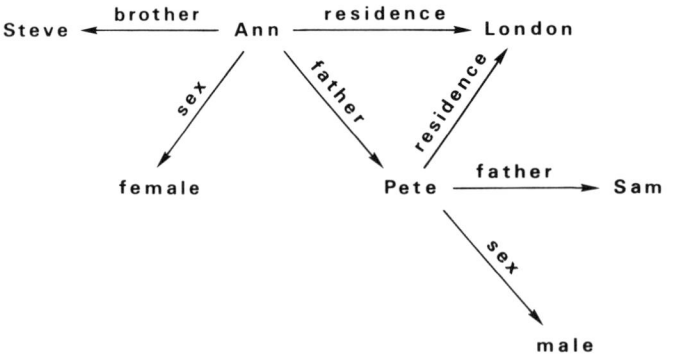

Fig. 1.2 A relational structure

graph they have been mentioned only once, in principle at least. Apparently the complexity of the graph depends on the number and type of facts (relations) declared.

It should be carefully noticed that the structure of the graph has in no way really been represented in memory; it is completely abstract or implicit, although its existence can be confirmed by tracing the cross-references. This may be understood as a pragmatic property. Retrieval of knowledge from this graph needs a computational process exemplified below.

For the search of relevant information, any implementation that is computable can be used. For instance, if all the stored triples shown in Table 1.1 are accessible by any of their elements, then, to answer a question of the type "Who is the father of Ann?" the following search could be executed: first, all triples with attribute "father" are retrieved, and temporarily recorded, then the triples with occurrences of "Ann" are found and finally the intersection of these sets of triples is computed, to find "Pete". Apparently, this is not a very natural process, although completely expedient for a computer. Retrieval as a dynamic process will be discussed in Subsection 1.1.3.

A more important application in automatic data processing than the above simple example may be the retrieval of all items which can be defined by partial structures, or which occur in a certain type of "structural context". For instance, a task with a data base may be to find all documents published in the USA after 1958, whose principal topic is artificial intelligence, and which have as descriptors at least three of the following: heuristic, problem-solving, theorem proving, inductive inference, deductive inference. (The logic to solve this task has been described in [6]. During the search process, auxiliary intervening relations of the type "x is an example of y" may be declared.)

On the Interpretation of Relations as Associations. Are the relations and associations one and the same thing? This question needs closer examination. Consider the following types of claims that occur in the literature: "An association is a two-termed relation, involving three symbols, one of which names the relation, the other two its arguments" [8]; "A relation consists of three components, an ordered pair of items and a link which specifies the type of association which relates items" [6]; and "An association is an ordered triple (A,O,V) of items...called the components of the association" [3]. What has been said above is essentially that a relation $O \xrightarrow{A} V$ is thought to link the terms O and V, or that all components in a triple (A,O,V) are mutually linked. Apparently a qualifier (A) cannot be understood as a simple link; a more expedient view might be that all elements A,O, and V that have been stored together in this specific order are associated. But since items may be linked by the cross-references in an abstract way which also can be thought to form associations, the concept of association must be defined in a more general fashion. One straightforward possibility to avoid confusion is to name the whole abstract structure "associative memory". The nature of the *process* which associates items together, however, may become more clear when discussion turns to physical models.

Relational Structures for a Semantic Memory. In order to understand a linguistic expression, one may try to parse it in various ways, for instance, by indicating the relational structures around some central words. In the ELINOR scheme [5], the attributes of these relations may describe properties, tools, actions, temporal relations, etc. A structure that describes the instance in which the word "crush" may occur, i.e., the sentence "The rock crushed the hut" is represented in Fig. 1.3.

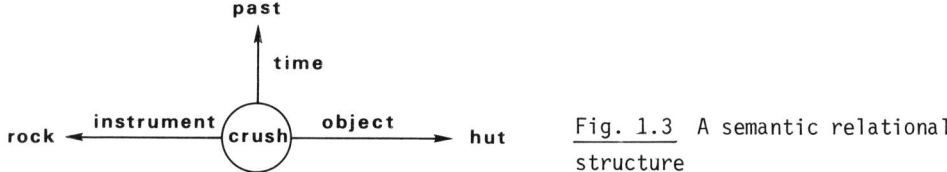

Fig. 1.3 A semantic relational structure

It has been reasoned, however, that a linguistic description of a concept or an instant cannot completely be understood unless all subordinate and superordinate relations associated with it are given. In an extreme case, a word must be considered in the context of a complete sentence which, again, is a part of a paragraph etc. What may essentially have been meant is that distinct items or symbol tokens usually do not have an invariant meaning, but they must be considered as more or less fuzzy subpatterns of larger patterns. This does not, of course, make it impossible to approximate semantic structures by simpler relations; a voluminous amount of research has been pursued on different systematics for semantic structures which are then expected to be implementable by machine analysis. As a review of these schemes would deviate the present discussion from its most central scope which is the discussion of associative mappings in adaptive physical systems, it may here suffice to refer to some thorough reviews of the computerized representation and analysis of semantic memory [1,2,7].

1.1.3 Acquisition and Retrieval of Knowledge as Structured Sequences

It is regrettable that information structures, especially the semantic ones, hitherto have been approached from the computational point of view only. As the digital computers provide efficient means for the search of information on a basis of solutions to partially specified relational structures, a view may have been held that the fundamental problem with the structures of knowledge, for instance, in question-answering and problem-solving tasks is to find out whether the solutions are computable or not. Much less attention has been paid to the aspect what are the types of natural *processes* by which acquisition and retrieval of structured knowledge can be implemented, whereby a question naturally arises of how knowledge ought to be acquired in such a process in order that it is retrievable in associative recall.

In this section, some primitive forms of acquisition and retrieval of knowledge in elementary dynamic processes are discussed; concrete facilities for the implementation of associative recall are introduced in Section 1.2 and Chapter 3.

System Model of a Simple Associative Memory. Human beings and animals learn facts about their environment and temporally related occurrences by association of rather restricted space-time-relations in their memories; knowledge about more complex information structures comes from the automatic linking of such elementary observations, perhaps in many repetitions. A hypothetical information process which might bear some resemblance to natural memorization is exemplified by the following model. Consider a physical implementation of memory (Fig. 1.4) which has four types of channel for information: three input channels through which information is simultaneously transferred into memory as spatial patterns, or sets of simultaneous signal values, and one output channel at which recollections of patterns appear.

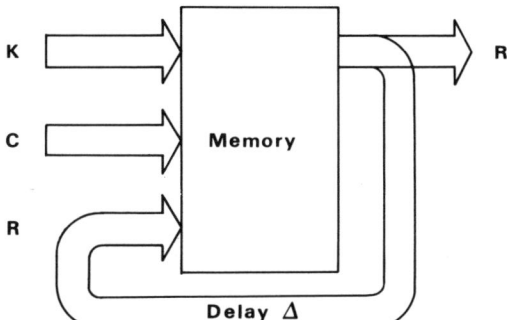

Fig. 1.4 Associative memory with feedback

Associative memory is here defined as any facility from which a stored data set, for instance, a set of concomitant patterns, can be recalled using any of its members as key excitation.

One of the input patterns is the representation of an object, here understood as a key pattern K(t) indexed by a time variable t. The second input channel carries a concomitant pattern C(t) (abbreviation for context or control) the role of which does not greatly differ from that of an attribute. If the output pattern at time t is denoted R(t) (abbreviation for response or recollection), then the third input is derived from R(t) through a delaying feedback channel. A similar arrangement with signal feedback connections has been used to implement the automatic operation in the well-known finite-state sequential machines, for instance in the Moore automaton. For a review of this and related principles, cf., e.g., [4].

This system model will now be shown to implement a memory in which structured knowledge can be represented. Its dynamic operation is discussed as a process in which the external patterns K(t) and C(t) arrive at uniform intervals corresponding to the feedback delay; the output response is obtained without delay. A generalization of the process for a time-continuous and asynchronous mode is straigthforward, although it leads to more complicated considerations. Suppose that the triple [K(t), C(t), R(t - Δ)] is regarded as a static pattern defined at time t, and there is a provision for transferring it as a whole into memory, in a single storage operation. In technological implementations, there are usually auxiliary control mechanisms by which the storage phase can be separated from the process of recall; in the adaptive physical systems discussed later, storage and recall may be simultaneous processes.

In particular, it is now supposed that the system structure is such that during storage, R(t) is identical to K(t). During recall, a replica of a stored K must occur as an output R.

Storage Phase. Assume that pairs of patterns K(t), C(t) are applied at the inputs as a synchronous sequence, and an output R(t) identical to K(t) simultaneously appears. After a delay, R(t - Δ) is available in synchronism at the third input. Every new triple that appears at the input is stored in memory. In most technological memories, the storage capacity ensues from spatially distinguishable memory locations. It will be pointed out in Section 1.2 that there also exist physical implementations of memory in which the patterns can be superimposed on a memory medium in spatially distributed form, i.e., as a kind of collective state change, without mutual interference of the stored items.

Acquisition of knowledge may be made in many independent subsequences during which the context C(t) is usually steady; the stored sequences are terminated with "empty" patterns which are not stored.

Recall Phase. By the application of key information that usually consists of a stimulus pattern K equal to an earlier stimulus, accompanied by its due context pattern C, an associative search process can be started. After this, the primary stimulus K can be switched off, but the context C is held steady. An output R = K is first obtained. According to the definition of associative recall, when the delayed output R(t - Δ) appears at the input, then, by virtue of the pair (C, R) used as the key, the next R(t) is obtained by associative recall. The new output, again, after a delay Δ acts as an input by which the third R(t) is recalled, etc. It is possible to deduce that a stored sequence with context pattern C is generated. It is moreover to be noted that although a key K may occur in many different sequences, only one particular sequence, specified by the context, is realized. A recalled sequence stops when it ends with an empty pattern (being the successor of itself). Processes that occur during storage and recall are illustrated by a simple example.

Example. The generation of a structured graph of knowledge is demonstrated when certain partial sequences of patterns formed of K(t) $\in$ {a,b,c,d,e,f,-} and C(t) $\in$ {A,B,-} are applied at the input of a memory of the type depicted in Fig. 1.4; the symbols a,b,..., A, B stand for spatial patterns of signals, and

(-) is an empty pattern with signal values zero. (It is assumed that empty patterns do not produce responses.) Assume that the following timed sequences of pairs [K(t), C(t)] have been presented at the input during storage phases:

{(a,A), (b,A), (d,A)};
{(b,A), (d,A), (e,A), (-,A), (-,-)};
{(a,B), (c,B)};
{(c,B), (d,B)};
{(d,B), (f,B), (-,B), (-,-)}.

If the earlier relation-type notations are used, these sequences might be described as triples $a \xrightarrow{A} b$, $b \xrightarrow{A} d$, $d \xrightarrow{A} (-)$, etc. This analogy now results in a structured graph of Fig. 1.5 which simultaneously constitutes a structured graph of knowledge, as well as a state graph of a sequential system (cf., e.g.,[1]). A dynamic

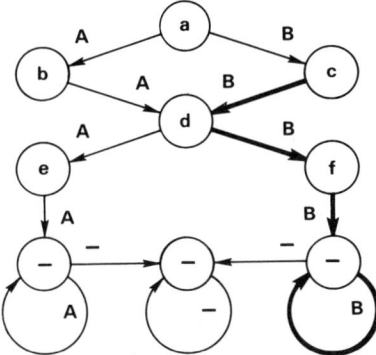

Fig. 1.5 A structured sequence

recollection can be triggered at any time later if the network is excited by one particular pattern that together with its context occurs in the graph; this will cause an output which in turn by means of the delayed feedback selectively evokes the next pattern in the sequence, and so on. For instance, if the pair (c,B) is applied at the input, then the sequence drawn in bold arrows is recalled. Notice that
    - this sequence was never stored in a complete form, and the learning of a sequence from shorter segments has thereby been demonstrated;
    - the order in which the segments are presented can be arbitrary;
    - the states a and d occur in different subsequences where they have a different context;
    - it is necessary to terminate the sequences by empty patterns; when the context pattern (A or B) has been switched off, the system enters the "empty" sequence (quiet state) where it waits for new key patterns.

More Involved Models. Apparently the triplet form of a relation is the most fundamental construct from which relational structures of arbitrary complexity can be built. Accordingly, the above physical system model for an associative memory might be regarded as the simplest paradigm. Nonetheless it is possible to imagine more complex relations and systems, too. A memory unit may have several inputs and outputs for patterns, for instance, for several distinct items which can be memorized in a single process. A memory system may be built of many units, interconnected by channels with different delays, etc. The activity in one channel may comprise the context to another, etc. Obviously the discussion then becomes very complicated and even more so if the patterns occur asynchronously. It may be possible to imagine, although difficult to analyze the behaviour of such systems.

1.2 Implementations of Associative Recall

1.2.1 Basic Characteristics of Associative Memories

Above, the concept of associative recall was used in a few instances. In general it may be understood as an action or operation with a set of input signals or other items considered as a *key*, and some sort of outcome which constitute the *recollection*. In the simplest form both the key and the recollection are spatial patterns of simultaneous signal values; sequential recall of a series of patterns may be regarded as a dynamic recollection. It should be noticed, however, that sequences may be composed of elementary recall actions, temporally linked by feedback couplings.

Various Cases of Associative Recall. The most characteristic property of associative recall is the following: if the totality of input signals, briefly called a pattern, is stored as such in memory, it is retrievable by any part of it. In some earlier examples a pattern consisted of a few subpatterns any of which, or any combination of which could be used as the key. It will now be useful to characterize the recall as *autoassociative* if the pattern is retrievable on a basis of an arbitrary fragment of it, provided that this fragment is large enough for its identification among the other patterns stored. (The possibility must be considered separately that the key may match with several stored patterns; this will lead to a conflict situation, whereby a unique outcome is not possible. With biological memories, multiple matches are not of central importance and they may be regarded as cases in which the outcome is a mixture of all matching items. In computer science, however, especially in the retrieval of information from data bases, multiple-match situation is the normal case. There are means to deal with multiple responses if they are temporarily stored and subsequently analyzed. Methods for the handling of multiple matches will be discussed in Secs. 2.1 and 2.2). Another case of associative recall may be named *heteroassociative*. In this mode of operation, an outcome which structurally does not correspond to any of the key items is obtained as a response to a specific key pattern. If an equivalent outcome had been stored earlier, the storage could have been made using specific inputs reserved for this purpose.

One case of associative recall is the *associative encoding* of patterns which may be an autoassociative or a heteroassociative process. A subpattern thereby takes on the role of symbolically representing the rest of the pattern; for instance a *code* or *tag field* in a pattern may be reserved for this purpose. The code need not necessarily be digital; a symbolic pattern of any kind, usually simple and clear in its features, can be made to represent the whole pattern. In memory, this is simply made by association of the "pictorial" and "symbolic" subpatterns. During recall, the "pictorial" part may recall the code, or vice versa. It will be pointed out in Section 2.3 that this paradigm has a bearing on pattern identification.

Local Memories. Almost without exception, the digital computer memories are of the *local* type in which every distinct data set is stored on its own piece of memory medium or a set of memory elements. For the designation and management of the stored representations, local memories need a control mechanism for the activation of a particular memory location into which information is written or from which it is read. This is normally done by means of the so-called address decoder mechanism which may take on various forms. Since the main principles of usual addressable computer memories may be well-known, at least on the programming level, their presentation is omitted here. Instead, more attention will be paid to an address selection principle that uses the so-called content-addressable memory (CAM) (Subsec. 1.2.2 and Sec. 2.2).

Distributed Memories. During recent years, plenty of evidence has been collected about biological nature using *distributed* memories in its information systems. In distributed memories, every memory element or fragment of memory medium holds traces from many stored items, i.e., the representations are superimposed on each other. On the other hand, every piece of stored information is spread over a large area. In order that information of one item not be lost in the storage by mixing with the other items, it is necessary that the state changes obey specific transformations of the primary signal patterns which preserve their interrelations without interference from the other stored items. In holographic memories, optical diffraction of coherent waves implements this transformation, and the proportionality of the photographic medium is utilized in superposition [11, 13, 15].

Implicitly referred to above is the possibility that distributed memories may not need a sophisticated control principle for the retrieval of information since there are no addressable memory locations for which a decoder mechanism would be necessary. For a long time it has been unclear, however, how a sufficient selectivity in distributed storages can be achieved; notice that if the patterns were superimposed as such, any recollection would be just a mixture of all the items. In this book this problem is of central importance. It will be shown that there are cases in which faultless recollections can be obtained from a distributed memory with a large number of stored patterns. In general, however, there is noise or other imperfection in the recalled patterns. The most important property of the devices suggested for associative memory is that *the imperfections are corrected in an optimal way with respect to all information that is available as the key.*

Information in distributed storages is spread throughout the memory medium by storage mappings. Consequently, the memory elements ought to be able to superimpose *continuous* state changes from very many items. The keynote of these principles is that when something is stored in memory, differentially small simultaneous changes take place in a very large number of memory elements; in this way the dynamic range of the variable memory elements can be utilized for many items. In recall, the stored information is reconstructed as a specific integral of these "memory traces" in a way which usually does not very much differ from the way in which messages can be reconstructed from their correlation functions. A particular advantage of the distributed memories may now be discernible: since the recollections are composed of very many differential elements, occasional defects in the memory traces of the key information are statistically smoothed out.

1.2.2 The Content-Addressable Memory (CAM)

In computer technology, the name *associative memory* has generally been adopted to mean a memory "... as a collection or assemblage of elements having data storage capabilities,... which are accessed simultaneously and in parallel on the basis of data content rather than by specific address or location" (HANLON [10]). The other generally used name for this type of device is *content-addressable memory* (CAM); this name ought to be preferred, because this device implements only an elementary operation in associative recall.

Such an "associative" memory relies on addressable memory locations, but there is an additional direct provision to check a search argument against all stored words. Upon partial agreement, a recall of the contents of the matching memory location is made.

The principle of associative recall of information from a simple content-addressable memory is described by the following example. The memory has a *directory* part with a content-addressable access, and for simplicity, in order to avoid the discussion of multiple responses, it is tentatively assumed that all entries are different. A data memory connected with the directory is a normal *linear-select-memory* in which one location is selected for writing or readout when the corresponding address line is made active. Data sets can be written into this memory in a normal way. The memory is organized as shown in Fig. 1.6.

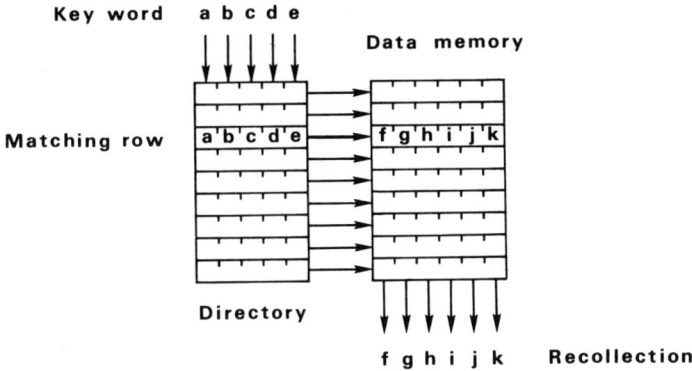

Fig. 1.6 Content-addressable memory (CAM)

The search is made by a search argument called key word which acts as a set of input signals in parallel and simultaneously over all respective bits of the entries; a comparison of these signals with the bits stored in memory elements is performed by means of special logic circuits built into the memory locations. If all the bits of an entry match with the key word, then the corresponding output line is activated. This line acts as an address line in a linear-select memory. The content-addressable memory thus replaces the address decoder circuit. The whole memory system can be regarded as a single logic circuit and hence the access time can be rather short (for instance, 50 ns). A usual version of this memory is controllable by a *mask word* which defines only a subset of bits in the key word used in the search. This is important for the implementation of *autoassociative recall* by this device. Other features may be added to this memory, too: for instance, if several matches must be allowed, a *multiple-response resolution logic* between the directory and the data memory becomes necessary.

1.2.3 Hash-Coding

The access to data in hardware implementations of associative memory is an extremely fast operation, and the search of an item on the basis of any fragment of it is possible, provided that this fragment is known exactly. A drawback of the CAM devices is the appreciable amount of electronic circuitry needed for every bit stored (cf. Sec. 2.2). For this reason, hardware constructs with more than a few thousand memory locations are not practicable, unless some radically new principles are invented.

If the key words on the basis of which information is searched are completely known and they always occur in the same form, a fast search may be implemented by pure programming techniques using conventional computer memories. These methods are named *hash-coding*, and in general it means that the address of a storage location

for data is a function of the data itself and it is determined by some mapping
algorithm applied to the data contents. During recall, the same algorithm is applied
to the key in order to find the storage location. Thus retrieval is normally made
in one readout operation. The name of this method comes partly from the random way
in which data are scattered into the memory area, partly from one particular algorithm
(hash-bit extraction, cf. Sec. 2.1). Fig. 1.7. illustrates the mapping of items,
denoted by rectangles, onto a memory area here shown as a linear array. In this example
every item is provided with a single key word.

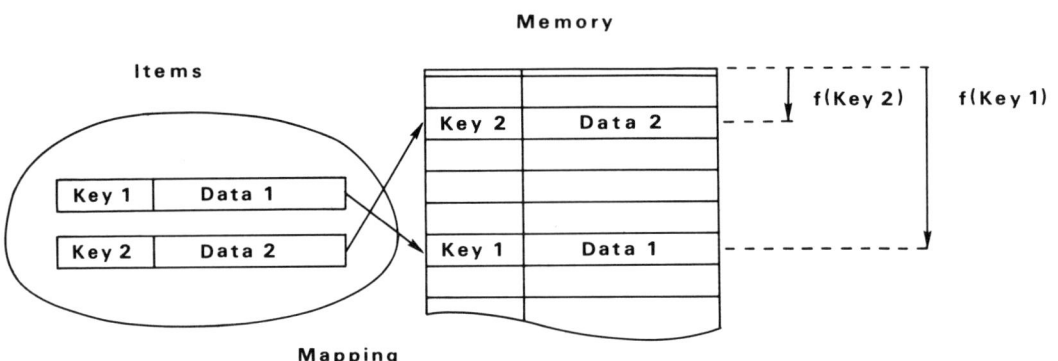

Fig. 1.7 Mapping of items in hash-coding

The most important condition for the applicability of hash-coding, the uniqueness
of the key word, was mentioned above. If the data must be encoded by several alternative key words, duplicates of the item must be stored at several memory locations
corresponding to all key words.

There is a characteristic problem which arises with the programmed implementations
of content-addressable memory, namely, a conflict situation named *collision*. It means
that two or more key words may have the same computed address, and only one of the items
can occupy it. The usual method for the handling of collision is to assign spare
locations for the computed location in which the colliding items are stored. A more
thorough discussion of collisions is made in Section 2.1.

As the programmed content-addressing methods allow the storage of almost unlimited
amounts of items in usual computer memories, they have become important in large-
scale implementations of associative memory. If, for instance, relational structures
are stored in memory as ordered triples, and every item in a triple must separately
be accessible, a straightforward implementation of programmed associative memory is to
store replicas of the triples encoded by all their items individually. Information
retrieval processes as discussed in Subsection 1.1.2 are then directly possible.

1.2.4 Holographic Associative Memories

Holographic memories are especially suitable for the storage of masses of pictorial information such as photographs, and in some special applications they offer an additional advantage of being tolerable to partial damage of memory media. Before a detailed discussion of the holographic principles for memories, it will be necessary to point out that spatial distributedness of memory traces, the central characteristic of holograms, may mean two facts: 1) Elements in a data set are spread by a transformation over a memory area, but different data sets are always stored in separate areas. 2) Several data sets are superimposed on the same medium in a distributed form.

Examples of the first type are holographic memories in which pieces of information, for instance photographs of documents, are stored on a photographic film in the form of their holograms, usually in a microscopic size; a typical density of information is one million bits per square millimeter. Nevertheless, all holograms are kept spatially separate, and to retrieve one document, a mechanical or optoelectronic control is necessary by which a beam of light used for reading is directed towards a particular area. An example of the second type of memory is a hologram which utilizes the crystalline properties of matter. The hologram is formed on a substrate which in effect is a lattice of atoms, and when waves of light pass through it, they can form images only at certain diffraction angles. If during exposure of the holograms, the direction of the reference ray necessary to form the hologram is different for every image, memory traces from many (up to some tens with the present techniques) images can be superimposed on the same photosensitive substrate, and one of the images can be chosen for readout if the reference beam during reading is selected respectively. However, neither of the above methods can yet be named *associative memory* because the set of possible reference beams is fixed and must be controlled by a selector mechanism; consequently, these are still *addressable* memories.

Associative Holographic Memories. A classical exemplification of a holographic memory, based on Fresnel diffraction, is the following. Fig. 1.8 a depicts a system with a coherent light source, laser L, the beam of which is split by a half-reflecting mirror M. The two beams are then scattered from objects A and B, respectively, and their wave fronts combine at the photographic plate P. The transmittance of plate P is changed in an exposure.

If, after development of the photographic plate, object B is removed but the wave fronts from object A are made to scatter from plate P, it is possible to perceive a "phantom" of object B in its due place (Fig. 1.8 b). This is the holographic image. The usual analysis of this phenomenon is delineated as follows (COLLIER [9], STROKE [17]): the periodicity in time of the wave functions is omitted, and the complex amplitudes of the electromagnetic fields of waves from objects A and B are denoted by $F_A(r)$ and $F_B(r)$, respectively, with r the spatial coordinate vector

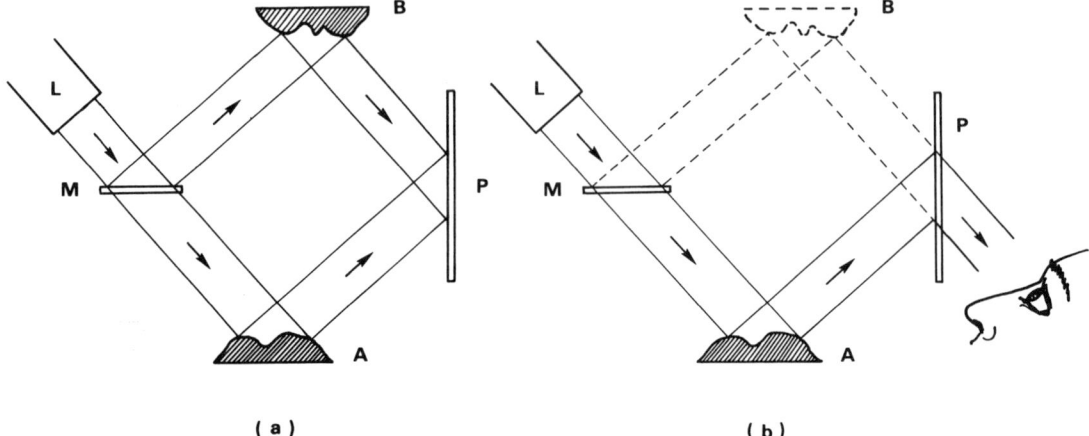

Fig. 1.8 Illustration of Fresnel holography

(especially referring to position at plate P). The change in transmittance $T(r)$ of plate P is assumed directly proportional to the light intensity, $\Delta T(r) = -\lambda[F_A(r) + F_B(r)] [F_A^*(r) + F_B^*(r)]$ where λ is a numerical constant and the star denotes the complex conjugate. After object B has been removed and plate P illuminated by waves from object A alone, the field intensity behind the plate (assumed very thin) is

$$F = [T(r) + \Delta T(r)] F_A(r)$$

$$= T(r) F_A - \lambda [F_A(r)F_A^*(r) + F_B(r)F_B^*(r)] F_A(r) \qquad (1.1)$$

$$- \lambda [F_A(r)F_B^*(r)F_A(r) + F_B(r)F_A(r)F_A^*(r)] \ .$$

Now $F_A(r)F_A^*(r)$ and $F_B(r)F_B^*(r)$ are the wave intensities due to the objects A and B, respectively, and they are assumed as constant with r over plate P. In addition to waves which are proportional to field $F_A(r)$ caused by object A, there are two additional components - $[\lambda F_A(r)F_A^*(r)] F_B(r)$ and $-\lambda F_A(r)F_B^*(r)F_A(r)$ of which the first is in effect a wave front caused by a virtual image of B; the last term has no structure and represents diffraction noise. The virtual image is equivalent to the *recollection* of object B.

Consider now that several exposures from pairs of different objects (A, B) are recorded on the same hologram. If one of the objects A could be restored in its original location maintaining the spatial relationships of the apparatus with extremely high accuracy, recall of the paired associate B will take place. The above analysis does not tell, however, whether the recall is exact (let alone the diffraction noise) or whether there is interference from other stored images. Experience has shown that if the beam via A is randomized by some kind of a diffusor in order to make the "key patterns" more orthogonal, a fair selectivity among a few patterns is achieved.

There are holographic schemes based on the so-called Fourier diffraction, too, in which the recollections are projected on a real image plane. It must be pointed out, however, that none of the holographic principles demonstrated so far really possesses features which are necessary for a large-scale implementation of an associative memory; even if the reference beam is derived from the picture itself, as made in the Fresnel diffraction, superposition of several patterns is not possible unless, for instance, auxiliary diffraction conditions are utilized. This shortcoming probably does not appear clear enough before contrasted with the optimal associative mappings discussed below. Then it will be found that recall from a true distributed associative memory can be implemented without auxiliary reference beams or other similar control.

1.2.5 Nonholographic, Distributed Associative Memories

It is necessary to point out that, contrary to a common view, the conventional digital content-addressing principles do not implement the operation of associative recall except in a very primitive and restricted form. Another common view held of associative recall implies that the search of information ought to be made on a basis of incomplete cues or "hunches" which have a higher or lesser correlation to the item to be found. Expressed in mathematical terms, this kind of search is a problem of statistical estimation on the basis of previously collected (and stored) statistics, and the facts that are available for the present. Apparently this is not what is done with content-addressable memories; in hash-coding, the key word which is compared with the stored items must be known exactly, and in hardware content-addressable memories, the parts selected for the search argument must be faultless, too. The computations in estimation are much more sophisticated and laborious.

In an attempt to implement associative memory in a statistical sense, the first task is to devise methods by which the statistical computations can be carried out with large patterns of data, without wasting too much time for it. As the highly parallel digital computers comprise a very complicated and expensive solution, it may be interesting to find out that this task has a much simpler but still powerful implementation by analog computing techniques. There exist adaptive systems, for instance, networks of simple physical components by which the matching of the search argument with the stored items is made in a single transformation operation, and the result is optimal in the sense of least squares. The system by which the transformation is implemented can then be characterized as an optimal estimator. As the discussion of such transformations needs some mathematical preliminaries presented in Section 1.3, the discussion of the theoretical foundations of these systems will be postponed to Section 2.3 and Chapter 3. As an introduction, in order to gain an idea of the physical embodiment of such systems, a simpler principle, completely realizable by the present technology, is presented.

The idea of a nonholographic, distributed associative memory was implicit in some models of adaptive networks studied around 1960 (cf., e.g., [18]) although their primary application was considered to be that of pattern classification. Several years later, a few distributed memory structures were suggested (cf. Subsec. 4.2.3). At that time there were also some other principles taken into consideration for the computation of convolution and correlation functions, thought to implement the distributed associative memories. Although representation of associations is without doubt implementable by such functions, no demonstration, even in a mathematical form, was able to show that such models have the needed degree of *selectivity* in recall (without crosstalk from the other items) that would make a mass memory for patterns feasible.

One feature of distributed memories, already mentioned above, is that information is stored as differential state changes of their memory elements. In photographic or other optic media with variable transmission properties, a sufficient proportionality of the state changes to signal values already has been achieved, statistically at least. (In photographic films, the silver grains are completely black but a variable transmittance of the medium can be defined in terms of the density of the grains.) Contrary to this, very little research has been pursued on electrical materials or components in which permanent linear changes proportional to the current through the device or the voltage over it would have been achieved. Electroplating has sometimes been suggested for the mass production of variable resistors but the arrangement of a sufficiently uniform plating process in a large signal network may be problematic. The detailed technological questions can be taken into consideration if such principles are found useful, for instance, in the extensive parallel computations that occur in the processing of patterned information. There is also a possibility to handle the technical problem by using digital computing principles for the evaluation of the transforms and the storage of information at the network elements, whereby large-scale integration technology offers powerful and yet relatively cheap solutions.

Resistor network as an analog associative memory. A linear mapping which selectively transforms a set of input patterns into output patterns can be implemented by a linear physical system, for instance by a resistor network with conductance values which must be computed separately for each family of data sets stored. After this, associative recall of the "stored" information is demonstrable. As mentioned above, there exist processes by which the network elements may be formed in an adaptive fashion. This problem will be postponed to Chapter 3.

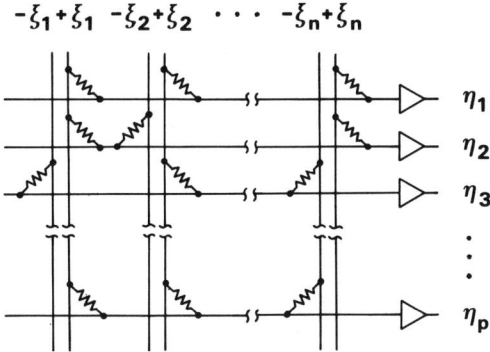

Fig. 1.9 Linear transformation in a resistor network

A network which implements a linear transformation is depicted in Fig. 1.9. Every horizontal line is provided with an output amplifier, similar to an operational amplifier which has a very low input impedance. A voltage output is obtained as a linear combination of the vertical inputs,

$$\eta_i = \sum_{j=1}^{n} \mu_{ij} \xi_j \tag{1.2}$$

whereby the μ_{ij} depend on the conductances at the crossings of the ith and jth lines. In order to avoid negative conductance values in the case that the coefficient μ_{ij} ought to be negative, the following method is used. Every input is represented by double signals, $+\xi_j$ and $-\xi_j$, respectively. If the coefficient μ_{ij} is positive, a conductance directly proportional to it is connected between the ith horizontal line and the line for $+\xi_j$. If the coefficient μ_{ij} is negative, a conductance which is directly proportional to its magnitude is connected between the ith horizontal line and the line for $-\xi_j$. Currents merging at every output amplifier are thereby added and transformed into output voltages according to (1.2).

The values μ_{ij} in (1.2) can be computed according to many different criteria; one of the choices corresponds to the least-square optimal estimator (cf. Subsec. 2.3.8). Another mapping which with suitably preprocessed data is not significantly inferior to the optimal case is the *correlation matrix network* ([12]; Subsec. 4.2.3) in which the μ_{ij} are computed from simpler formulas. Let us define an input pattern as an ordered set $x_t = (\xi_{1t}, \xi_{2t}, \ldots, \xi_{nt})$, with the second index denoting a particular pattern. Similarly an output pattern is denoted by $y_t = (\eta_{1t}, \eta_{2t}, \ldots, \eta_{nt})$. The μ_{ij} are now computed as the unnormalized correlation matrix of a set of pairs (x_t, y_t), with $t = 1, 2, \ldots, m$:

$$\mu_{ij} = \sum_{t=1}^{m} \eta_{it} \xi_{jt} \ . \tag{1.3}$$

It can easily be found from (1.2) and (1.3) that if a key pattern
$x = (\xi_1, \xi_2, \ldots, \xi_n)$ is applied at the input, then the recollection at the output has elements

$$\eta_i = \sum_{t=1}^{m} \left(\sum_{j=1}^{n} \xi_j \xi_{jt} \right) \eta_{it} = \sum_{t=1}^{m} w_t \eta_{it} \tag{1.4}$$

where the coefficients w_t depend on the *inner products* (cf. Subsec. 1.3.1) of the key pattern x with the respective stored patterns x_t. If the key was very similar to one of the stored patterns, partly at least, and dissimilar from the other patterns, then it is expected that only one η_{it} predominates in the recollection; the other terms represent crosstalk between the items.

Demonstration of Associative Recall by a Linear Mapping. The purpose of the following computer simulation was to demonstrate selective associative recall from a linear system characterized by (1.2-1.4), with no reference to a network that may underlie it. As the nonholographic schemes are most effective with very large patterns, the demonstration was performed with two-dimensional optical images, produced by a special image digitizer. The photographs, 500 in number, were converted into raster format in which every raster point had a numerical value. These points were then put to correspond to the pattern elements.

In the following computer simulation the purpose was to demonstrate *autoassociative recall* of patterns. This would have meant that the patterns x_t and y_t ought to have been selected identical. As the selectivity in recall, however, primarily depends on the inner products w_t which again are functions of the input patterns, it was found more advantageous to derive the key patterns x_t from the y_t in the following way: referring to Fig. 1.10, the y_t were *preprocessed* by an operation which increased selectivity.

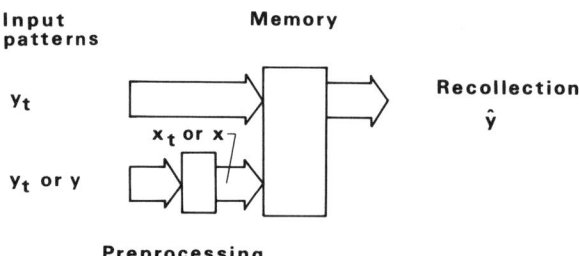

Fig. 1.10 System model of an associative memory with preprocessing

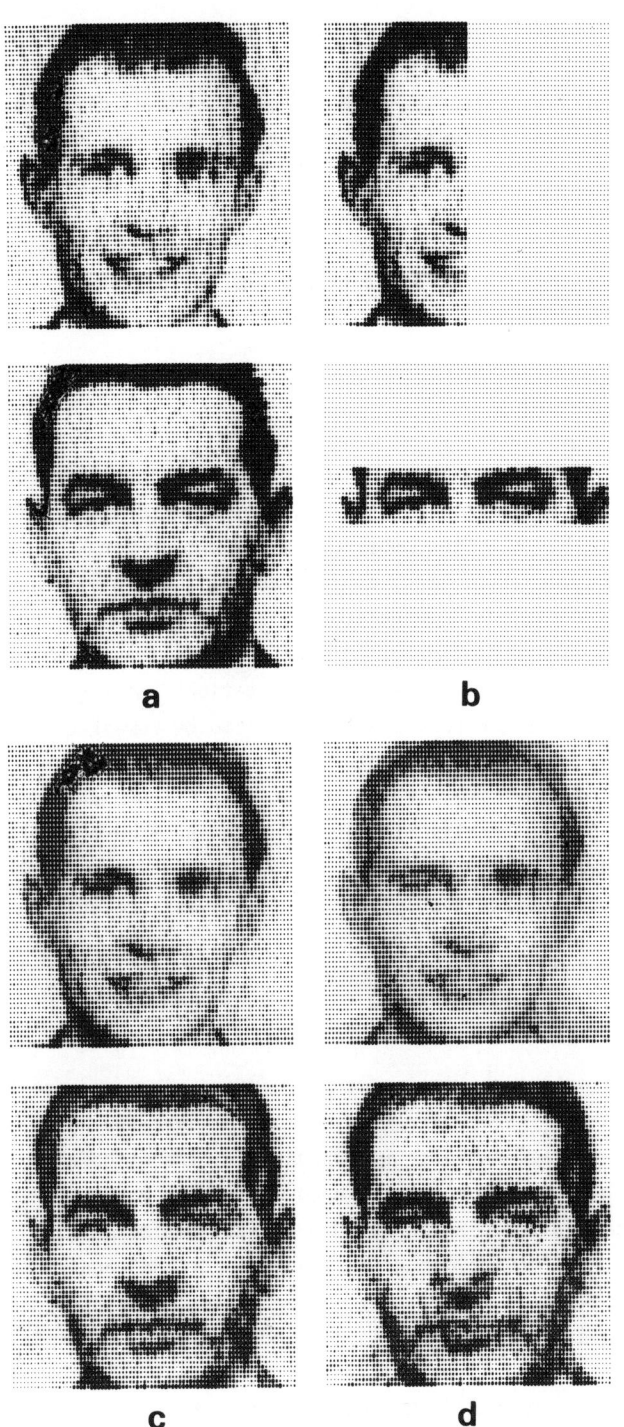

Fig.1.11
Demonstration of associative recall from a linear system

a. Samples of original images
b. Key patterns
c. Recollections from a memory with 160 stored images
d. Recollections from a memory with 500 stored images

As different preprocessing operations will be discussed in more detail in Sections 2.3 and 2.4, it may suffice to mention here that the x_t were obtained from the y_t by a high-pass filter which in effect performed a second-order spatial differentation. A similar preprocessing operation was applied to the key pattern y used for the recall of information from this "memory".

After these considerations the results of the following experiment may be conceivable. In Fig. 1.11, pictures a represent samples of the 500 stored images, pictures b are key patterns (before spatial differentation), and the pictures c and d represent the recollections.

1.3 Mathematical Notations and Methods

When dealing with spatially or temporally related samples of signal values that represent "information", one needs a mathematical framework for the description of their quantitative interrelations. This is often provided by the vector formalism. The operations in vector spaces, on the other hand, can conveniently be manipulated by matrix algebra. These topics form the main contents of this section.

As a mathematical representation, this section is more referential than formally complete; it is intended solely to serve as a collection of notations and results used elsewhere in the book, for their better readability. It is to be remarked that especially in matrix algebra plenty of alternative notations are used. The nomenclature and symbols selected for this text are used by the majority of writers in these fields. For the application of the results it is urged that the reader familiarize himself with some central works on modern matrix algebra of which the excellent book of ALBERT [19] perhaps better than any other single text covers the formalism used here.

1.3.1 Vector Space Concepts

Representation Vectors. Especially in the physical theory of information processes, spatially or temporally adjacent signal values are thought to form *patterns* which can be understood as ordered sets of real numbers. In pursuance of the methods developed in the theory of pattern recognition (cf. references in Sec. 2.4) such sets are described by *representation vectors* which are generalizations of the vectors of plane and space geometry. If there are n independently defined and somehow related real numerical values $\xi_1, \xi_2, \ldots, \xi_n$, they can be understood as coordinates in a space which has n dimensions. This space is denoted R^n and it is the set of all possible n-tuples of real numbers each of which is from the interval $(-\infty, +\infty)$. (Note that a scalar is defined in the space $R^1 = R$.) Hereupon the scalars are denoted by lower-case Greek letters and vectors by lower-case Roman letters, respectively, unless otherwise stated. All indices and exponents, however, are denoted in Roman. A vector x is a point in R^n (expressed $x \in R^n$), the coordinates of which are

$\xi_1, \xi_2, \ldots, \xi_n$. To visualize a vector (although this may be difficult in a multidimensional space) it may be imagined as a directed line from the origin to the point in question.

Consider a representation vector which is put to stand for optical patterns. These are usually composed of picture elements like a mosaic, and every picture element attains a scalar real value. The indexing of the elements can now be made in an arbitrary fashion. In Fig. 1.12, three different examples of indexing are shown;

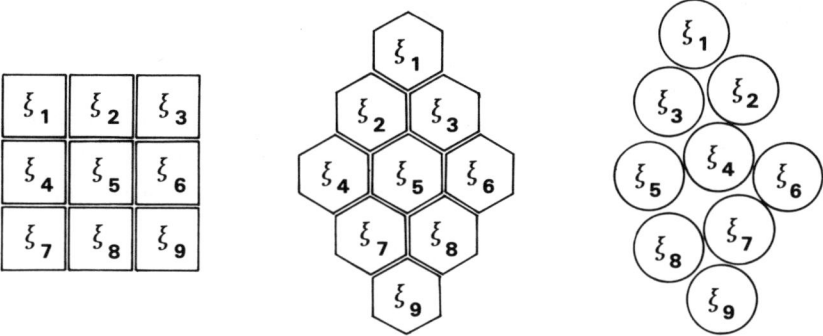

Fig. 1.12 Examples of pattern "vectors"

in all of them, the formal representation vector then attains fhe form $(\xi_1, \xi_2, \ldots, \xi_9)$. It should be noticed that this is a *linear array of numbers* in spite of the original images being two-dimensional.

Linear Vector Spaces. For analytical purposes, it will be necessary to define the concept of a vector space. A *linear vector space* $\mathcal{V}$ (over the reals) is generally defined as a set of elements, the vectors, in which the operations of vector addition (+) and (scalar) multiplication (.) have been defined, and the following facts hold true: if $x,y,z \in \mathcal{V}$ are vectors and $\alpha, \beta \in R$ are scalars, then

A 1) $x + y = y + x \in \mathcal{V}$ (commutativity)
A 2) $\alpha \cdot (x + y) = \alpha \cdot x + \alpha \cdot y \in \mathcal{V}$ ⎫
A 3) $(\alpha + \beta) \cdot x = \alpha \cdot x + \beta \cdot x$ ⎬ (distributivity)
A 4) $(x + y) + z = x + (y + z)$ ⎫
A 5) $(\alpha \cdot \beta) \cdot x = \alpha \cdot (\beta \cdot x)$ ⎬ (associativity)
A 6) There exists a zero vector 0 such that for every $x \in \mathcal{V}$, $x + 0 = x$.
A 7) For scalars 0 and 1, $0 \cdot x = 0$ and $1 \cdot x = x$.

An example of $\mathcal{V}$ would be R^n. The sum of two vectors is then defined as a vector with elements (coordinates, components) which are obtained by summing up the respective elements of the addends. The scalar multiplication is an operation in which all elements of a vector are multiplied by this scalar. (For simplicity of notation, the dot may be dropped.)

Inner Product. The concept of *inner product* refers to a two-argument, scalar-valued function which has been introduced to facilitate an analytic description of certain geometric operations. One very important case of inner product of vectors $x = (\xi_1, \ldots, \xi_n)$ and $y = (\eta_1, \ldots, \eta_n)$ is their *scalar product* defined as

$$(x,y) = \xi_1 \eta_1 + \xi_2 \eta_2 + \ldots + \xi_n \eta_n \; , \tag{1.5}$$

and unless otherwise stated, the inner product is assumed to have this functional form. It should be pointed out, however, that there are infinitely many choices for inner products, for instance, variants of (1.5) where the elements of the vectors are weighted differently, or enter the function (x,y) with different powers.

In general, the inner product of two elements x and y in a set, by convention, must have the following properties. Assume that the addition of the elements, and multiplication of an element by a scalar have been defined. If the inner product function is now denoted by (x,y), there must hold

B1) $(x,y) = (y,x)$
B2) $(\alpha x, y) = \alpha (x,y)$
B3) $(x_1 + x_2, y) = (x_1, y) + (x_2, y)$
B4) $(x,x) \geq 0$ where equality holds if and only if x is the zero element.

Metric. In practice, all observable vectors must be represented in a space which has a *metric*. The latter is a property of any set of elements characterized by another function called *distance* d(x,y) between all pairs of elements. For the choice of the distance function, the following conditions must hold:

C1) $d(x,y) \geq 0$ where equality holds if and only if $x = y$.
C2) $d(x,y) = d(y,x)$
C3) $d(x,y) \leq d(x,z) + d(z,y)$.

An example of distance is the *Euclidean distance* in a rectangular coordinate system, which is almost exclusively used in this book: for the vectors $x = (\xi_1, \ldots, \xi_n)$ and $y = (\eta_1, \ldots, \eta_n)$,

$$d(x,y) = \sqrt{(\xi_1 - \eta_1)^2 + (\xi_2 - \eta_2)^2 + \ldots + (\xi_n - \eta_n)^2} \; . \tag{1.6}$$

Another example of distances is the *Hamming distance* which has been defined for binary vectors; a binary vector has elements which are either 0 or 1. The Hamming distance indicates in how many positions (elements) the two vectors are different. Apparently the rules C1 to C3 are valid for Hamming distances, too.

Norm. The magnitude of a vector can be defined in different ways. The name *norm* is used for it, and in general, the norm, in a set of elements for which scalar multiplication, addition, and the zero element have been defined, is a function $\|x\|$ of an element x for which the following rules must be valid:

D1) $\|x\| \geq 0$, and the equality holds if and only if x = 0.
D2) $\|\alpha x\| = |\alpha| \, \|x\|$ where $|\alpha|$ is the absolute value of α.
D3) $\|x_1 + x_2\| \leq \|x_1\| + \|x_2\|$.

The *Euclidean norm* can be defined by the scalar product:

$$\|x\| = \sqrt{(x,x)} = \sqrt{\xi_1^2 + \xi_2^2 + \ldots + \xi_n^2} \; . \tag{1.7}$$

Notice that the Euclidean distance $d(x,y)$ is equivalent to the Euclidean norm $\|x - y\|$. A space in which Euclidean distance and norm have been defined is called Euclidean space.

Angles and Orthogonality. Generalization of the usual concept of angle for higher-dimensional spaces is straightforward. The angle θ between two Euclidean vectors x and y is defined by

$$\cos\theta = \frac{(x,y)}{\|x\| \, \|y\|} \; . \tag{1.8}$$

Accordingly, the two vectors are said to be *orthogonal* and denoted $x \perp y$ when their inner product vanishes.

Linear Manifolds. The vectors $x_1, x_2, \ldots, x_k$ are said to be *linearly independent* if their weighted sum, or the linear combination

$$\alpha_1 x_1 + \alpha_2 x_2 + \ldots + \alpha_k x_k \tag{1.9}$$

cannot become zero unless $\alpha_1 = \alpha_2 = \ldots = \alpha_k = 0$. Accordingly if the sum expression can be made zero for some choice of the α-coefficients all of which are not zero, the vectors are *linearly dependent*. Some of the vectors then can be expressed as linear combinations of the others. Examples of linear dependence can be visualized in the three-dimensional space R^3: three or more vectors are linearly dependent if they lie in a plane that passes through the origin, because then each vector can be expressed as a weighted sum of the others (as shown by the dashed-line constructions in Fig. 1.13).

Consider all possible linear combinations of the vectors $x_1, x_2, \ldots, x_k$ where k is at most the dimensionality n; they are obtained when the α-coefficients take on all real values from $(-\infty, +\infty)$. The set of all linear combinations is called a *subspace* in R^n and denoted by $\mathcal{L}$. Examples of subspaces are planes and straight lines in R^3 which pass through the origin. In higher-dimensional spaces, very important linear subspaces are those *hyperplanes* which are defined as linear

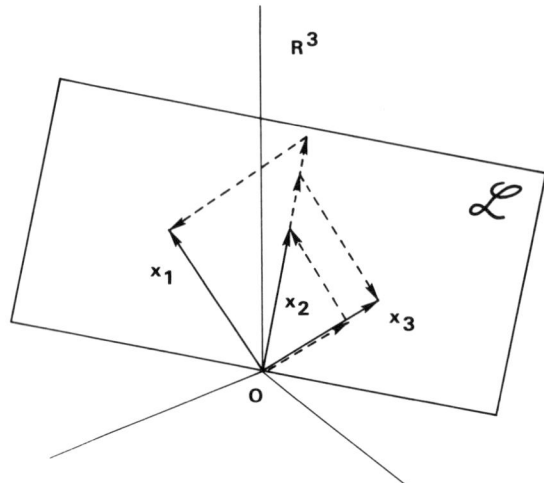

Fig. 1.13 Exemplification of linear dependence

combinations of n-1 linearly independent vectors, and which divide R^n into two half-spaces. Now all linear subspaces, including R^n, are also named *linear manifolds*, and the set of vectors which define the manifold is said to *span* it. It is to be noted that the manifold spanned by the above vectors is k-dimensional if the vectors are linearly independent. In this case the vectors $x_1, x_2, \ldots, x_k$ are called the *basis vectors of* $\mathcal{L}$.

Orthogonal Spaces. A vector x is said to be orthogonal to subspace $\mathcal{L}$ if it is orthogonal to every vector in it (abbreviated $x \perp \mathcal{L}$). Two subspaces $\mathcal{L}_1$ and $\mathcal{L}_2$ are said to be orthogonal to each other ($\mathcal{L}_1 \perp \mathcal{L}_2$) if every vector of $\mathcal{L}_1$ is orthogonal to every vector of $\mathcal{L}_2$. An example of orthogonal subspaces in R^3 are a coordinate axis and the plane of the two other axes of a rectangular coordinate system.

Orthogonal Projections. Below it will be pointed out that if $\mathcal{L}$ is a subspace of R^n, then an arbitrary vector $x \in R^n$ can be uniquely decomposed into the sum of two vectors of which one, $\hat{x}$, belongs to $\mathcal{L}$ and the other, $\tilde{x}$, is orthogonal to it.

Assume tentatively that there exist two decompositions

$$x = \hat{y} + \tilde{y} = \hat{z} + \tilde{z} \tag{1.10}$$

where $\hat{y}$ and $\hat{z}$ belong to $\mathcal{L}$ and $\tilde{y} \perp \mathcal{L}$, $\tilde{z} \perp \mathcal{L}$. Now $\tilde{z} - \tilde{y} \perp \mathcal{L}$, but since $\tilde{z} - \tilde{y} = \hat{y} - \hat{z}$, then $\tilde{z} - \tilde{y} \in \mathcal{L}$. Consequently $\tilde{z} - \tilde{y}$ has thus been shown to be orthogonal to itself, or $(\tilde{z} - \tilde{y}, \tilde{z} - \tilde{y}) = 0$ which cannot hold in general unless $\tilde{z} = \tilde{y}$. This proves that the decomposition is unique.

The proof of the existence of the decomposition will be postponed until an orthogonal basis has been introduced. Let us tentatively assume that the decomposition exists,

$x = \hat{x} + \tilde{x}$ where $\hat{x} \in \mathcal{L}$ and $\tilde{x} \perp \mathcal{L}$. (1.11)

Hereupon $\hat{x}$ will be called the *orthogonal projection* of x on $\mathcal{L}$; it will also be useful to introduce the space $\mathcal{L}^\perp$ which is named the *orthogonal complement* of $\mathcal{L}$; it is the set of all vectors in R^n which are orthogonal to $\mathcal{L}$. Then $\tilde{x}$ is called the orthogonal projection of x on $\mathcal{L}^\perp$. The orthogonal projections are very fundamental to the theory of optimal associative mappings discussed in this book.

The Projection Theorem. One particular property of the orthogonal projections is important for the discussion of approximations: of all decompositions of the form $x = x' + x''$ where $x' \in \mathcal{L}$, the one into orthogonal projections has the property that $\|x''\|$ is minimum. This is called the *projection theorem*. To prove it, use is made of the definition $\|x'\|^2 = (x',x')$ and the facts that $\hat{x} - x' \in \mathcal{L}$, $x - \hat{x} = \tilde{x} \perp \mathcal{L}$, whereby $(\hat{x} - x', x - \hat{x}) = 0$. The following expansion then yields

$$\|x - x'\|^2 = (x - \hat{x} + \hat{x} - x', x - \hat{x} + \hat{x} - x')$$
$$= \|x - \hat{x}\|^2 + \|\hat{x} - x'\|^2 .$$
(1.12)

Because the squared norms are always positive or zero, there can be written

$$\|x - x'\|^2 \geq \|x - \hat{x}\|^2$$
(1.13)

from which it is directly seen that $x'' = x - x'$ is minimum for $x' = \hat{x}$ whereby $x'' = \tilde{x}$. Orthogonal projections in a three-dimensional space are visualized in Fig. 1.14.

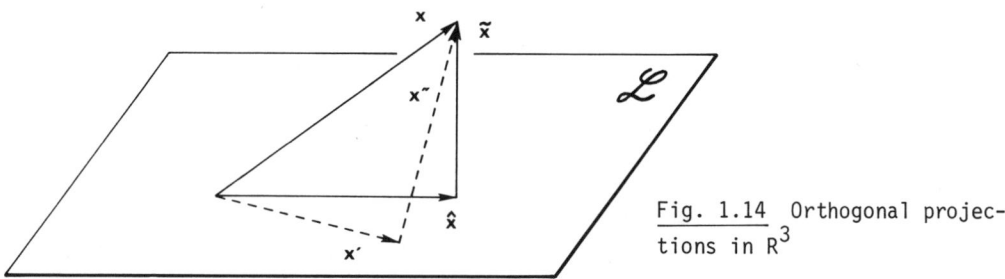

Fig. 1.14 Orthogonal projections in R^3

The Gram-Schmidt Orthogonalization Process. For the computation of the orthogonal projections, and to prove that an arbitrary vector can be decomposed as discussed above, a classical method named *Gram-Schmidt orthogonalization process* can be used.

Its original purpose is to construct an *orthogonal vector basis* for any linear space R^k, i.e., to find a set of basis vectors which are mutually orthogonal and which span R^k.

To start with, consider the nonzero vectors $x_1, x_2, \ldots x_p$, $p \geq k$ which span the space R^k. For a vector basis, one direction can be chosen freely whereby the first new basis vector is selected as $h_1 = x_1$. Unless x_2 has the same direction as x_1, it is easily found that the vector

$$h_2 = x_2 - \frac{(x_2, h_1)}{\|h_1\|^2} h_1 \qquad (1.14)$$

is orthogonal to $h_1 = x_1$; the inner product (h_2, h_1) is zero. Therefore, h_2 can be chosen for the new basis vector. If, on the other hand, x_2 had the same direction as x_1, it would be represented by x_1, and can thus be ignored. Consider now the sequence of vectors $\{h_i\}$ where each new member is constructed according to the recursive rule

$$h_i = x_i - \sum_{j=1}^{i-1} \frac{(x_i, h_j)}{\|h_j\|^2} h_j \qquad (1.15)$$

where the sum over j shall include terms with nonzero h_j only. In this way a set of vectors h_i is obtained. To prove that all the h_i are mutually orthogonal, the method of complete induction can be used. Assume that this rule is correct up to i-1, i.e, the $h_1, h_2, \ldots, h_{i-1}$ are mutually orthogonal, which means that for all $q < i$, and for nonzero $h_j, h_q, (h_j, h_q) = \|h_j\| \cdot \|h_q\| \cdot \delta_{jq}$ where δ_{jq} is the Kronecker symbol (=1 for j=q, =0 for j≠q). By a substitution there follows

$$(h_i, h_q) = \begin{cases} (x_i, h_q) - (x_i, h_q) = 0 & \text{if } h_q \neq 0 \\ (x_i, h_q) = 0 & \text{if } h_q = 0 \end{cases} \qquad (1.16)$$

Therefore the rule is correct up to i, and thus generally.

From the way in which the h-vectors were constructed, there directly follows that the $h_1, \ldots, h_i$ span exactly the same space as the $x_1, \ldots, x_i$ do. When the process is carried out for the vectors $x_1, x_2, \ldots x_p$ among which there are known to exist k linearly independent vectors, the space R^k will be spanned exactly.

If a further vector $x \in R^n$ that may or may not belong to space R^k shall be decomposed into its orthogonal projections $\hat{x} \in R^k$ and $\tilde{x} \perp R^k$, the Gram-Schmidt process is simply continued one step further whereby $\tilde{x} = h_{p+1}$, $\hat{x} = x - h_{p+1}$.

Since the above process is always possible, and it was earlier shown that the decomposition is unique, the so-called *decomposition theorem* can now be stated: an arbitrary vector $x \in R^n$ can uniquely be decomposed into two vectors of which one is in a subspace $\mathscr{L}$ of R^n and the other is orthogonal to it.

Hyperspheres. Examples of vector sets which are not linear spaces are hyperspheres and their surfaces. These concepts are important in the discussion of projective mappings of pattern vectors. In the N-dimensional Euclidean space R^N, a hypersphere with radius ρ, is the set of all points which lie within a distance ρ from the origin. The N-dimensional volume is a straightforward generalization of the three-dimensional one, being an integral of the volume elements $d\xi_1 d\xi_2 \ldots d\xi_N$, as expressed in a rectangular coordinate system.

Hyperspheres have been discussed in statistical mechanics. The volume of an N-dimensional sphere with radius ρ is (cf., e.g., [26])

$$V_N = \frac{\pi^{N/2}}{\left(\frac{1}{2}N\right)!} \rho^N \quad \text{for even N} ,$$

$$V_N = \frac{2^N \pi^{(N-1)/2} \left(\frac{1}{2}N - \frac{1}{2}\right)!}{N!} \rho^N \quad \text{for odd N} ,$$

(1.17)

or, in general, of the form $V_N(\rho) = \alpha_N \rho^N$ where α_N is a numerical constant. Eqs. (1.17) can also be expressed recursively,

$$V_{N+2}(\rho) = \frac{2\pi\rho^2}{N+2} V_N(\rho) ,$$

(1.18)

and two series of formulas (for N even and odd, respectively) can be computed starting with $V_2(\rho) = \pi\rho^2$ and $V_3(\rho) = 4\pi\rho^3/3$. The surface area of a hypersphere is obtained from $V_N(\rho)$ by differentiating it with respect to ρ.

Some of the lowest-order expressions for $V_N(\rho)$ and surface area have been represented in Table 1.2.

Table 1.2 Formulas for hyperspheres

Dimensionality N	Volume $V_N(\rho)$	Surface area $dV_N(\rho)/d\rho$
0	1 (point)	0
1	2ρ (line segment)	2 (two points)
2	$\pi \rho^2$	$2\pi\rho$
3	$4\pi\rho^3/3$	$4\pi\rho^2$
4	$\pi^2 \rho^4/2$	$2\pi^2\rho^3$
5	$8\pi^2\rho^5/7$	$40\pi^2\rho^4/7$
6	$\pi^3\rho^6/6$	$\pi^3\rho^5$

Mass Projection of a Homogeneous Hypersphere. (The following discussion relies on a geometrical imagination of spaces which can be represented by illustrations only for R, R^2, and R^3, but may be difficult to visualize in a higher-dimensional case. Although the results are important for the discussion of associative mappings, their derivation may be skipped here without affecting the reading of the rest.)

One of the central features of the optimal associative mappings discussed below is that they orthogonally project representation vectors on subspaces of R^n, spanned by a set of *reference vectors*. If a representation vector happens to be of the form $x = x_i + v$ where x_i is one of the reference vectors which span a space $\mathscr{L}$ and v is a random vector from R^n, then apparently x_i is not changed in a projection operation because it already lies in $\mathscr{L}$. On the other hand, since v is a general vector of R^n, it is probable that its projection is shorter. The central question is how much on the average the norm is reduced in the projection. This will be qualitatively shown for a simple distribution of v.

Consider a hypersphere with radius ρ in R^n that has a homogenous mass distribution, i.e., in which the hypothetical number of vectors or points per differential n-dimensional volume element is constant within the sphere and zero outside. The projection of the sphere on subspace $\mathscr{L}$ is obtained when every point is separately projected, and the density of the projections is computed. In order to keep track on the argumentation, it may be useful to consult the two examples of Fig. 1.15 that can be illustrated.

In Fig. 1.15a, a sphere is projected on a straight line; in Fig. 1-15b, the subspace onto which the projection is due is a plane. If the original space was n-dimensional and the subspace k-dimensional, respectively, then the set of all vectors which are orthogonal to $\mathscr{L}$ is an (n-k)-dimensional space named $\mathscr{L}^\perp$. Consider a point in $\mathscr{L}$ the distance of which from the origin is ρ_k, being less than or equal to the

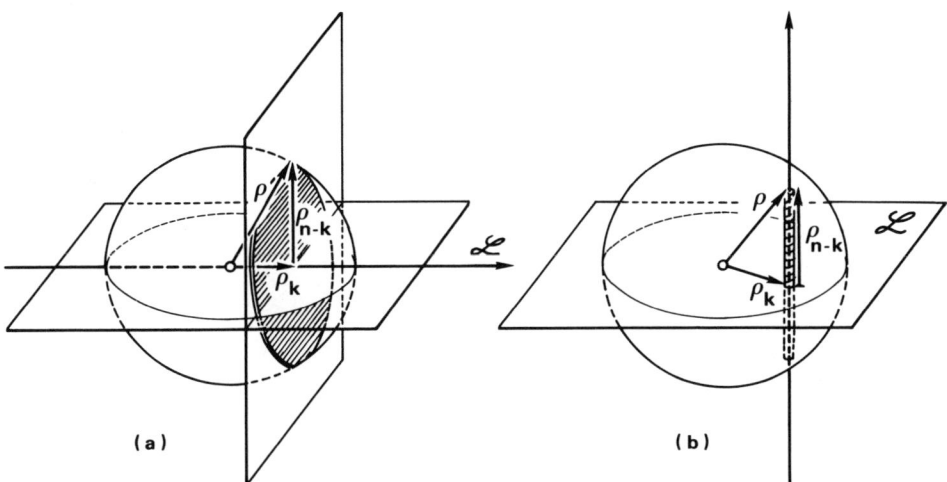

Fig. 1.15 Projections of a sphere on subspaces of R^3

radius ρ. Consider further a differential volume element dV_k in $\mathscr{L}$ at this point (line element in Fig. 1.15a, surface element in Fig. 1.15b); the *projection density* $\mu(\rho_k)$ is now defined as the number of points in a slice of the original sphere which have their projection on dV_k. Since dV_k was assumed infinitesimal, apparently the following generalized Pythagoran formula is valid (it was in fact derived in (1.6)):

$$\rho^2 = \rho_k^2 + \rho_{n-k}^2 \qquad (1.19)$$

with notations which may be obvious from Fig. 1.15. Now, although a strict mathematical proof is not given here, it may be obvious on account of spherical symmetry that the above slice of the original hypersphere is also a hypersphere, albeit of a lower dimension n-k. (It is a circular plate in Fig. 1.15a, and a line segment in Fig. 1.15b.) Consequently, the projection density on dV_k, denoted by $\mu(\rho_k)$, is obtained by using (1.17):

$$\mu(\rho_k) = \alpha_{n-k}(\rho^2 - \rho_k^2)^{\frac{n-k}{2}} . \qquad (1.20)$$

The next task is to compute the root-mean-square (rms) distance of the points of the original hypersphere from the origin, and to compare it with the corresponding rms distance of the mass projection in $\mathscr{L}$. In averaging, it should be carefully noticed that all points in $\mathscr{L}$ which have the distance ρ_k from the origin must lie on a k-dimensional spherical shell with radius ρ_k. After these considerations, the rms distances in R^n and $\mathcal{L}$, denoted by σ_n and σ_k, respectively, can be computed:

$$\sigma_k^2 = \frac{\int_0^\rho \rho_k^2 \, \mu(\rho_k) k \, \alpha_k \, \rho_k^{k-1} d\rho_k}{\int_0^\rho \mu(\rho_k) k \, \alpha_k \, \rho_k^{k-1} d\rho_k}$$

(1.21)

$$\sigma_n^2 = \frac{\int_0^\rho \rho^2 n \, \alpha_n \, \rho^{n-1} d\rho}{V_n(\rho)}$$

or, after substitution of $\zeta = \rho_k/\rho$ and some simplification,

$$\sigma_k^2 = \rho^2 \frac{\int_0^1 \zeta^{k+1} (1-\zeta^2)^{\frac{n-k}{2}} d\zeta}{\int_0^1 \zeta^{k-1} (1-\zeta^2)^{\frac{n-k}{2}} d\zeta}$$

(1.22)

$$\sigma_n^2 = \frac{n}{n+2} \rho^2 \; .$$

The numerator and denominator in σ_k^2 can be expressed in terms of the *beta function* which is defined as

$$B(a,b) = 2 \int_0^1 \zeta^{2a-1} (1-\zeta^2)^{b-1} d\zeta$$

(1.23)

whereby

$$\sigma_k^2 = \frac{B(\frac{k+2}{2}, \frac{n-k+2}{2}) \rho^2}{B(\frac{k}{2}, \frac{n-k+2}{2})} \; .$$

(1.24)

By application of the following generally known formulae

$$B(a,b) = \frac{\Gamma(a) \, \Gamma(b)}{\Gamma(a+b)} \; ,$$

$$\Gamma(a+1) = a \, \Gamma(a) \qquad (a > 0)$$

(1.25)

where $\Gamma(.)$ is the *gamma function*, there is obtained

$$\sigma_k^2 = \frac{k\rho^2}{n+2} \qquad (1.26)$$

and finally

$$\sigma_k/\sigma_n = \sqrt{k/n} \qquad (1.27)$$

The result of this analysis has even more generality because it can be shown that it holds exactly for other spherically symmetrical mass distributions, too, for instance for a spherical shell or for a multivariate symmetric Gaussian distribution. The validity for a distribution which is uniform in a hypercube centered around the origin (nonspherical case) has been demonstrated in [24]. Other nonspherical distributions give values for σ_k/σ_n which qualitatively comply with the $\sqrt{k/n}$-law.

1.3.2 Matrix Notations

Matrices, Their Sums, and Matrix Products. The concept of a matrix may be generally known. It might be necessary to point out that formally matrices are ordered sets of numbers or scalar variables indexed by a pair of indices. If index k runs through $(1,2,...p)$, ℓ through $(1,2,...,q)$, and m through $(1,2,...,r)$ the following ordered sets of elements $\alpha_{k\ell}$ and $\beta_{\ell m}$ can be named matrices. The sum of two matrices (of the same dimensionality) is a matrix in which every element is a sum of the respective elements of the addends. The *matrix product* is defined by

$$A \cdot B = C \qquad (1.28)$$

where C is a further ordered set (γ_{km}) with elements defined by

$$\gamma_{km} = \sum_{\ell=1}^{q} \alpha_{k\ell}\beta_{\ell m} \quad . \qquad (1.29)$$

The definition of the matrix product is not as arbitrary as it seems; it has been introduced for the description of linear transformations by operator products.

For brevity, the dot symbol in matrix products may be dropped. A matrix product is defined only for such pairs of indices in which an element like ℓ above is common. Multiplication by a scalar is defined as multiplication of all elements with it.

Matrix-Vector Products. A vector is an ordered set, and can be understood as a matrix with one-index elements. Consider the matrix $A = (\alpha_{k\ell})$, and four vectors $b = (\beta_k)$, $c = (\gamma_\ell)$, $d = (\delta_\ell)$, and $e = (\varepsilon_k)$, where k runs through $(1,2,\ldots,p)$ and ℓ through $(1,2,\ldots,q)$. The following matrix-vector products are then defined:

$$c = b \cdot A \text{ where } \gamma_\ell = \sum_{k=1}^{p} \beta_k \alpha_{k\ell} ,$$

$$e = A \cdot d \text{ where } \varepsilon_k = \sum_{\ell=1}^{q} \alpha_{k\ell} \delta_\ell$$

(1.30)

Notice again the compatibility of indices.

Linear Transformations. The main reason for the introduction of matrices is a possibility to denote and manipulate with linear transformation operations on vectors. The transformation of vector x into vector y is generally denoted by function $y = T(x)$. In order that T be called *linear transformation*, it is a necessary and sufficient condition that for $x_1, x_2 \in R^n$,

$$T(\alpha x_1 + \beta x_2) = \alpha T(x_1) + \beta T(x_2) .$$

(1.31)

The general linear transformation of vector $x = (\xi_1, \xi_2, \ldots, \xi_n)$ into vector $y = (\eta_1, \eta_2, \ldots, \eta_n)$ can be expressed in the element form as

$$\eta_i = \sum_{j=1}^{n} \alpha_{ij} \xi_j$$

(1.32)

with the α_{ij} parameters defining the transformation.

Eq. (1.32) can be expressed symbolically as a matrix-vector product. If A is an ordered set of parameters (α_{ij}), there follows from the above definitions that

$$y = A \cdot x .$$

(1.33)

The above definition of the matrix-vector product makes it possible to describe successive transformations by transitive operators: if $y = A \cdot x$ and $z = B \cdot y$, then $z = B \cdot A \cdot x$.

Array Representation for Matrices. For better visualization, matrices can be represented as rectangular arrays of numbers. Below, only matrices consisting of real numbers are considered. The dimensionality of a matrix is expressed by the product of rows and columns; for instance an m × n matrix has m (horizontal) rows and n (vertical) columns. Matrices are denoted by capital Roman letters, and when they are written explicitly, brackets are used around the array.

The *transpose* of any matrix is obtained by rewriting all columns as rows, whereby a notation X^T is used for the transpose of X. For instance,

$$X = \begin{bmatrix} 1 & 5 \\ 2 & 1 \\ 3 & 3 \end{bmatrix}, \quad X^T = \begin{bmatrix} 1 & 2 & 3 \\ 5 & 1 & 3 \end{bmatrix}.$$

Row and Column Vectors. Since one-row and one-column matrices are linear arrays of numbers, they can be understood as vectors, called *row* and *column vectors*, respectively. Such vectors can be denoted by lower-case letters. In a matrix-vector product, the row vector always stands on the left, and the column vector on the right. For reasons which become more apparent below, representation patterns are normally understood as column vectors. For better clarity, column vectors are normally denoted by simple lower case letters like x whereas row vectors are written in the transpose notation as x^T. Within the text, for typographic reasons, column vectors are usually written in the form $[\xi_1, \xi_2, \ldots, \xi_n]^T$ where the commas are used for clarity.

Symmetric, Diagonal, and Unit Matrices. A matrix is called symmetric if it is identical with its transpose, i.e., it is symmetric with respect to the main diagonal whereby it also must be square. A matrix is called diagonal if it has zeroes elsewhere except on the main diagonal. If all diagonal elements of a diagonal matrix are unities, the matrix is a *unit matrix*, denoted by I.

Indexing and Partitioning of the Matrices. The matrix elements, denoted by Greek letters, are identified by double indices for the rows and columns, respectively. Sometimes it will be necessary to compose a rectangular matrix from rows or columns which have a special meaning: for instance, in a so-called observation matrix X, representation vectors $x_1, x_2, \ldots x_n$ may appear as columns and the matrix can then be written as $X = [x_1 \ x_2 \ \ldots \ x_n]$.

Partitioning of the matrices can also be made more generally into rectangular submatrices. In the transposition of a partitioned matrix, the submatrices change their positions like the scalars in a normal matrix, and in addition they are transposed:

$$\begin{bmatrix} A & B \\ C & D \end{bmatrix}^T = \begin{bmatrix} A^T & C^T \\ B^T & D^T \end{bmatrix}.$$

For typographic reasons, the dotted lines are often dropped within the text and possibly replaced by a comma. For instance, an observation matrix can be written $X = [x_1, x_2, \ldots, x_n]$.

In the product of partitioned matrices, submatrices are operated according to the same rules as elements in matrix products. Submatrices then must have dimensionalities for which the matrix products are defined. For instance,

$$\begin{bmatrix} A & B \\ C & D \end{bmatrix} \begin{bmatrix} E \\ F \end{bmatrix} = \begin{bmatrix} AE + BF \\ CE + DF \end{bmatrix} .$$

Comment. It is possible to regard an m × n matrix as an element of the real space $R^{m \times n}$.

Some Formulas for Matrix Operations. In general, matrix products are not commutative, but they are associative and distributive. The following formulas can be proven when written in component form:

E 1) $IA = AI = A$
E 2) $(AB)C = A(BC)$
E 3) $A(B+C) = AB+AC$
E 4) $(A^T)^T = A$
E 5) $(A+B)^T = A^T + B^T$
E 6) $(AB)^T = B^T A^T$

It should be noticed that in a product of two matrices the former one must always have as many columns as the latter one has rows, otherwise the summation over all indices is not defined.

Hadamard Products. There exists another type of matrix product which has a simpler multiplication rule, and which has applications in some nonlinear problems. The *Hadamard product* $C = (\gamma_{ij})$ of matrices $A = (\alpha_{ij})$ and $B = (\beta_{ij})$ is defined as

$$C = A \otimes B \text{ where } \gamma_{ij} = \alpha_{ij} \beta_{ij} . \quad (1.34)$$

In other words, the respective matrix elements are mutually multiplied.

1.3.3 Further Properties of Matrices

The Range and the Null Space of a Matrix. The *range* of a matrix A is the set of vectors Ax for all values of x. This set is a linear manifold denoted $\mathcal{R}(A)$, and it is the subspace spanned by the columns of A. This can be shown by writing $A = [a_1, a_2, \ldots a_k]$ and $x = [\xi_1, \xi_2, \ldots, \xi_k]^T$ and noticing by (1.30) that

$Ax = \xi_1 a_1 + \xi_2 a_2 + \ldots + \xi_k a_k$ whereby Ax is found to be the general linear combination of the columns of A.

The *null space* of matrix A is the set of all vectors x for which $Ax = 0$. It has at least one element, namely, the zero vector. The null space is a linear manifold, too, denoted as $\mathcal{N}(A)$.

Rank of a Matrix. The rank of matrix A, abbreviated $r(A)$, is the dimensionality of the linear manifold $\mathcal{R}(A)$. Especially an $m \times n$ matrix A is said to be *of full rank* if $r(A) = \min(m,n)$. Without proof it is stated that for any matrix A,

$$r(A) = r(A^T) = r(A^T A) = r(AA^T) \ . \tag{1.35}$$

In particular, $r(A) = r(A^T A)$ implies that if the columns of A are linearly independent, then $A^T A$ is of full rank. In a similar way, $r(A^T) = r(AA^T)$ implies that if the rows of A are linearly independent, then AA^T is of full rank.

Singular Matrices. If A is a square matrix and if its null space consists of the zero vector only, then A is called *nonsingular*. A nonsingular matrix has an inverse (cf. Subsec. 1.3.4). Otherwise a square matrix A is *singular*. If $Ax = b$ is a vector equation which, when written for each element of b separately, can be regarded as a set of linear equations in the elements ξ_i of vector x, then the singularity of A means that in general a unique solution for this system of equations does not exist.

The determinant formed of the elements of a singular matrix is zero. All square matrices of the form ab^T are singular which can be easily verified when writing out its determinant explicitly.

When dealing with matrix equations, extreme care should be taken when multiplying matrix expressions by matrices which may become singular. There is a possiblility to end up with false solutions, in a similar way as when multiplying the sides of scalar equations by zeros.

Eigenvalues and Eigenvectors of Matrices. Consider a vector equation of the type

$$Ax = \lambda x \tag{1.36}$$

where A is a square matrix of dimensionality $n \times n$; any solutions for x are called the *eigenvectors* of A. Notice that the "direction" of an eigenvector corresponding to the relative magnitudes of its elements is not changed in the multiplication by A.

Eq. (1.36) is solved in the following way. Let the determinant formed of the elements of a square matrix M be denoted $|M|$. If equation $(A - \lambda I)x = 0$ must have solutions other than the trival one $x = 0$, the familiar condition known from systems of linear equations is that

$$|A - \lambda I| = 0 \ . \tag{1.37}$$

Apparently the determinant can be written in powers of λ, and (1.37) must be of the form

$$\lambda^n + \gamma_1 \lambda^{n-1} + \ldots + \gamma_n = 0 \qquad (1.38)$$

where the γ_i are parameters that depend on matrix A. This polynomial equation, also called the *characteristic equation* of A, has n roots $\lambda_1, \lambda_2, \ldots, \lambda_n$ some of which may be equal. These roots are the *eigenvalues* of A. Methods for the construction of eigenvectors can be found in numerous textbooks of linear algebra and will be skipped here. In this book an inverse problem, the construction of a matrix from a set of its eigenvectors is more central (cf. Sec. 2.3). The *spectral radius* of matrix is defined as $\rho(A) = \max_i |\lambda_i(A)|$, where the $\lambda_i(A)$ are the eigenvalues of A.

Idempotent Matrices. A matrix is called *idempotent* if $P^2 = P$; from the iterative application of this condition it follows that for any positive integer n then holds $P^n = P$. Notice that $(I - P)^2 = I - P$ whereby $I - P$ is idempotent, too. The identity matrix I is idempotent trivially. Examples of idempotent matrices which are named *projection operators* will be discussed in Subsection 1.3.5.

Positive Definite and Positive Semidefinite Matrices. If A is a square matrix and for all nonzero $x \in R^n$ there holds that the scalar expression $x^T A x$ is positive, then by definition A is *positive definite*. If $x^T A x$ is positive or zero, then A is called *positive semidefinite*. The expression $x^T A x$ is named *quadratic form* in x.

Without proof it is stated (cf. [19]) that any of the following conditions can be applied for the definition of a positive semidefinite (also named nonnegative definite) matrix, where the definition is restricted to symmetric matrices only.

F 1) $A = HH^T$ for some matrix H.
F 2) There exists a symmetric matrix R such that $R^2 = A$, whereby $R = A^{1/2}$ is the square root of A.
F 3) The eigenvalues of A are positive or zero.
F 4) $x^T A x \geq 0$, as already stated.

If A is further nonsingular, it is positive definite.

Positive semidefinite matrices occur, for instance, in linear transformations. Consider the transformation $y = Mx$ which yields a vector; the inner product $(y,y) = y^T y$ must be nonnegative, whereby $x^T M^T M x$ is nonnegative, and $M^T M$ is a positive semidefinite matrix for any M.

Elementary Matrices. There exist matrices which have been used extensively in the solution of systems of linear equations and also occur in the projection operations discussed in this book. They are named *elementary matrices*, and in general, they are of the form $(I - uv^T)$ where u and v are column vectors of the same dimensionality.

In this book elementary matrices of the form $U = I - \alpha uu^T$, where $\alpha \in R$, $u \in R^n$, are applied. In the case that $\alpha = (u^T u)^{-1}$, U is idempotent and its null space, denoted as $\mathcal{N}(U) = \mathcal{L}(u)$, is the straight line spanned by u. The range of U is $\mathcal{R}(U) = \mathcal{L}^\perp(u)$.

Matrix Norms. The norm of a matrix can be defined in different ways, and apparently it must satisfy the general requirements imposed on the norm in any set. The *Euclidean matrix norm* is by definition the square root of the sum of squares of its elements.

The *trace* of a square matrix S, denoted tr(S), is defined as the sum of all diagonal elements. The Euclidean norm of any matrix A is then easily found, by writing out explicitly by elements, to be $\|A\|_E = \sqrt{tr(A^T A)}$.

Another definition of matrix norm which is different from the Euclidean norm can be derived from any definition of vector norm denoted by $\|\cdot\|$. Such a matrix norm is said to be consistent with the vector norm, and the definition reads

$$\|A\| = \max_{\|x\|=1} \|Ax\| \ . \tag{1.39}$$

Notice that the Euclidean matrix norm is not consistent with the Euclidean vector norm.

1.3.4 Matrix Equations

Inverse of a Matrix. The usual definition of the inverse of a (square) matrix A, denoted by A^{-1}, is that $A A^{-1} = A^{-1} A = I$. In order that A^{-1} exist, A must be nonsingular.

Determination of the inverse of a matrix can be made in many different ways. In elementary matrix algebra it is frequently made by the determinant method. An alternative is the following: consider the solution of the matrix equation $AX = I$ where it is assumed that A is square and of full rank. If X and I are written in partitioned forms $X = [x_1, x_2, \ldots, x_n]$ and $I = [e_1, e_2, \ldots, e_n]$ then, according to the rules of matrix multiplication, the matrix equation is obviously equivalent to a set of vector equations

$$Ax_k = e_k \text{ for } k = 1, 2, \ldots, n \ . \tag{1.40}$$

Take one of these equations and write it explicitly. For every fixed k this is a system of linear equations in n unknown scalar variables $\xi_{1k}, \xi_{2k}, \ldots, \xi_{nk}$:

$$\sum_{j=1}^{n} \alpha_{jk} \xi_{jk} = \varepsilon_{ik} \text{ for } k = 1, 2, \ldots, n \ . \tag{1.41}$$

Each of these systems of equations has a unique solution if and only if the determinant of the coefficients α_{ij}, or $|A|$, is nonzero. The solution can be carried out, for instance, by the Gauss elimination method. In this way there is obtained a solution for every x_k separately which together constitute matrix X. This procedure, however, yields only the so-called *right inverse* of A. The *left inverse* is obtained by solving the matrix equation $XA = I$. The right and left inverses, however, will be found identical for a nonsingular matrix, and denoted by $X = A^{-1}$.

The Matrix Inversion Lemma. The following identity, usually called *matrix inversion lemma*, is frequently utilized in regression, estimation, and related problems. Assume that A and C are arbitrary matrices for which the inverses exist and B is a further matrix such that BCB^T has the same dimensionality as A. Then identically

$$(A + BCB^T)^{-1} = A^{-1} - A^{-1}B(B^TA^{-1}B + C^{-1})^{-1} B^TA^{-1} . \qquad (1.42)$$

The proof follows after multiplication of the right-hand side by $A + BCB^T$ and regrouping of the terms (hint: $B(\ )^{-1} \equiv BCC^{-1}(\ )^{-1}$), whereby I results. Notice that usually C is of lower dimensionality than A whereby the computation of C^{-1} is lighter that that of A^{-1}.

The Pseudoinverse. Suppose that A and B are general rectangular matrices. Then, apparently, the above methods for the solution of matrix equations of the type $Ax = c$ or $x^TB = c^T$ do not apply even if it were assumed that solutions exist; moreover, the case must be considered that there do not exist any solutions. All such cases shall be discussed within the context of matrix equations of the form $AXB = C$. For their treatment, however, the concept of pseudoinverse, or the Moore-Penrose generalized inverse [27,28] must first be introduced.

By definition, X is the *pseudoinverse* of matrix A (with real or complex elements) if all of the following conditions are valid:

G 1) $AXA = A$
G 2) $XAX = X$
G 3) AX and XA are Hermitian matrices

where a *Hermitian* matrix is defined as one having the property that it is identical with the complex conjugate of its transpose. The complex conjugate of a complex matrix has elements which are complex conjugates of the original elements. For a real matrix, the property of being Hermitian simply means that the matrix is *symmetric*.

It can be shown that *there exists a unique pseudoinverse for every matrix*. Although pseudoinverses are very fundamental to many sections of this book, the above existence theorem is skipped and the reader is asked to consult the original work of PENROSE [27], or some textbooks [19-21]. It may here suffice to point out how pseudoinverses can be constructed, and to find out that the constructions fulfil the definition.

A Preliminary Example of Pseudoinverse; Vector Equation. Consider the vector equation

$$Ax = b \qquad (1.43)$$

where A is an m × n matrix, and x,b are column vectors, $x \in R^n$, $b \in R^m$. Suppose that $r(A) = m \leq n$. It can be proven by substitution in (1.43) that the following expression constitutes the solution:

$$x = A^T(AA^T)^{-1}b + (I - A^T(AA^T)^{-1}A)y \qquad (1.44)$$

where y is an arbitrary vector of the same dimensionality as x.

The condition $r(A) = m$ implies that AA^T which is an m × m matrix then has an inverse and x is immediately conceived as a solution; the fact that the solution is also general will become more obvious below.

The expression $A^T(AA^T)^{-1}$ will now be shown to comply with the definition of pseudoinverse. If it is tentatively denoted by X, then $AXA = A$ and $XAX = X$ are immediately found valid. Since $AX = I$, this expression is symmetric. To show that XA is symmetric, one further identity of usual matrix inverses is needed, namely, for any matrix A^{-1}, there holds $(A^{-1})^T = (A^T)^{-1}$. The simplest proof of this formula follows by noticing that $(A^{-1})^T$ is the solution of $XA^T = (AX)^T = I$. By the application of this identity to X^T it is found that $(XA)^T = A^T X^T = AX$, which completes the proof for that X is the pseudoinverse of A, of course provided that $r(A) = m$ as assumed.

In an analogous way it can be shown that if $r(A) = n \leq m$, then the expression $(A^T A)^{-1} A^T$ is the pseudoinverse of A. For the rank $r(A) = n < m$, however, the above vector equation (1.43) does not always have a solution.

Some Basic Formulas for Pseudoinverses. If α is a scalar, its pseudoinverse, denoted by α^+, is

$$\alpha^+ = \begin{cases} \alpha^{-1} & \text{if } \alpha \neq 0, \\ 0 & \text{if } \alpha = 0, \end{cases} \qquad (1.45)$$

which can directly be verified by the definitions. From this simplest case one fundamental property of the pseudoinverse can be seen; the pseudoinverse in general is not a continuous function of the original matrix; in the scalar case, for instance, it makes an infinitely high jump when $\alpha \to 0$.

The pseudoinverse of a general vector a can be expressed in simple forms, too, as seen when substituting these forms into the definitions. Denoting the pseudoinverse by a^+,

$$a^+ = \begin{cases} a^T/a^Ta & \text{if a is a nonzero vector,} \\ 0^T & \text{(zero vector) otherwise.} \end{cases} \tag{1.46}$$

For a general matrix A, either of the following formulas yields the correct expression for the pseudoinverse, denoted by A^+. Sometimes these formulas have been used for the definition of pseudoinverses [19]:

$$\begin{aligned} A^+ &= \lim_{\delta \to 0} (A^TA + \delta^2 I)^{-1} A^T \\ &= \lim_{\delta \to 0} A^T(AA^T + \delta^2 I)^{-1}. \end{aligned} \tag{1.47}$$

The proof will be omitted here. Notice that these expressions exist even if A^TA and AA^T do not have inverses. If the columns of A are linearly independent, then δ in the upper expression can immediately be put zero since $(A^TA)^{-1}$ then exists. If the rows of A are linearly independent, δ can be put zero in the lower expression.

A diagonal matrix can be denoted as diag $(\alpha_1, \alpha_2, \ldots, \alpha_n)$ where the α-parameters are its diagonal elements. Since the product rules for diagonal matrices are simple, it can be seen from the definition of pseudoinverses that

$$[\text{diag}(\alpha_1, \alpha_2, \ldots, \alpha_n)]^+ = \text{diag}(\alpha_1^+, \alpha_2^+, \ldots, \alpha_n^+). \tag{1.48}$$

The Theorem of Greville. There exist several methods for the computation of the pseudoinverse of a general matrix [19,20]. Some of them use library programs of large computer systems. One nice compromise between computational efficiency and programming simplicity is the recursive algorithm known as *Greville's theorem.* The idea is to partition the original matrix into columns and recruit them one at a time, thereby computing the pseudoinverse of the new submatrix from the already computed pseudoinverse of a smaller submatrix and the new column ([23]; cf. also [22, 78]).

If a matrix A, with k columns, is denoted by A_k and partitioned as $A_k = [A_{k-1} \vdots a_k]$, with A_{k-1} a matrix having k-1 columns, then the theorem of Greville states:

$$A_k^+ = \begin{bmatrix} A_{k-1}^+ (I - a_k p_k^T) \\ \hline p_k^T \end{bmatrix}$$

where

$$p_k = \begin{cases} \dfrac{(I - A_{k-1}A_{k-1}^+)a_k}{\|(I - A_{k-1}A_{k-1}^+)a_k\|^2} & \text{if the numerator is} \neq 0 \\[2ex] \dfrac{(A_{k-1}^+)^T A_{k-1}^+ a_k}{1 + \|A_{k-1}^+ a_k\|^2} & \text{otherwise.} \end{cases} \quad (1.49)$$

The initial value A_1 is equal to the first column of A whereby $A_1^+ = a_1^T(a_1^T a_1)^{-1}$, provided that a_1 is a nonzero vector; if a_1 is a zero vector, then $A_1^+ = 0^T$.

The proof of this theorem is a bit elaborate and will be omitted. It may be carried out by a direct substitution in the definition of pseudoinverse.

Some Useful Identities. A few formulas for the manipulation with pseudoinverses are listed below. For complex matrices, these formulas are valid if the transpose is replaced by the complex conjugate of the transpose.

H 1) $\quad 0^+ = 0^T$ $\qquad$ (0 is a matrix full of zeroes)
H 2) $\quad (A^+)^+ = A$
H 3) $\quad (A^T)^+ = (A^+)^T$
H 4) $\quad (\alpha A)^+ = \alpha^{-1} A^+$ $\qquad$ if $\alpha \neq 0$
H 5) $\quad A^+ = (A^T A)^+ A^T = A^T (AA^T)^+$
H 6) $\quad A^+ = A^{-1}$ $\qquad$ if A is square and nonsingular
H 7) $\quad A^+ = (A^T A)^{-1} A^T$ $\qquad$ if the columns of A are linearly independent
H 8) $\quad A^+ = A^T (AA^T)^{-1}$ $\qquad$ if the rows of A are linearly independent
H 9) $\quad \mathcal{R}(A^+) = \mathcal{R}(A^T)$
H 10) $\quad r(A^+) = r(A) = r(A^T)$
H 11) $\quad A^T A A^+ = A^T$
H 12) $\quad (A^+)^T A^T A = A$
H 13) $\quad A^+ A A^T = A^T$
H 14) $\quad A A^T (A^+)^T = A$

Solution of the Matrix Equation $AXB = C$. Consider the matrix equation given in the heading; A, B, and C may have any dimensionalities for which the matrix products are defined. It is first claimed that a necessary and sufficient condition for this equation to have solutions is that

$$AA^+ C B^+ B = C . \quad (1.50)$$

At first glimpse this seems a severe restriction. We shall see below, however (cf. Subsec. 1.3.5), that if the rows of any matrix A are linearly independent, then $AA^+ = I$; and if the columns of any matrix B are linearly independent, then $B^+ B = I$.

The validity of both of these conditions already guarantees the existence of solutions to AXB = C, and the condition stated in (1.50) is in fact still milder. To show that (1.50) is a necessary condition, suppose that X is a solution. Using the definition of pseudoinverse, it is then found that $C = AXB = AA^+AXBB^+B = AA^+CB^+B$; the existence of a solution thus implies (1.50). To show that (1.50) is a sufficient condition, there is found a particular solution, namely, A^+CB^+, implicit in the condition itself.

The most important task, however, is to solve the equation. It is known from the theory of linear equations that the general solution is obtained if a) one particular solution is found and b) the general solution of the corresponding homogeneous equation (AXB = 0) is then added to it. Now A^+CB^+ was shown to be a particular solution; and by the identity $M = MM^+M$ for any matrix M, all expressions of the form $Y - A^+AYBB^+$ for an arbitrary Y of the same dimensionality as X are found to be solutions of the homogenous equation. On the other hand, the identity $X = X - A^+AXBB^+$ (for AXB = 0) implies that if X is any solution of the homogenous equation, it is *of the form* $Y - A^+AYBB^+$. Consequently, the general solution of the original equation must then be of the form

$$X = A^+CB^+ + Y - A^+AYBB^+ . \qquad (1.51)$$

The above result is due to PENROSE [27].

The Minimum-Norm Solution of AXB = C. In the case that there are many solutions to the above equation, the one with minimum norm is of particular interest. Consider the following identity

$$\| A^+C B^+ + Y - A^+AYBB^+ \|_E^2 = \|A^+CB^+\|_E^2 + \|Y - A^+AYBB^+\|_E^2 . \qquad (1.52)$$

For the proof of (1.52), the following hint is given. Both sides are first written in explicit matrix form. Let us recall that the Euclidean matrix norm of any matrix A is $\sqrt{tr(A^TA)}$. To show that the trace of the terms on the left-hand side in excess to those shown on the right is zero, the recently established Identities H 11 and H 12 are first applied where possible. Next, the generally valid identity $tr(PQ) = tr(QP)$ is utilized in order to facilitate the application of Identities H 13 and H 14. Since the norms are always positive semidefinite, it is then possible to write

$$\| A^+CB^+ \|_E \leq \|A^+CB^+ + Y - A^+AYBB^+\|_E , \qquad (1.53)$$

the strict equality holding for Y = 0. Therefore, the minimum-norm solution of AXB = C is $X = A^+CB^+$.

The Best Approximate Solution of a Matrix Equation. A solution to any task can be "best" only in the sense of a chosen criterion. If a matrix equation $F(X) = 0$, where F is a matrix-valued function, does not have solutions, substitution of a value $X = X_0$ yields the residual $F(X_0)$ for which the minimum may be sought. The minimum for a matrix can be expressed in terms of any norm. Two cases may now occur:
1) There is a unique value X_0 which yields the minimum, e.g., $\|F(X)\| \geq \|F(X_0)\|$ the strict inequality holding for $X \neq X_0$. Then X_0 is called the best approximate solution of $F(X) = 0$. 2) There are many, perhaps infinitely many values of X for which the equality in the above condition holds; they are all named approximate solutions. The *best approximate solution* X_0^* is then defined as the minimum-norm approximate solution; $\|X_0\| \geq \|X_0^*\|$.

The Best Approximate Solution of XA = B. In another work [28], PENROSE has pointed out that the best approximate solution of $AXB = C$ in the sense of Euclidean matrix norm for the case in which exact solutions do not exist is $X_0 = A^+CB^+$. For the purpose of this text, a derivation is carried out for the matrix equation $XA = B$ which occurs in the associative mappings (Sec. 2.3).

When the Euclidean norm of $XA - B$ is to be minimized, an equivalent task is to minimize $tr(R)$ where $R = (XA - B)(XA - B)^T$. To solve this problem, the following trick is used: it can be verified, by the application of Identities H 13 and H 14 of Subsection 1.3.4 that R may be written in the form

$$R = (BA^+ - X)AA^T(BA^+ - X)^T + B(I - A^+A)B^T \quad . \tag{1.54}$$

Now $(BA^+ - X)AA^T(BA^+ - X)^T$ is positive semidefinite on account of its form, and $tr(BA^+ - X)AA^T(BA^+ - X)^T$ becomes zero for $X = BA^+$. This must then be its minimum. On the other hand, since R in this problem is always positive definite, then $B(I - A^+A)B^T$ is positive definite, and $X = BA^+$ has thereby been shown to minimize $tr(R)$, or the Euclidean norm of the residual $XA - B$.

1.3.5 Projection Operators

It will be shown that the decomposition of an arbitrary vector $x \in R^n$ into its orthogonal projections $\hat{x} \in \mathscr{L} \subset R^n$ and $\tilde{x} \perp \mathscr{L}$ can be expressed in terms of linear transformations whereby there always exists a symmetric matrix P such that $\hat{x} = Px$, $\tilde{x} = (I - P)x$. Then P is called the orthogonal projection operator on $\mathscr{L}$, and $I - P$ the orthogonal projection operator on the space $\mathscr{L}^\perp$ that is the orthogonal complement of $\mathscr{L}$. Let us recall that $\mathscr{L}^\perp$ was defined as the set of all vectors in R^n which are orthogonal to $\mathscr{L}$.

Consider the matrix X with $x_1, x_2, \ldots, x_k$, $k < n$ its columns. The vectors $x_i \in R^n$, $i = 1, 2, \ldots, k$ shall span the space $\mathscr{L}$. The decomposition $x = \hat{x} + \tilde{x}$ is unique and $\tilde{x}$

may be determined by the condition that it must be orthogonal to all columns of X or,

$$\tilde{x}^T X = 0 \qquad (1.55)$$

under the normalizing condition $(x,\tilde{x}) = (\tilde{x},\tilde{x})$ which directly follows from the orthogonality of $\tilde{x}$ and $\hat{x}$. The Penrose solution of (1.55) for $\tilde{x}^T$ is

$$\tilde{x}^T = y^T(I - XX^+) \qquad (1.56)$$

with y an arbitrary vector of the same dimensionality as $\tilde{x}$. Using the symmetry of XX^+ and the properties of pseudoinverse, the following derivation then follows:

$$x^T\tilde{x} = x^T(I - XX^+)y = \tilde{x}^T\tilde{x} = y^T(I - XX^+)^2 y = y^T(I - XX^+)y \quad . \qquad (1.57)$$

Now y = x is a possible choice whereby

$$\tilde{x} = (I - XX^+)x \quad . \qquad (1.58)$$

Because $\tilde{x}$ is unique, then $I - P = I - XX^+$, and $P = XX^+$.

The above orthogonal projection operators are found symmetric and idempotent. In general, a matrix is called *projection matrix* if it is idempotent (although it were not symmetric).

If it is denoted $X^T = Y$, then the rows of Y are the columns of X. The projection operator on the space spanned by the rows of Y is

$$I - XX^+ = I - Y^T(Y^T)^+ = I - Y^T(Y^+)^T = (I - Y^+Y)^T = I - Y^+Y$$

where the last result follows from the symmetry of Y^+Y. We are now in a position to state the following rule: XX^+ is the orthogonal projection operator on the space spanned by the columns of X, and X^+X the orthogonal projection operator on the space spanned by the rows of X. The matrices $I - XX^+$ and $I - X^+X$ are the orthogonal projection operators on the spaces which are the orthogonal complements of the column space and the row space of X, respectively.

Computational Forms of Orthogonal Projection Operators. If it becomes necessary to express the projection operators in explicit forms, any pseudoinverse algorithm can be applied. A simple formula can be derived from Greville's theorem: if X_k is a matrix with $x_1, x_2, \ldots, x_k$ its columns, and it is partitioned as $[X_{k-1} \vdots x_k]$, it then follows from (1.49) that

$$X_k X_k^+ = X_{k-1} X_{k-1}^+ (I - x_k p_k^T) + x_k p_k^T \qquad (1.59)$$

where p_k is the expression in (1.49) with the a-vectors replaced by the corresponding x-vectors. If now $(I - X_{k-1} X_{k-1}^+) x_k$ is a zero vector, the above formula yields $X_k X_k^+ = X_{k-1} X_{k-1}^+$; for a nonzero vector, the upper expression of p_k holds, whence for both cases it can be written

$$I - X_k X_k^+ = (I - X_{k-1} X_{k-1}^+) - \frac{(I - X_{k-1} X_{k-1}^+) x_k x_k^T (I - X_{k-1} X_{k-1}^+)}{\|(I - X_{k-1} X_{k-1}^+) x_k\|^2} \qquad (1.60)$$

It should be noticed that $I - X_{k-1} X_{k-1}^+$ is the orthogonal projection operator on the space that is orthogonal to the space spanned by the $x_1 \ldots x_{k-1}$; $I - X_k X_k^+$ is the corresponding projection operator with $x_1 \ldots x_k$ the spanning vectors. Eq. (1.60) can be put into a form

$$\phi_k = \phi_{k-1} - \frac{\tilde{x}_k \tilde{x}_k^T}{\|\tilde{x}_k\|^2} \qquad (1.61)$$

where

$$\tilde{x}_k = \phi_{k-1} x_k \qquad (1.62)$$

and the recursion starts with $\phi_0 = I$. After k steps, the orthogonal projection operator on $\mathcal{R}(X_k)$ is $P = I - \phi_k$.

The above algorithm also results from the Gram-Schmidt orthogonalization formulae written as

$$\tilde{x}_1 = x_1$$
$$\tilde{x}_k = x_k - \sum_{j=1}^{k-1} \frac{\tilde{x}_j (\tilde{x}_j^T x_k)}{\|\tilde{x}_j\|^2} \qquad k = 2, 3, \ldots \qquad (1.63)$$

where the sum is taken over those indices j that correspond to nonzero $\tilde{x}_j$. Eqs. (1.63) directly yield (1.61) and (1.62) when it is denoted

$$I - \sum_{j=1}^{k-1} \frac{\tilde{x}_j \tilde{x}_j^T}{\|\tilde{x}_j\|^2} = \phi_{k-1} \;, \qquad (1.64)$$

and

$$\tilde{x}_k = \phi_{k-1} x_k \quad . \tag{1.65}$$

A further formula is useful, too: if q_j, $j = 1,2,\ldots,k$ are *orthonormal basis vectors* of $\mathcal{R}(X_k)$, i.e., they are orthogonal and of unit norm and span the space $\mathcal{R}(X_k)$, then

$$X_k X_k^+ = \sum_{j=1}^{k} q_j q_j^T \tag{1.66}$$

which directly follows from (1.61).

Fourier Expansion. By writing

$$x = \hat{x} + \tilde{x} = \sum_{j=1}^{k} (q_j, x) q_j + \tilde{x} \quad , \tag{1.67}$$

vector x has been expanded in terms of orthogonal "functions" q_j and a residual $\tilde{x}$ the norm of which is minimized. This is the general form of *Fourier expansion* for vector functions, and the (q_j, x) are named the Fourier components of x.

1.3.6 Matrix Differential Calculus

It was demonstrated above that the existence of solutions to algebraic matrix equations may be more problematic than in the scalar case. In the similar way it may be expected that matrix differential equations behave differently from the scalar equations. This is due to several reasons: matrix products in general do not commute, matrices may become singular, and first of all, a matrix differential equation is a system of coupled equations of the matrix elements whereby stability conditions are more complicated. Extreme care should therefore be taken when dealing with matrix differential equations.

Derivatives of Matrices. If the matrix elements are functions of a scalar variable, for instance time, then the derivative of a matrix is obtained by taking the derivatives of the elements. For instance, for a matrix A,

$$A = \begin{bmatrix} a_{11} & a_{12} \\ a_{21} & a_{22} \end{bmatrix}, \quad dA/dt = \begin{bmatrix} da_{11}/dt & da_{12}/dt \\ da_{21}/dt & da_{22}/dt \end{bmatrix} . \tag{1.68}$$

Partial derivatives of a matrix are obtained by taking the partial derivatives of the elements.

In the differentiation of products of matrices and other matrix functions, the noncommutativity must be kept in mind. For instance,

$$d(AB)/dt = (dA/dt)B + A(dB/dt) \ . \tag{1.69}$$

This restriction is important in the derivatives of the powers of matrices: e.g., if A is square,

$$dA^3/dt = d(A \cdot A \cdot A)/dt = (dA/dt)A^2 + A(dA/dt)A + A^2(dA/dt) \ , \tag{1.70}$$

and in general the above form cannot be simplified because the terms are not combinable.

The formulas of derivatives of general integral powers are found if the following fact is considered: if A^{-1} exists whereby $AA^{-1} = I$, then it must hold

$$d(AA^{-1})/dt = (dA/dt)A^{-1} + A(dA^{-1}/dt) = 0 \quad \text{(the zero matrix)};$$

$$dA^{-1}/dt = - A^{-1}(dA/dt)A^{-1} \ . \tag{1.71}$$

In general it is obtained:

$$dA^n/dt = \sum_{i=0}^{n-1} A^i (dA/dt) A^{n-i-1} \quad \text{when } n \geq 1 \ ,$$

$$dA^{-n}/dt = \sum_{i=1}^{n} -A^{-i}(dA/dt)A^{i-n-1} \quad \text{when } n \geq 1, \ |A| \neq 0 \ . \tag{1.72}$$

The *gradient* of a scalar is a vector. In matrix calculus, the gradient operator is a column vector of differential operators of the form

$$\nabla_x = [\partial/\partial \xi_1, \partial/\partial \xi_2, \ldots, \partial/\partial \xi_n]^T \ , \tag{1.73}$$

and differentiation of a scalar α is formally equivalent to a matrix product of vector ∇_x and α:

$$\nabla_x \alpha = [\partial \alpha/\partial \xi_1, \partial \alpha/\partial \xi_2, \ldots, \partial \alpha/\partial \xi_n]^T \ . \tag{1.74}$$

If a scalar-valued function is a function of vector x, then the differentation rules are most easily found when writing by elements, e.g.,

$$\nabla_x(x^T x) = [\partial/\partial\xi_1, \partial/\partial\xi_2, \ldots, \partial/\partial\xi_n]^T (\xi_1^2 + \xi_2^2 + \ldots + \xi_n^2)$$
$$= 2x \ . \tag{1.75}$$

Since ∇_x is a vector, it is applicable to all row vectors of arbitrary dimensionality, whereby a matrix results. For instance, $\nabla_x x^T = I$. In some cases it is applicable to products of vectors or vectors and matrices if the expression has the same dimensionality as that of a scalar or row vector. The following examples can be proven when writing by elements: if a and b are functions of x, and p and q are constants,

$$\nabla_x[a^T(x)b(x)] = [\nabla_x a^T(x)]b(x) + [\nabla_x b^T(x)]a(x) \ , \tag{1.76}$$

$$\nabla_x(p^T x) = p \ , \tag{1.77}$$

$$\nabla_x(x^T q) = q \ . \tag{1.78}$$

Consider a quadratic form $Q = a^T(x) \psi a(x)$ where ψ is symmetric. Then

$$\nabla_x Q = 2 [\nabla_x a^T(x)] \psi a(x) \tag{1.79}$$

which can be proven by writing $\psi = \psi^{1/2} \psi^{1/2}$, whereby $\psi^{1/2}$ is symmetric.

Chapter 2
Associative Search Methods

2.1 Addressing by the Contents

"Names, to name effectively, must stand still, and so must the entities they name."
(Aristotle)

As the digital computers have become indispensable tools in various tasks involving intelligent operations, one would have expected that their basic functional principles had acquired features from natural information processing. But although computers are extremely effective in numerical and Boolean computing and inference on the basis of deterministic set relations, their efficiency is severely impaired if the data are incomplete or ill-defined; biological systems, however, are well-trained to deal with incomplete information. The primary reason for the inferiority of computers in this respect lies in the discrete representation of information. In most cases the computing operations cannot be executed effectively by means of machine instructions unless the variables are identifiable on the basis of unique names or codes; even minor errors in the representations may break down the computing processes.

Another characteristic limitation of the digital computers is their memory organization. The principle of local or addressable storage restricts the representations of the primary data to lists, tables, and elementary cross-references between them. More complex relational structures (such as the representations of knowledge in associative memory) must be managed by sophisticated programming techniques. Large hardware constructs for associative or content-addressable memory have not been realized; almost all data banks with partial associative access have been implemented by software.

If it is possible to rest content with variables with unique names, then their values can be stored in memory locations the addresses of which are obtained from the names by the application of some simple and fast algorithm; all names are mapped onto the set of available memory addresses by the same algorithm, in a one-to-one fashion. Every particular item, together with other items connected with it, is then accessible if the same algorithm is applied to the search argument. This principle works in memory systems of almost arbitrary size, and the search process very much resembles associative recall. This kind of encoding of data by its content has turned out to be effective in the management of large archives and data bases, and in the implementation of interpreters and translators for high-level programming languages where large symbol tables must be kept up [31-37].

2.1.1 Hash-Coding Principles

Methods of storing data sets in conventional addressed computer memories in such a way that they can be rapidly accessed by symbolic names have been studied since the introduction of the first powerful computers [35]. The basic principle underlying these methods that are named *hash-coding*, *hash-addressing*, *scatter addressing*, etc., is to store a data set at an address which is a function of its symbolic name, or of a specified portion of the data set itself used as the search argument. If there is a need to encode a data set by several alternative names, a separate address can be computed for each of them, and duplicates of the data set can be stored at all the computed addresses. In this way, for instance, the searching for documents on the basis of alternative descriptors becomes feasible. Instead of storing a large data set at several locations, it may be stored at one location only, but the address of this location (*pointer*) is stored at all computed addresses corresponding to the different names; during search, when the pointer is read out, the location of the data set is immediately known.

A problem which is characteristic of all programmed content-addressing methods is the occurrence of an event called *collision*. Let s_1 and s_2 be two different search arguments, and let $f(s_1)$ and $f(s_2)$ be the computed addresses, respectively. It would be desirable that $f(s_1) \neq f(s_2)$, and this indeed happens with a high probability if function f is such that it scatters the computed addresses at random, and if the number of available memory locations is much larger than the number of all occurring search arguments. In principle, however, there is always a finite nonzero probability for the occurrence $f(s_1) = f(s_2)$ which is the collision. A remedy is now to store one of the colliding data sets, usually the latter one, at a reserve location which is determined by some rule relative to the computed address; very often the address next to the computed address will do. If there is a stored item at this reserve location, then the next address is taken, etc. It is necessary to have some kind of marker, e.g., an extra bit in the memory locations which is turned on when the location is occupied by a stored item. As long as the available memory space is not filled up, the process of finding an empty location converges. The last reserve location in a chain of reserve addresses must be marked somehow, too. A new problem arises when a search is to be performed: how can it be known which one of the stored data sets resides at the computed address, and what is there in the reserve locations? The simplest solution is to have an additional field in every memory location in which copies of the associated search arguments $s_1, s_2, \ldots$, called *tags*, are stored. If the data set now resides at the computed address, a tag identical with the search argument is found from the computed address; unless this is true, the reserve locations are studied until a tag is found which agrees with the search argument, or until the stop marker is found.

The efficiency of the algorithm used for the computation of the content-addressing function f depends on two factors: computational simplicity, especially if the memory is accessed frequently, and the uniformity by which the algorithm spreads the computed addresses over the available memory space. Both of these depend on the type of search arguments, and no general criteria can be given.

One of the oldest hashing algorithms and by far the simplest one is the *hash-bit extraction*. Let us assume that the available memory space consists of 2^N locations the addresses of which can be defined by N-bit binary numbers. The digital representations of the search arguments shall be strings of M bits. It is desirable to choose the names in a random way, and M should be much greater than N. The computed address is now formed by extracting the values of N bits from the M-bit representation at predetermined bit positions, and concatenating these bits into a single binary number, the N-bit address. The associated data set is now stored at this address or at its reserve locations. The hash bit extraction is so simple that special hardware for its implementation is easily added to conventional computers. Its drawback is that the distribution of the computed addresses sometimes may not be very uniform.

Examples of Hashing Algorithms.

Because of the practical importance of hash-coding, some generally used hashing algorithms are reviewed here in more detail.

Hashing Algorithm 1. This is in fact one version of hash-bit extraction. Let us assume that programmers have an affection for "natural" names for data sets. Therefore, the statistical distribution of the beginnings and endings of search arguments is expected to be very uneven. When the alphabetical representation is replaced by character codes and the latter are concatenated into a binary string, the bits chosen for the address must be extracted from positions in the middle part of the string.

Hashing Algorithm 2. If the search arguments consist of several words, a better algorithm than the former one is based on the so-called multiplicative congruence. Assuming that each word has a numerical value in some representation, the product of these values is first formed. The smallest positive residue modulo 2^N of the product is then used for the N-bit address. This method can also be applied to single-word arguments multiplying them by a large, suitably chosen constant and extracting specified bits from the product. Sometimes this procedure might be improved by first adding a numerical constant to the word or words before multiplication.

Hashing Algorithm 3. In order to obtain an N-bit calculated address for an argument string of variable length, the string is first divided into N-bit sections and the modulo 2^N sum of these sections is then used as the calculated address.

Hashing Algorithm 4. The digital representation of the search argument, understood as an integer, is divided by the number of locations of the available memory space, n. The remainder which is an integer from the range [0,n-1] is then used as the computed address. This method is not restricted to tables whose size is a power of two, and it may be implemented moderately fast in machines having a fast fixed-point division algorithm.

Handling of Collisions

When a collision between computed addresses occurs, another location must be found for one of the entries by a trial-and-error method. If the first trial fails, the search must be continued, and so on. This procedure is called *probing*, and the first, second, etc., reserve locations for a computed address must be determined by a unique algorithm which is applied during the storing process as well as in the retrieval. The efficiency of hash-coding depends not only on the hashing algorithm but on the probing, too. It can be shown for the collision handling methods reviewed in this chapter that if the memory is no more than half full, the average number of look-ups for a data set does not exceed 1.5 (including the first look-up at the computed address).

There are two principal algorithms in use to probe for a reserve location. In the simpler one, called *linear probing*, the reserve location is the one next to the computed address, and if it is occupied, the probing is continued with the location next to it, etc. The second method, called *random probing*, makes use of pseudo-random numbers which are added to the computed address. These are numbers that are generated by special arithmetic algorithms, and they are distributed almost uniformly over a given range of numbers; the number sequence appears fairly random. A property of pseudo-random numbers is that, when initialized with a fixed number, the same sequence is always obtained. Therefore, the order of a number in a pseudo-random sequence uniquely defines the number itself.

Let us denote a pseudo-random number (an integer) generated at the kth step by $R^{(k)}$. The following formula generates an almost uniform distribution of these numbers on the range [0,c]:

$$R^{(k+1)} = (a R^{(k)} + b) \bmod c \qquad (2.1)$$

where a and b are suitably chosen constants. For less stringent requirements, b can be dropped.

Some improvement in the uniformity of the distribution is obtained by the following modified formula, with c a power of two, and d another small power of two, e.g., d = 4:

$$R^{(k+1)} = integer \{d^{-1} (a R^{(k)} + b) \mod cd\} \ . \tag{2.2}$$

Deletion of Items from Memory

If a hash-coded memory is maintained for a long time, sooner or later there comes a need to delete useless items in order to give room for new ones. Useless data also delay the search process unnecessarily. In the hash-addressing scheme, deletion of items causes extra problems because if a memory location is marked empty, probing is stopped at it and there is no access to the reserve locations behind it. For this reason, the gap in the chain of reserve addresses must be closed up by moving the latter items one step upwards in the chain. This operation is easily implemented with linear probing but moving items in a randomly probed store may be a cumbersome task, because the pseudo-random number algorithms usually do not work in the reverse direction. If there is no lack of space but one wants to avoid unnecessary search operations, the empty locations may be retained in the chain, and skipped during probing. For this end, a special marker can be used to denote whether a location, when found empty, is followed by other items or not. Such a marked location can be used as a new computed address, too, and its reserve locations are those that are appended to the old chain of reserve locations.

Linked-List Organization in Hash-Addressing

With minor expenditures in additional memory space, and using only a few rearrangement operations during storage, the search process can be made significantly faster by the application of the so-called *linked-list* organization of the reserve locations. In this organization, an additional field in every memory location is reserved for an extra pointer. This is the address at which the next item in the chain can be found and immediately read out. When data sets are stored in the memory, the pointers of the reserve locations are constructed by the probing program. So, instead of applying the probing algorithm every time when a new search is initiated, the address of the first reserve location, when once computed, is permanently stored as a pointer in the computed location. The address of the second reserve location becomes the pointer stored at the first reserve location, etc. When an item is read, the list is scanned by following the pointers, starting at the computed address, until the stored tag matches with the search argument. When this is done, the item is read out. If all checks fail, the item does not exist in the list. The last item in a list must be indicated by a special pointer (for instance, by the address of the item itself).

If a collision occurs during storage, any probing algorithm can be used to find a reserve location for the new item. This item must become part of that list with which the collision occurred. Therefore, the pointer found at the address where the collision took place is taken for the pointer in the new item, and the probed address shall replace the old pointer in the target of collision. This rearrangement of pointers is illustrated in Fig. 2.1.

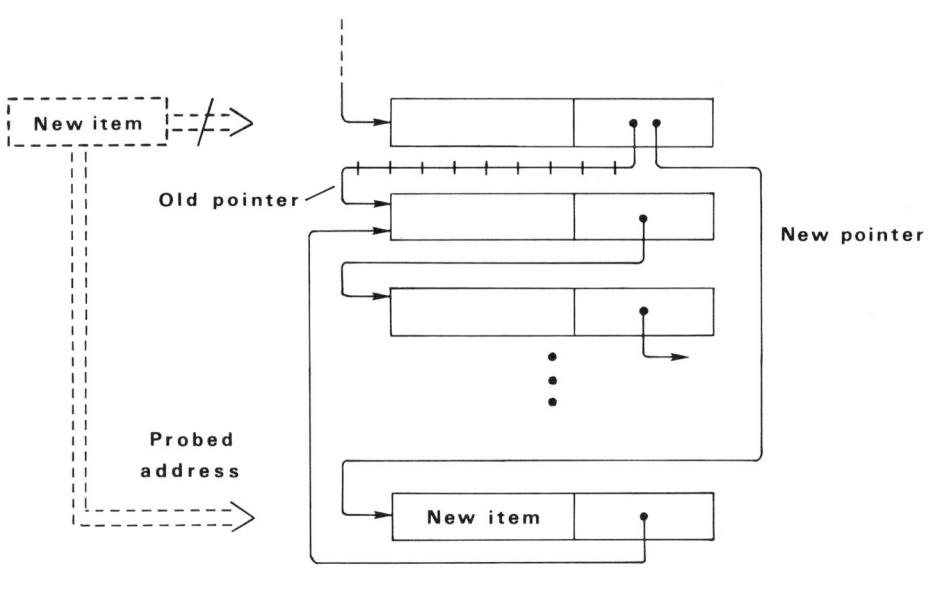

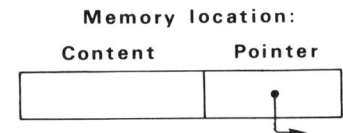

Fig. 2.1 Linked-list organization of the reserve locations

With list memories, in order to avoid probing, it is customary to use an *overflow area* that is an auxiliary area in memory reserved for this purpose. The colliding item is inserted in the overflow area which is filled in the numerical order; the pointers are chained through this area.

Deletion of items from a list is a fast operation. The item that is next in the chain is moved in place of the deleted item whereby its own pointer automatically follows with it. The memory location of this *latter* item is then marked empty, and the rest of the list need not be touched.

Comparison of the Average Number of Probes with Different Methods.

The number of trials to find an empty slot for a new item depends primarily on the filling ratio F.R., i.e., the fraction of the memory locations that is occupied. Moreover, the number of trials depends on the distribution of occupied addresses which depends on the probing algorithms as well as on the management of the data structure. The average number of trials (including the first one) has been represented in Table 2.1. The numbers given have been analyzed in [32-36].

Table 2.1

Filling ratio F.R.	Average number of trials		
	Usual memory		List memory
	Linear probing	Random probing	
0.1	1.06	1.05	1.05
0.5	1.50	1.39	1.25
0.75	2.50	1.83	1.38
0.9	5.50	2.56	1.45

The strikingly small increase of probings in the list memory with a growing value of F.R. is due to the use of the overflow area.

Hash Table and Hash Index Table

The hash-coded memory may be organized in two principal ways. In one of them, the tags and the associated items are kept in the same memory area. This is called *hash table*. An alternative to it is to store the items in a separate memory area, and only pointers to this area are held in the hash-coded memory. Such an organization is called *hash index table*. The former method is more straightforward to manage but the latter has many advantages over the former and should be used whenever possible. There is no marked difference in programming load between these two methods.

Of course, if a linked-list organization is used, extra pointers must be used that link the list items together.

2.1.2 An Example of Hash-Coding: Multiple-Keyword Search

Document retrieval is an application where an astonishing efficiency can be achieved by the use of hash-coding techniques. The following illustrative example has been programmed for a minicomputer system provided with a disk cassette memory, but similar principles are directly amenable to implementation on much larger computers, too. In this example the problem was to store and retrieve up to 5000 documents (e.g., customer files), each one consisting of a maximum of 68 alphanumerical character codes, and provided with one to ten key words (descriptors). It should be pointed out that application of this principle to longer documents is a trivial generalization since they can be stored in archives, for instance, on magnetic tape, whereby a fraction of those 68 characters describing the content is reserved for a pointer by which the full document can be located. The key words were arbitrary strings of characters of which the six first characters were taken into account. This retrieval was intended to be carried out interactively in real time as a so-called *combination search*: when the user types in a combination of key words (or single words), the system responds by writing out all those documents (or their identifying codes) which include the key words given. Search on more complex functions of the key words is performed in several combination search operations. In the solution described in this section, one search is carried out in less than 200 milliseconds. This value might not become essentially larger although the volume of the storage were greater by an order of magnitude.

Fig. 2.2 illustrates the memory areas used in the manipulation of data. Table A is the hash index table for key words in which the location relative to the

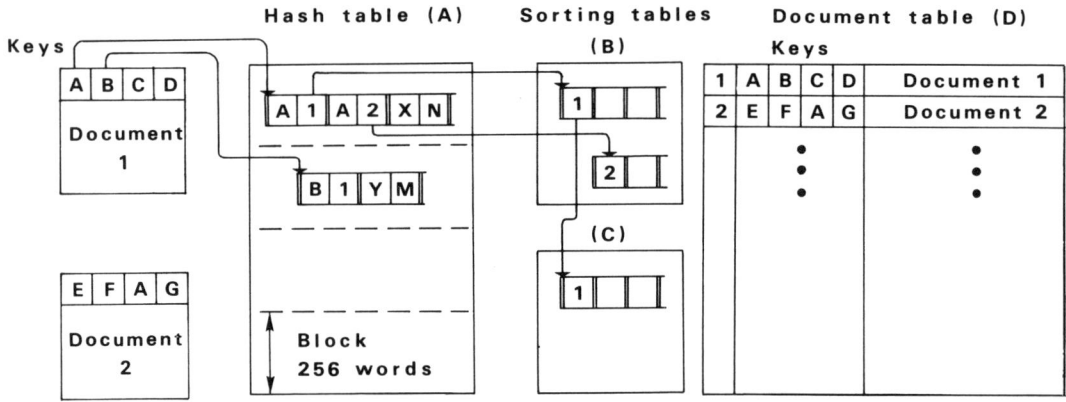

Fig. 2.2 Memory areas in a multiple-keyword search

beginning address r_A is given by Hashing Algorithm 4 (division method) that was described earlier in this chapter. For a key word with content x, the computed address is $r_A + f(x)$, where f is the function defined by the hashing algorithm. The index associated with the key word in Table A is a pointer to Table D which is a memory area for the documents; each document is provided with key words of which only four are shown. A pointer in Table A indicates the address of Table D at which the corresponding record begins. As all documents must be accessible by any of their key words, a pointer to a document must be stored in Table A in as many places as there are key words associated with the respective document. Consequently, because the same key word may occur in a large number of documents, the number of collisions at a computed address is expected to be high. For this reason, it is desirable to keep the filling ratio F.R. of the hash addressed memory low. This can be achieved by reserving a very large area, in this example 2^{20} words (on the disk) for the hash index table. In accordance with the operating system used, the disk memory is divided into *pages* of 256 words. At every search in Table A, the whole page on which the computed address is located is transferred to the fast memory, where the comparison of the tags is made. In order to have a high probability for finding the reserve locations to a computed address on the same page, linear probing is used. Now it might seem as if the probed addresses (relative to r_A) might profitably be numbers modulo 256, in order to keep the reserve locations on the same page. However, as it is not wanted to set restrictions on the frequency with which a particular key word may occur in the documents, the chain of reserve locations must be allowed to continue on the next pages. In our application the time needed to swap a page is only 180 milliseconds, and in most cases, all reserve locations are found on the same page anyway.

Many computers have operating systems with the so-called *virtual storage* feature: a set of those pages that are accessed most frequently is buffered in the fast memory, and a search from the backing storage (e.g., disk) is necessary only if the page is not found in the fast storage.

In addition to the hash index table and the document area, three other tables are used. Two of them, named Table B and Table C, respectively, are special memory areas reserved for immediate results in combination search, and they are hash-addressed with respect to *pointers* in the following way. The key word given first picks up the set of all pointers in Table A the tags of which agree with the first key word. These pointers are stored in Table B at an address that is computed by the hashing algorithm from the pointer itself. The second key word picks up another set of pointers from Table A regardless of whether they correspond to the same documents that were found in the first search or not. By virtue of hash coding used to address Table B, it is now an easy task to check whether a pointer picked up by the second key word is in Table B or not; in the former case both key words occur in the document. Only such pointers which agree in both searches are stored in Table C, again using hash coding. If a third key word is used, it is checked whether the pointers found for it exist in Table C, and if this is the case, the pointers are again stored in Table B (which was cleared before the third search). In this way the set of candidates left in Table B or Table C is reduced and the corresponding documents are read out at the same time when the last search is performed. It is convenient to use a *stack* area where the found pointers are buffered until the documents are typed out; a stack is a list of numbers which is filled in the order of their entrance, with the last one on the top, and from which the last number is always read first.

In our example the Tables B,C, and the stack were in the fast memory. The complete search, not including the time to write out the documents, was always completed in less than 200 milliseconds.

2.1.3 A Processing Language for Associative Data Structures

There have been developed many high-level computer languages for artificial intelligence research [30]. Not only has it thereby become possible to create complex and efficient program codes by automatic programming aids, for instance, by the use of implicitly defined local variables that satisfy certain set-inclusion properties, but the execution of a program can also be made to cope with a given task optimally. One feature which is found in many high-level languages is a provision for the management of relational structures.

One of the first languages designed for the management of associative structures was named LEAP [3]. In its design it was reasoned that the smallest elementary construct by which arbitrary data structures yet can be defined is the relational ordered triple (A,O,V) = (attribute, object, value). One of the items (V) names the relation, or gives a value to it, while the other two are arguments.

A semantic content can be given to the triple. A construct of this type is equivalent to a statement, read as

(A,O,V) "*attribute* of *object* is *value*",
e.g.   "*colour* of *apple* is *red*".

Experience has shown that this rather restricted form of statement can still be used effectively in interactive computer-aided design (even more conveniently than the statements in conventional algorithmic languages) whereas such simple relations may not be sufficient for the analysis of natural languages.

Structures are formed from relations when one or several of the elements are substituted by other relations. The value V of the triple must then be understood as *equivalent* to the pair of its arguments (A,O); substitution simply means that either of these parts can be made to stand for the element to be replaced. In order to clarify this operation, let us study the following two-level structure:

"*father* of (*father* of *Steve* ≡ *Bill*) is *John*"

where, for clarity, the verb "is" in the inner relation has been replaced by the sign of identity, indicating that "*Bill*" and "*father* of *Steve*" are alternatives. The principle of formation of more complicated structures may be self-evident.

In automatic search there is a definite purpose of effectively locating all and nothing but that information which matches the given key definition; therefore one of the elementary tasks is to survey the memory for all items which match a given partial specification of a relation. For instance, assume that the following triples have been stored in memory:

"*father* of *Pete* is *Joe*",
"*father* of *John* is *Jim*",
"*father* of *Ann* is *Joe*".

If a search criterion is defined using an item variable X, e.g.,
"*father* of X is *Joe*", the memory can be retrieved associatively in a combination search, on the basis of the symbols *"father"* and *"Joe"* as the search arguments, and there are to be listed all solutions X = *Pete* or *Ann*. It might be clear from the foregoing that the most effective principle to organize an associative data base is to apply hash-coding, as was done with the implementation of multiple-keyword search; the idea is to encode every relation by all its elements separately, and to store corresponding duplicates of the relations in a hash table, or duplicate pointers in a hash index table.

The results of such a search operation, or the values of X that satisfy the search criterion, now form an unordered set, with X a *set variable*. The above system makes it possible to define sets of items, and to iterate computer programs on parameter values corresponding to the set variable.

Combinations of partial specifications can be used in search, too, as the following example shows in which the purpose is to find all brothers of Steve defined implicitly:

"(*child* of (*father* of *Steve*) is X) & (*sex* of X is *male*)".

In LEAP, a search on the basis of all of the following partial specifications or their arbitrary combinations can be performed (Table 2.2.).

Table 2.2 Partial specifications of relations

Form	Example	Interpretation
(A,O,X)	"*son* of *John Doe* is X"	Any son of John Doe
(A,X,V)	"*son* of X is *Don Doe*"	Father of Don Doe
(X,O,V)	"X of *John Doe* is *Don Doe*"	Any relation of John Doe to Don Doe
(A,X,Y)	"*son* of X is Y"	Any (father, son) -pair
(X,Y,V)	"X of Y is *Don Doe*"	Any association with Don Doe as value
(X,O,Y)	"X of *John Doe* is Y"	Any association with John Doe as object.

2.2 Content-Addressable Memories

A problem of constant interest in computer science and its applications is that of rapid searching of all items which satisfy a given criterion from a data base. One frequently occurring task is to locate all items which match a given search argument in specified portions. With numerical data, another common problem is to find all items which satisfy given magnitude relations, for instance, which have one or several of their attributes confined between specified limits. Comparison operations of this kind can be performed simultaneously and in parallel on all memory locations, if special electronic hardware or other technological (e.g., optical) methods are used. In computer technology, the name *associative memory* has therefore been coined for such devices; this name is then used in a rather restricted sense. We shall later discuss the possibility that associative recall in biological memories may mean more than just location of an item by its contents.

In order to check a search argument against all memory words, three types of operations are needed: 1) There must be a method of broadcasting the argument to all memory locations. 2) A separate comparison of the search argument with every stored word must be performed. 3) The matching information must be recollected.

In the electronic circuit implementations, the only practicable broadcasting method is the use of parallel signal lines for the search argument on which all the memory locations are hooked up. The line signals are compared with the states of the memory locations using built-in logic circuits as discussed in Subsections 2.2.2 and 2.2.3. The matching words are transmitted through another set of parallel lines to the common output buffer circuits. This is an expensive solution, and if the number of circuits hooked up to a line becomes appreciable (say, more than a few thousand) there may arise noise problems. For this reason there might exist appreciable interest in other memory principles, for instance, in so-called iterative organizations in which the various locations pass information to each other; or perhaps electromagnetic fields for the broadcasting of information might be a solution. Something like this has been used in some experimental optical memories; nevertheless, such implementations are not yet commercially available.

2.2.1 Associative Recall by the Partial Match Operation

There have been attempts since 1956 to create hardware memory structures in which the search argument is compared in parallel with all memory locations, using electronic logic circuits or other corresponding technological principles. Extensive reviews have been published, for instance, by HANLON [10], MINKER [39], and PARHAMI [14], with many literature references.

Such *content-addressable memories* (CAM's) have been based on various principles: cryogenic, magneto-optical, magnetic core, thin-film magnetic element, and active or semiconductor circuit principles. It seems that most of these structures will be implemented in coming years by large-scale integrated semiconductor circuits. For the time being, there exist CAM structures with only a few thousand addresses, although rather long memory words (up to hundreds of bits) have been used. With the development of large-scale integrated semiconductor circuit memories, it seems that CAM structures will be commonplace in general-purpose computers, at least in the buffer memories of their central processing units, or in microprogrammed control circuitry. The implementation of extensive data bases by means of content-addressable hardware is still beyond sight, partly on account of problems that are caused in complicated circuitry by a progressively increasing probability for failures with the growing size of memory, partly due to the addressing problem; at least in the existing electronic solutions, every memory location must be provided with a separate address line (linear addressing).

In this context it may suffice to review a couple of the logic descriptions of content-addressable memories, in order to give an idea of the circuit complexity. The basic operation in CAM structures is *bit match*. If the Boolean values of two binary variables are denoted by X and Y, respectively, then the Boolean function which has the value 1 (*true*) for *logical equivalence* (match) of X and Y, and 0 (*false*) otherwise is

$$(X \equiv Y) = (X \mathbin{\&} Y) \lor (\bar{X} \mathbin{\&} \bar{Y}) \; , \tag{2.3}$$

where & is the logical *and*, $\lor$ is the logical *or* - function, and $\bar{X}$ is the logical *negation* of X. Alternatively, the *mismatch* of the values X and Y is indicated by the *exclusive or* - function,

$$X \oplus Y = (X \mathbin{\&} \bar{Y}) \lor (\bar{X} \mathbin{\&} Y) \; . \tag{2.4}$$

In *masked search*, only a set of specified bits in the search-argument word is used for comparison with respective bits of all memory words. Those stored words which agree in the specified bits with the search argument are read out. For that purpose, each bit position in the memory is equipped with circuit logic which implements either (2.3) or (2.4), together with an indication whether this bit is involved in the comparison or not. If the ith memory word $(S_{i1}, S_{i2}, \ldots, S_{in})$, with the S_{ij} the Boolean values of its respective bits, agrees with the Boolean search argument $(A_1, A_2, \ldots, A_n)$ in all bit positions where the *mask word* $(C_1, C_2, \ldots, C_n)$ has the Boolean value 0, a function which indicates this kind of match by the Boolean value 1 is the following:

$$M_i = [(A_1 \equiv S_{i1}) \lor C_1] \mathbin{\&} \ldots \mathbin{\&} [(A_n \equiv S_{in}) \lor C_n] \; . \tag{2.5}$$

Note that if the jth bit is masked ($C_j = 1$), then the respective factor $(A_j \equiv S_{ij}) \lor C_j$ is identically 1. Alternatively, the mismatch of the ith word is indicated by Boolean function

$$\bar{M}_i = [(A_1 \oplus S_{i1}) \mathbin{\&} \bar{C}_1] \lor \ldots \lor [(A_n \oplus S_{in}) \mathbin{\&} \bar{C}_n] \; . \tag{2.6}$$

2.2.2 Hardware Implementation of the CAM Structure

A logic structure that generally has been accepted in various semiconductor circuit implementations of CAM is shown in Fig. 2.3 using the conventional circuit notation. The horizontal line with signal A_i is an *address line* for writing and reading data. If $A_i = 1$, then $\bar{B}_j$ tells the state of the addressed *bit storage* (its negation).

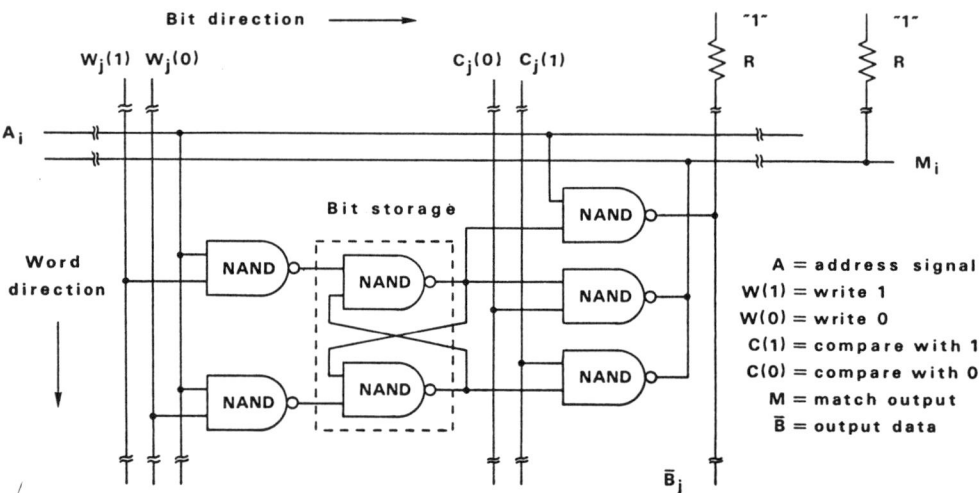

Fig. 2.3 Memory cell for a content-addressable memory

Notice that the outputs of the bit storage (the bistable circuit) indicate the bit value and its negation; as the external control signals with their negations can be connected to this circuit using double lines, too, it becomes possible to implement the search logic with a minimum number of logic operations. Another special feature of this circuit is the method by which the Boolean *or*-functions, with a very large number (maybe thousands) of variables, may be implemented. The parallel connections of logic gates on the M and $\bar{B}$ lines are equivalent to the so-called *wired-or* electric operation: by a particular electronic design, a property has been achieved that the outputs of the logic circuits act in the similar way as a set of parallel switches connected from the line to a common potential with value 0. The electrical potential of the line now attains the potential level "1" by means of the resistor R, unless any of the outputs of the circuits connected to this line has the Boolean value 0, whereby the line potential takes on the value "0". The double control lines marked by $C_j(0)$ and $C_j(1)$ combine the search and masking: if the purpose is to find a bit value 0 from this memory cell, then $C_j(0)$ is taken equal to 1 and $C_j(1) = 0$. If, on the other hand, a bit value 1 has to be searched from the memory cell, then it is taken $C_j(0) = 0$ and $C_j(1) = 1$. Finally, if this bit position must be masked in the search operation, then the corresponding control signals are $C_j(0) = C_j(1) = 0$. As a result, $M_i = 1$ if and only if matching values are found in the bit storages.

For the writing of information into the bit cell, the bit control lines $W_j(0)$ and $W_j(1)$ that are common to all memory words are used. A memory word is selected by the address line, and if "1" is to be written, then $W_j(0) = 0$ and $W_j(1) = 1$. Respectively, for the writing of "0", there must be $W_j(0) = 1$ and $W_j(1) = 0$. In all other cases $W_j(0)$ and $W_j(1)$ are held at the value 0.

A parallel content-addressable memory organization is shown in Fig. 2.4. An array of cells of the type depicted in Fig. 2.3 constitutes the central block (memory array).

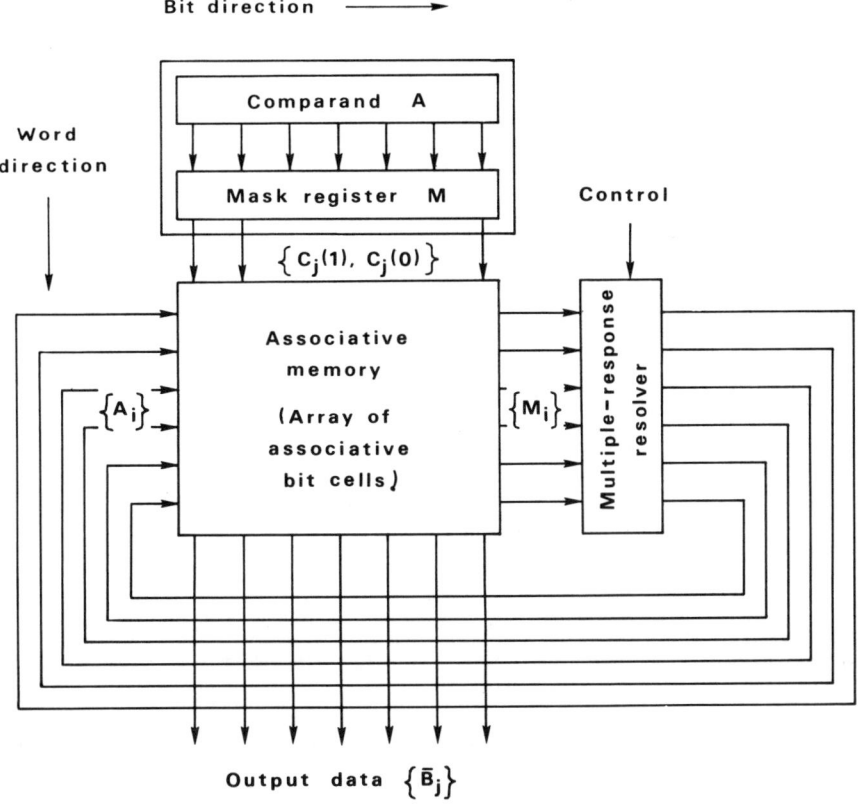

Fig. 2.4 Organization of a content-addressable memory

The search argument (comparand) is stored in the A register, and the mask word in register M. The double control lines $C_j(0)$ and $C_j(1)$ obtain their values in a system unit with A and M parts of it. Another system unit called *multiple-match-resolver* is shown on the right and it has the following function: because several memory words may yield a response, this block reads out the corresponding memory words one at a time. The multiple-match resolver has as many output lines as inputs, and by means of logic-circuit control, it is possible to select one of the actively responding lines to the outputs; this operation is then repeated for all active lines in turn. When the output of the multiple-match-resolver is connected to the corresponding address line A_i of the content-addressable memory array, the memory word at A_i is read out at the data outputs as its binary complement $(\bar{B}_1,\ldots,\bar{B}_n)$.

Priority-Logic for Multiple-Match Resolution

A simple resolver circuit which outputs only the uppermost of the responding signals is shown in Fig. 2.5. The M_i signals, corresponding to matching words, are outputs from auxiliary bistable circuits, set to value 1 by the responding M-lines.

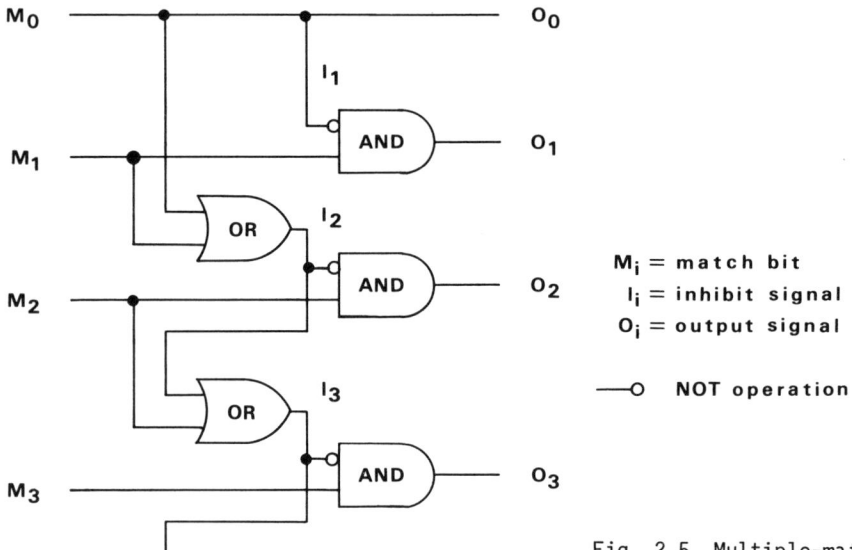

M_i = match bit
I_i = inhibit signal
O_i = output signal

—o NOT operation

Fig. 2.5 Multiple-match resolver

The idea is to inhibit all lower signals so that only one output at a time can be active. When the contents of the responding memory location have been read out, the corresponding bistable circuit is reset to 0 whereby a new active signal appears at the output lines, and so on.

A drawback of this simple circuit is that the output signals settle down to their due value in cascade. If the delay per stage were, for instance, 10 ns, it would take 10 μs in a 1000-word store to reach stationary logic levels. Although this time may seem small, faster circuits may sometimes by applied in order to avoid slowing down of the search time due to this circuit only [38].

Associative memories have been built using the so-called *bit-serial* comparison principle, too: the comparison of memory words is performed in parallel, but only one bit position at a time, in a sequence. An auxiliary register in the multiple-match resolver collects the results from the successive bit comparisons. These method may have importance in search with long numerical arguments, but since their logic does not differ very much from all-parallel operations, they are not treated here.

2.2.3 Parallel Comparison of Magnitudes

Inequality Search

Another important operation in content-addressable search is to locate all memory words the numerical value of which is greater or less than that of the search argument. A combination of these two searches can also be performed, whereby all items that lie between two specified limits can be found. For simplicity, it is assumed that the values are represented as positive binary numbers.

A paradigm of logic circuits, the so-called *iterative circuit* of Fig. 2.6 is here used to exemplify magnitude-comparison by hardware logic.

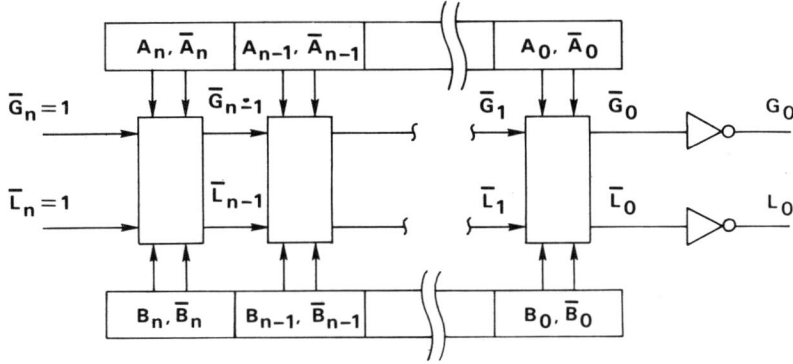

Fig. 2.6 Circuit for the comparison of magnitudes

Register A is assumed to hold the search argument; for simplicity, no masking provisions are incorporated. Every bit value is assumed to be available as its binary complement signal, as the case usually is if bistable electronic circuits are used. Another register B may represent, for instance, one of the locations in a memory. There is now an identical (iterative) logic circuit between every pair of bit positions (A_i, B_i) of the registers A and B, respectively, and information from one circuit to another is propagated by the pairs of signals G_i and L_i. The basic idea of iterative comparison is the following: let us assume that a hypothetical process of comparison is started at the left-hand (numerically most significant) end of the registers, and it has proceeded to the ith position. If it has been possible to produce the signals G_i and L_i which uniquely tell whether one of the following situations is true: A is greater than B, A is less than B, or the result is still unconfirmed (because all respective bits to the left from the ith position are pairwise equal), then, based on the values A_i, B_i, G_i, and L_i it is logically possible to resolve and propagate similar information to the (i-1)th position by means of the signals G_{i-1} and L_{i-1}. Namely, it is self-evident that if two numbers disagree in their bits to the left from the ith position, one of them is uniquely greater, whatever the less significant bits are. It can now be shown that if the iterative circuits satisfy the following equations, the problem has been solved:

$$\text{for all } i, \; G_{i-1} = G_i \vee (A_i \; \& \; \bar{B}_i \; \& \; \bar{L}_i) ,$$

$$L_{i-1} = L_i \vee (\bar{A}_i \; \& \; B_i \; \& \; \bar{G}_i) ,$$

(2.7)

with the initial values $G_n = L_n = 0$. If, namely, $A_n = 1$ and $B_n = 0$, then it is obvious that A is greater than B, and it can be computed from (2.7) that for all $i < n$, $G_i = 1$, $L_i = 0$. If, on the other hand, $A_n = 0$ and $B_n = 1$, then, for all $i < n$, $G_i = 0$, and $L_i = 1$. But if $A_n = B_n$, then $G_{n-1} = L_{n-1} = 0$, and the magnitude relation must be solved on the basis of the less significant bits. In the latter case, the same deductions are carried out on the bits A_{n-1} and B_{n-1}, and so on, proceeding up to the rightmost position which yields the final output signals G_0 and L_0. If now $G_0 = 1$, $L_0 = 0$, then A was greater than B; if $G_0 = 0$, $L_0 = 1$, then B was greater. If $G_0 = L_0 = 0$, the numbers were equal.

Maximum (Minimum) Search

In the search for the maximum among stored numbers, the CAM organization of Fig. 2.4 can be applied. The search is carried out in several passages by studying the successive bits of the binary numbers starting from the left, one bit at a time. The idea is to find a set of candidates for the maximum, from which each passage drops a subset until only the largest are left. In order to keep track on the intermediate results, every memory location is provided with an additional match bit that can be controlled properly. These bits are connected with the multiple-match resolver. There is also a possibility to mask any argument bits.

In the beginning, all match bits are set to 1. The leftmost argument bit is set to 1 and all other argument bits to the right from it are masked out, whereby a logical equivalence search on the masked argument is performed. If there are memory words with 1 in the first position, they are candidates for the maximum, and they are indicated with $D_j = 1$. All other words are dropped out from this subset by resetting their match bits to 0. In the next passages, the argument bit keeps the value 1. If, however, the search shows that there are no memory words with 1 in this position, the first argument bit is reset to 0. Now, with the value for the first argument bit obtained in the first passage, the next bit is set to 1, and all bits to the right from it are masked out, whereafter a new equality search is carried out. The idea used in the continuation may now be discernible: when the search for candidates at the ith bit position is due, the bits to the left of this position attain those values obtained in the previous passages, and the ith argument bit is tentatively taken as 1 for finding candidates with 1 in this position. If none are found, the argument bit is reset to 0 and the next bit position is examined. This process is continued until all bits of the search argument have been exhausted, whereby the match bits in the multiple-match resolver with value 1 indicate the maxima.

The search for the minimum amongst the memory words is the dual of the maximum search. It is started with the bit value 0 in the search argument, and if no candidates are found, the bit is set to 1. As the next argument bit, a 0 is tried, etc.

Search for the Nearest-Below (Nearest-Above) to the Argument

By a combination of search for memory words that are less than the argument, and a selection of maximum in this subset, those memory words which are nearest below the argument are found. In a similar way, a combination of the greater-than and minimum searches yields the memory words that are nearest above the argument.

2.3 Optimal Associative Mappings

It was mentioned above that digital computers are particularly effective in numerical and discrete-valued computations. When dealing with patterned information, however, the data variables are usually incomplete or ill-defined, although the amount of available information may be very great. For such computations, highly parallel computers, perhaps based on analog methods, would be more suitable. It is an intriguing observation that nature seems to have solved the principles of computing and memory in an analog way, by the use of large adaptive networks for the processing of information (cf. Chap. 4). The biological memories very probably operate like *adaptive filters*, and their primary purpose seems to be to correct random errors that occur in sensory experiences. As the search of information from natural memories is made associatively, it therefore becomes necessary to study their possible functional principles in this context.

It is now pointed out that error-tolerant associative memories can be implemented by simple signals-transforming physical systems without the use of any logic circuits or operations. The mathematical mappings that describe such "analog associative memories" have a fundamental bearing on the mathematical formalisms of estimation theory and regression analysis. It will be shown below that optimal estimation and optimal associative recall of stochastic information may be unified in the same formalism, as two different cases of it.

One further interesting property of the optimal associative mappings is that in the first place they always describe the operation of *distributed memories*.

2.3.1 System Model for an Analog Associative Memory

Consider the system of Fig. 2.7 which is a linear physical system that transfers parallel signal patterns. The linear system is the simplest representative of a class

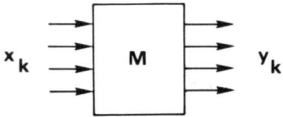

Fig. 2.7 System model for an associative memory

of analog physical systems. A method for the analysis of nonlinear systems will be given in Subsection 2.3.6.

Let us describe the input signals by pattern vectors x_k in a representation space R^n, and let the output signals y_k be vectors in R^p. The patterns are assumed to be transformed linearly by a transfer relation

$$y_k = M x_k \tag{2.8}$$

where M is a p × n matrix. We are concerned with the existence of solutions to this *paired-associate problem*: does there exist an M such that for a finite set of arbitrarily selected pairs $\{(x_k, y_k)\}$, $k = 1, 2, \ldots, m$, we can always have (2.8) satisfied? This problem will be discussed in Subsection 2.3.5, and let us tentatively assume that it has been solved. We may then regard y_k as the memorized *data*, and x_k as the *search argument* (also called *key*) by which y_k is encoded and retrieved. The excitation of the system by x_k and the subsequent observation of y_k is comparable to table lookup in computational operations.

Another question is what happens if such a system is excited by an erroneous or incomplete search argument. It shall further be shown in Subsection 2.3.5 that there exist solutions to the paired-associate problem which are *optimal* in the sense of least squares; if, in such a system, the input excitation resembles any of the stored patterns, then the output is a corrected approximation of the associated pair.

It may also be asked whether both autoassociative and heteroassociative memory (cf. Subsec. 1.2.1) can be described by the optimal mappings. Let us recall that in autoassociative memory, an item is retrieved by its fraction, that is, the recollection comprises a set of data elements of which a fraction is used as the key. In heteroassociative memory, arbitrary keys can be paired with arbitrary responses. Both of these schemes will be discussed below.

Finally it may be remarked that systems of the above kind can be characterized as *memories* if and only if the value of the transfer operation M is formed in an *adaptive process*, by the influence of the occurring signals. Possibilities for the adaptive formation of analog associative memory are discussed in Chap. 3 in more detail. It has been found that the asymptotic transfer properties of such adaptive systems are very often equivalent to *orthogonal projection operators*. On the other hand, it has been intriguing to find that optimal autoassociative recall can be implemented by the orthogonal projection operators, too. Therefore, in the hope that this would constitute a new formalism in the context of associative memory, the next sections are first devoted to associative mappings that are implemented by the orthogonal projection operators.

2.3.2 Autoassociative Recall as an Orthogonal Projection

Orthogonal Projections

Let there be m distinct Euclidean vectors denoted by $x_1, x_2, \ldots, x_m \in R^n$ which span a subspace $\mathcal{L} \subset R^n$. As mentioned in Subsection 1.3.1, it can be shown that an arbitrary vector $x \in R^n$ is uniquely expressible as the sum of two vectors $\hat{x}$ and $\tilde{x}$ of which $\hat{x}$ is a linear combination of the x_k; in particular, $\hat{x}$ is the orthogonal projection of x on the space $\mathcal{L}$, while $\tilde{x}$ is the remaining contribution in x which is orthogonal to $\mathcal{L}$. So $\hat{x}$ is the best linear combination of the x_k that approximates x in the sense of least squares. Let us denote

$$\hat{x} = \sum_{k=1}^{m} \gamma_k x_k \tag{2.9}$$

with γ_k being scalar factors; they represent the linear regression of the x_k on x.

Hereupon the vectors x_k are understood as the representations of m distinct *memorized items*, also named *reference patterns*, and x is the (possibly incomplete) *key pattern* by which information is associatively searched from the memory. If the key x bears a close correlation with one of the stored items, say x_r, then it is expected that the term $\gamma_r x_r$ of $\hat{x}$ will predominate. If this is the case, it can be said that x_r is *associatively recalled* by x. Notice further that x_r is one of the stored patterns in a perfect form. On the other hand, the other terms in the linear mixture $\hat{x}$ represent a residual which is the noise contribution, with no content other than cross-talk arising from the other stored patterns.

The classical computational method for the evaluation of orthogonal projections is the Gram-Schmidt process; for the subspace $\mathcal{L}$ spanned by the x_k, a new orthogonal vector basis is defined by the recursion

$$\tilde{x}_1 = x_1$$

$$\tilde{x}_k = x_k - \sum_{i=1}^{k-1} \frac{(x_k, \tilde{x}_i)}{\|\tilde{x}_i\|^2} \tilde{x}_i \quad (k = 2, 3, \ldots, m) \quad , \qquad (2.10)$$

where $(x_k, \tilde{x}_i)$ is the inner product of x_k and $\tilde{x}_i$, and the sum must be taken only over such terms for which $\tilde{x}_i \neq 0$. The decomposition of the key vector x into the projections $\hat{x}$ and $\tilde{x}$ is obtained by continuation of the above recursion one step further, whereby $\tilde{x} = \tilde{x}_{m+1}$, $\hat{x} = x - \tilde{x}_{m+1}$.

Error-Correcting Properties of Orthogonal Projections

The purpose of the following discussion is to show that orthogonal projection operations have the property of correcting and standardizing incomplete key patterns towards "memorized" reference patterns. This fact may result in practical applications as such, for instance, in the correction of broken fonts in character reading, in the filtering of noisy messages, and so on. If the key x is a noisy version of one of the reference patterns x_r,

$$x = x_r + v \qquad (2.11)$$

where v is a stochastic error, then in general, $\hat{x}$ is an improved approximation of x_r. This can be demonstrated analytically in a simple case in which v has a constant length $\|v\| = v_0$ and a direction that is uniformly distributed in R^n. It is a straightforward matter to generalize the result for the case in which v has an arbitrary radial distribution in R^n, for instance a symmetrical multivariate Gaussian one. Notice, first, that the orthogonal projection of x_r on $\mathcal{L}$ is equal to x_r. On the other hand, it has been shown in Subsection 1.3.1 that the projection $\hat{v}$ of v on $\mathcal{L}$ has a distribution with a variance that is m/n times the square of the norm of v, where m is the number of patterns, and n their dimensionality. In other words, the noise occurring in the key pattern is attenuated in the orthogonal projection operation if $m < n$: its standard deviation is

$$\text{var}^{1/2}(\|\hat{x} - x_r\|) = \sqrt{\frac{m}{n}} \|x - x_r\| \quad . \qquad (2.12)$$

Recall of Missing Fragments

By definition of associative recall, elements lacking from a data set that is otherwise complete ought to be recalled by the rest. If now a defective version of one of the reference patterns, say x_r, is used as the key x, then $x_r - x$ can be regarded as stochastic noise. Its statistics, however, depend upon pattern x_r, and as a result are difficult to define. If it is tentatively assumed, again, that the noise attenuation factor is < 1, then $\hat{x}$ is an improved approximation of x_r, and it is said that autoassociative recall of the missing portion has taken place.

Example

A straightforward demonstration of the error-correcting properties of optimal associative mappings can be performed by computer simulation using real patterns. A computer system, described in [24], was applied in the following experiment. An optical test pattern, consisting of a few thousand picture elements, here discretized to eight gray levels, could be prepared in digital form and transferred to the computer files automatically by a special scanner. For this study, a rectangular display of 54 by 56 picture elements was chosen. The pictures were treated as 3024-component real pattern vectors. A phototype-setting machine was used for the preparation of reproductions of the eight-shade pictures, using oval dots with corresponding intensities. Fig. 2.8.summarizes the results of the demonstrations of

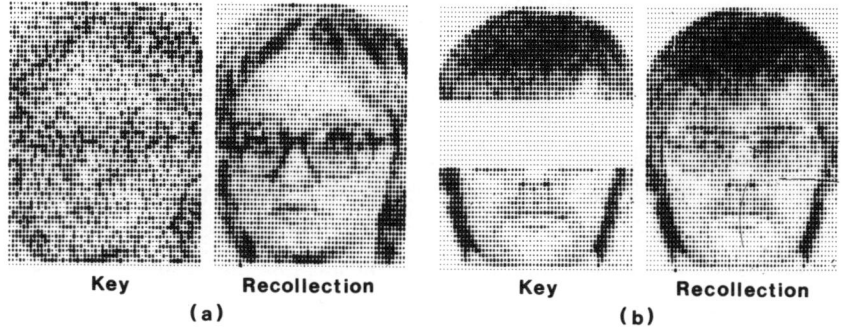

Fig. 2.8 Demonstration of noise suppression and autoassociative recall in the orthogonal projection operation

noise suppression and autoassociative recall. In the first pair of images, Fig. 2.8a, the key was one of the original patterns, with white noise superimposed on all picture elements. The norm of the noise vector was 1.6 times that of the pattern, and the noise was derived from a uniform distribution. (Actually, such a noise has not a spherical but a cubic distribution.) There is illustrated the corresponding recollection from a "memory" in which 100 reference patterns were stored, giving a conception of the noise suppression ability of this mapping.

Another experiment in which the key was derived from another pattern, by masking 25 per cent of it, is shown by the pair of images in Fig. 2.8b.

2.3.3 The Novelty Filter

The component $\tilde{x}$ of vector x which is orthogonal to subspace $\mathcal{L}$ can be understood as the result of a particular information processing operation resulting in very interesting properties. If it is recalled that $\tilde{x}$ is the residual that is left when the best linear combination of the "old" patterns is fitted to the input data x, it is possible to think that $\tilde{x}$ is the amount that is "maximally new" in x. It may be justified to call this component the "novelty", and the name Novelty Filter is hereupon used for a system which extracts $\tilde{x}$ from input data x and displays it at the output without the $\hat{x}$ component. In Chapter 3, an adaptive scheme is discussed, the asymptotic properties of which reflect the features of Novelty Filter.

Two Examples of Novelty Filter

Applications of the Novelty Filter are demonstrated in the following by two examples. It should be noticed that the filter is opaque to familiar input patterns. In the first one, there were *defects* in some input patterns. Accordingly the filtered outputs displayed these defects as their negatives. For the clarity of representation, the outputs were made binary by discriminating them properly. In the second example, the anomalies in the patterns were positive, and accordingly only they were displayed as positive signals at the output.

Fig. 2.9 illustrates 10 two-dimensional patterns comprised of 35 dots in which the blank areas have a value of 0, and the black dots attain a value of 1. These patterns are now regarded as 35-component representation vectors x_k (cf. Subsec. 1.3.1). The orthogonal projection operator is computed with the x_k used as "old" patterns. A number of old and novel input patterns x are then applied at the input, and multiplied by the projection operator to yield the outputs $\tilde{x}$. For graphic display,

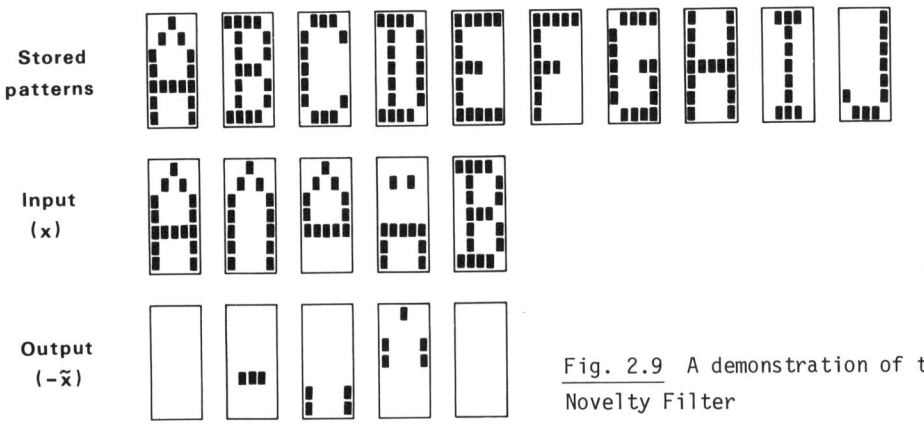

Fig. 2.9 A demonstration of the Novelty Filter

the outputs $\tilde{x}$ have been represented as their negatives, and made binary by their being discriminated at a level 0.4. In general, the true outputs are not binary. The input patterns, and the respective output patterns which represent novelty in the input patterns, are indicated on the two lower rows of Fig. 2.9.

Another demonstration introduces a new method for the processing of radiographic images that were obtained by a special device called gamma camera. Fig. 2.10 is a map of radioactive accumulation in patients who have been given Tc-99m isotope. The upper row of illustrations shows lateral images of the brain; the corresponding data were available in numerical form, too. A region of interest, a half-elliptical area about the cerebrum, was bordered and the various images were first standardized so that this area was transformed to the same shape and size. A number of numerical samples, 1300 points from this area, were selected as the components of a pattern vector to represent it. In the first phase of experiment, 30 images (not shown in Fig. 2.10) from normal cases were collected; although these too looked rather different mutually, they were classified as normal cases by a clinical diagnosis. The normal patterns were then used as the "old" or reference patterns x_k for which a Novelty Filter mapping was computed. (In numerical analysis, it is advisable to use the Gram-Schmidt orthogonalization process.) In the second phase of experiment, the new images

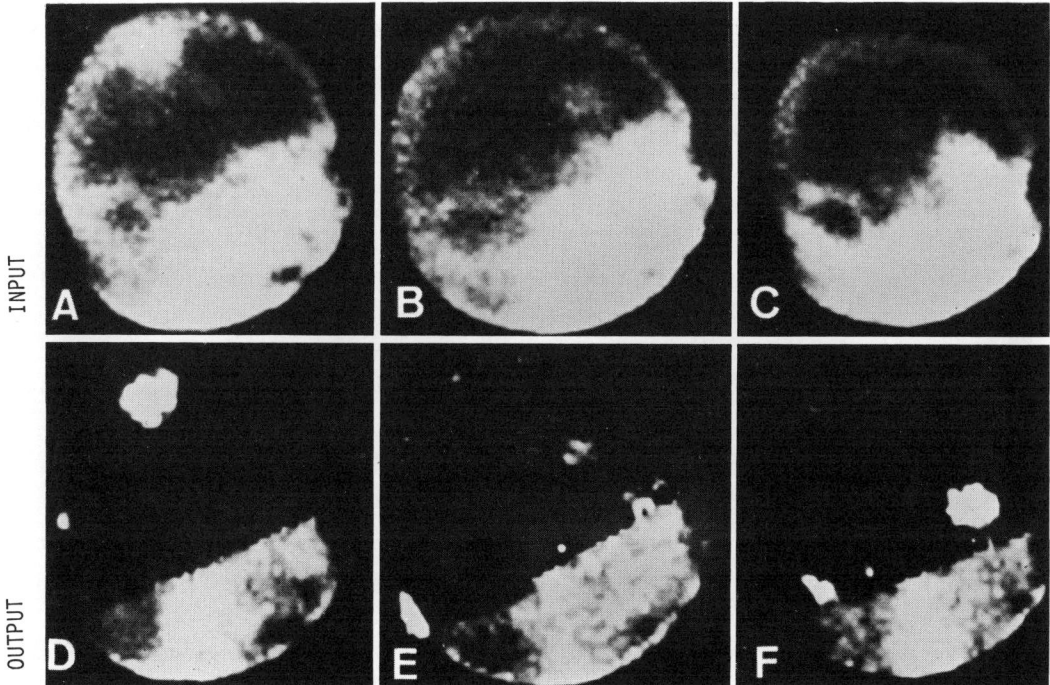

Fig. 2.10 Enhancement of abnormalities in autoradiographic brain images

to be analyzed were used as the input patterns x using similar standardization for them. The output patterns $\tilde{x}$ yielded by the Novelty Filter were then transformed to their original shape and size and displayed on a cathode-ray tube screen; for visual inspection, discontinuities due to the discretization of the signal values were smoothed out. The lower row of illustrations of Fig. 2.10 shows the outcomes of three abnormal cases. The intensity in the region around the bordered area was left unaltered, let alone some differences due to rescaling, whereas within this area, only the novelty component is visible. Picture A represents an image of an arteriovenous malformation; picture B shows a vascular glioma, and picture C the meningioma of olfactorius. Pictures D,E, and F are the filtered counterparts of images A,B and C, respectively [48].

Novelty Filter as an Autoassociative Memory

It is discernible, e.g., from the demonstration of Fig. 2.9 that missing parts in patterns that were used as the input to the Novelty Filter are recalled associatively; the main difference of the orthogonal projection $\tilde{x}$ with respect to $\hat{x}$ is that the missing parts are reproduced as negatives, and the portion used as the key is depressed.

2.3.4 Autoassociative Encoding

As the patterns were defined as a collection of component data, this definition is general enough to allow special meaning to be given for the various components of the patterns. The pattern vector may be formed as a combination of vectors of a smaller dimension, each one representing a subpattern. In particular, one subpattern can be a symbolic representation, a *code* or a *tag* of the rest.

Let us first consider a case where pictorial patterns x_k and symbolic patterns y_k are combined into vectors $x'_k = [x_k^T, y_k^T]^T$ in which all elements are treated equally irrespective of their meaning. If this model has to bear any connection with biological memory, then a similar effect would be the merging of different sensory signals in the same neural area. Now the orthogonalization process is carried out on the x'_k to yield the new base vectors $\tilde{x}'_k$. If, during recall, a pictorial pattern x is used as the key, the key vector attains the form $x' = [x^T, 0^T]^T$. The orthogonal projection $\hat{x}'$ of x' is then expected to contain the missing code: if x was an approximation of, say, x_r, then the recollection in the code part $\hat{y}$ is expected to be an approximation of that code vector y_r which was associated with x_r.

An Example of Autoassociative Encoding

Unit vectors, i.e., orthonormal coordinate vectors which have one element equal to 1 and all the other elements equal to 0, are the simplest code vectors to be used as the tags y_k. Let us denote a unit vector corresponding to the kth pattern vector by u_k. A computer simulation was carried out in which an extra tag field corresponding to the u_k was attached to the patterns which attained the form $x'_k = [x_k^T, u_k^T]^T$. As the patterns x_k, digitized optical images consisting of 53 by 56 picture elements were used. The values of the pattern elements were indicated by the dot size; the display was made in an eight-shade scale. (The value of 0 was indicated by the smallest dot size.) In the display, the extra horizontal row of points at the bottom shows the 56 first elements of the unit vector; the rest were not shown in the pictures. There was a dot corresponding to a numerical value of 1 in the dot position that corresponded to the identification number of the picture. When a picture was recalled, the code vector in the key pattern was set equal to 0; after formation of the orthogonal projection of the augmented pattern x', a recollection of the code part was obtained, too. For a successful identification of the pictures it was expected that the correct element in the tag field of the recollection would have a significantly higher intensity than the others. In the demonstration, some results of which are shown in Fig. 2.11, the left half of the patterns was

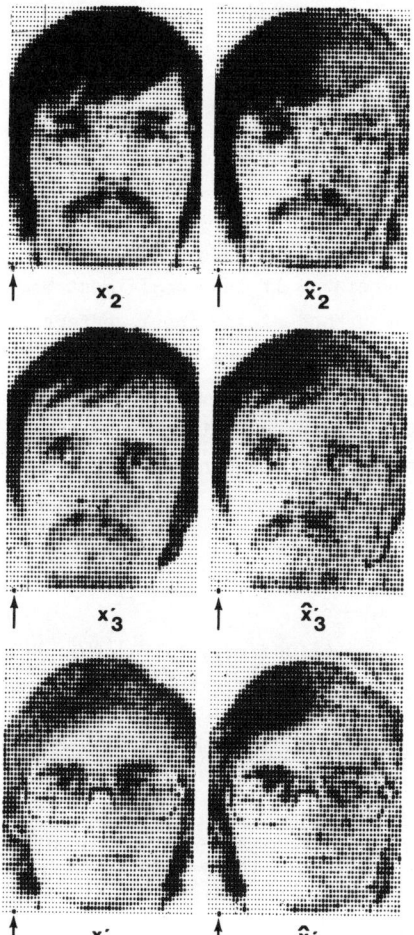

Fig. 2.11 Pairs of stored images and their recollections. There were 100 images stored in this memory, and the *left half* of the images was used as the key. Notice the tags on the bottom row. (The quality of the recollections is worse than, e.g., in Fig. 1.11 since no preprocessing was used.)

used as the key and identification of one of 100 patterns was successfully demonstrated: an arrow shows the position in the tag field where a large element is found.

The reliability of this associative identification method was checked numerically, too. The values given in Table 2.3 tell the quality of recall when the key was 50 per cent and 10 per cent of the picture area, and the number of images to be identified was 10 and 100, respectively. The recognition was made by comparing the relative values of the elements of the recalled unit vector $\hat{u}$, and the average ratio of its two largest elements here indicates the "safety margin". In all cases studied, identification was correct.

Table 2.3 Average ratio of the two largest elements in $\hat{u}$ in a recall experiment

10 reference patterns		100 reference patterns	
Key 50%	Key 10%	Key 50%	Key 10%
7.68	2.16	4.96	1.88

2.3.5 Optimal Linear Associative Mappings

Associative recall may in general be defined as a mapping in which a finite number of input vectors is transformed into given output vectors. If the recall must be error-tolerant, all vectors which lie in the neighbourhood of the input vectors in the sense of some metric are mapped into the neighbourhood of the corresponding output vectors. In Subsection 2.3.2, when dealing with orthogonal projection operations, it was shown that random deviations from the reference patterns were optimally corrected in the recall operation; it is now expected that the general linear associative mappings have this same property, too.

The General Linear Associative Mapping

The basic linear recall problem was formulated in Subsection 2.3.1 as follows: What is the matrix operator M by which a pattern $y_k \in R^p$, for every $k = 1, 2, \ldots, m$ is obtained from the pattern $x_k \in R^n$ as

$$y_k = M x_k \quad \forall k \in \{1, 2, \ldots, m\}? \tag{2.13}$$

By the introduction of the rectangular matrices Y and X with the y_k and x_k as their columns, respectively,

$$X = [x_1, x_2, \ldots, x_m], \quad Y = [y_1, y_2, \ldots, y_m] \quad , \tag{2.14}$$

(2.13) can be put in the matrix form [43, 45]

$$\underset{p \times n}{M} \underset{n \times m}{X} = \underset{p \times m}{Y} . \tag{2.15}$$

A formal solution for the unknown M, with X and Y known matrices, is obtained by the Penrose method (Subsec. 1.3.4) whereby the least-square approximate solution reads

$$\hat{M} = Y X^+ . \tag{2.16}$$

With arbitrary Y, a sufficient condition for an exact matrix solution to exist is that

$$X^+ X = I \tag{2.17}$$

which means that the x_k are linearly independent.

Various procedures for the computation of $Y X^+$ will be derived in Section 3.3.

The error-correcting properties of the linear associative mapping can be seen from the following analysis. Assume that the x_k are linearly independent whereby YX^+ is the exact solution denoted by M. If x is a pattern vector which is an approximation of x_r, $r \in \{1, 2, \ldots m\}$, then $\hat{y} = M x$ is expected to be an approximation of y_r. Now $\hat{y}$ is derived into a form which enables direct discernment of the quality of the recollection. If it is recalled that $X^+ = X^+ \cdot XX^+$, then $\hat{y} = Y X^+ x = Y X^+ (X X^+ x)$. But $X X^+ x = \hat{x}$, since $X X^+$ is the orthogonal projection operator on space $\mathcal{L}$. Then, from (2.16), (2.9), and (2.13) it follows that

$$\hat{y} = M \hat{x} = \sum_{k=1}^{m} \gamma_k (M x_k) = \sum_{k=1}^{m} \gamma_k y_k \tag{2.18}$$

so that the relative magnitudes of the terms in mixture $\hat{y}$ directly correspond to the relative magnitudes of the corresponding terms in mixture $\hat{x}$. The statistical analysis which was carried out in Subsection 2.3.2 to find the variance of the projection of a spherically distributed random vector on subspace $\mathcal{L}$ is now transferable to the space in which the y_k are defined. Because the coefficients γ_k in the recollections $\hat{x}$ and $\hat{y}$ are identical, it can be deduced that if one of the terms $\gamma_r y_r$ represents the correct recollection and the other terms $\gamma_k y_k$ together are regarded as noise, the $(m/n)^{1/2}$-law for noise attenuation applies with minor modifications to the output vectors, too.

Optimal Linear Identification

If the purpose of associative recall is only that of identification of a stored item without a need to reconstruct the "stored" image, the linear associative mapping can directly be applied to the generation of identification tags for each pattern, in the same ways as in the autoassociative encoding. The simplest identification tags are unit vectors. Denoting $u_1 = [1,0,\ldots,0]^T$, $u_2 = [0,1,0,\ldots,0]^T$, etc., and introducing the matrix $U = [u_1, u_2, \ldots, u_m]$, the problem in optimal identification of patterns is to find a solution to the equations

$$u_k = M x_k \text{ for all } k \ , \qquad (2.19)$$

or, alternatively, a solution to the matrix equation

$$U = M X \ . \qquad (2.20)$$

The least-square solution for M is

$$\hat{M} = U X^+ \ . \qquad (2.21)$$

Again, if the x_k are linearly independent, and an unknown vector x is to be identfied, it is operated by UX^+, whereby according to (2.18),

$$\hat{u} = \sum_{k=1}^{m} \gamma_k u_k = [\gamma_1, \gamma_2, \ldots, \gamma_m]^T \ . \qquad (2.22)$$

The values γ_k in the recollection correspond to the relative intensities of the patterns x_k in the vector $\hat{x}$ which is the orthogonal projection of the key x on the space spanned by the x_k .

Improvement of Identifiability by Spatial Differentiation

It ought to be noticed that the above identification methods characterized as optimal were optimal only with respect to random errors that occur in the key patterns. However, a characteristic situation in associative recall is one in which a pattern has to be identified from a *fragment*, whereby random noise can yet be superimposed on it.

In general, it has become evident that the selectivity of the associative mappings is better with reference patterns which are mutually more orthogonal. This may give an idea that the quality of associative recall in general is good if arbitrary fragments of the reference patterns are as orthogonal as possible with respect to the corresponding fragments in all the other patterns. Chances of this occurring are higher if only high spatial frequencies occur in the patterns. In order to achieve this property, the reference patterns, as well as the key, can be *preprocessed* before application of the mappings. Functional operators which enhance high frequencies and thus increase the orthogonality are derivatives or difference operators of various orders.

In the following demonstration we are dealing with optical patterns. Three different preprocessing methods to improve the orthogonality were tried: 1) Subtraction of the mean from the elements of the reference patterns x_k and the key x. 2) Formation of the absolute value of the two-dimensional gradient of the patterns. 3) Operation of the patterns by the two-dimensional Laplace operator ("Laplacian") $\partial^2/\partial\zeta_h^2 + \partial^2/\partial\zeta_v^2$, where ζ_h and ζ_v are the horizontal and vertical coordinates in the image plane, respectively.

Since the images were defined at discrete lattice points, the derivative operators had to be replaced by their difference approximations. Assuming that the lattice had a unity spacing in the horizontal and vertical direction (this assumption was not quite exact, but does not significantly affect the results), the *gradient* can be computed, for instance by the following formula. Denoting the primary picture elements in the grid by $\xi_{i,j}$, where i is the horizontal and j the vertical index, respectively, and the corresponding picture elements of the transformed picture by $n_{i,j}$, respectively, the first differences yield

$$n_{i,j} = \sqrt{C^2 + D^2}_+ \qquad (2.23)$$

where

$$C = 1/2\, (\xi_{i+1,j} - \xi_{i-1,j}) \text{ and } D = 1/2\, (\xi_{i,j+1} - \xi_{i,j-1}) \,.$$

Diagonal differences, or differences averaged over a larger portion of the grid, might also be used.

The *Laplacian* is obtained by the second differences, whereby

$$n_{i,j} = -4\xi_{i,j} + \xi_{i,j+1} + \xi_{i,j-1} + \xi_{i+1,j} + \xi_{i-1,j} \,. \qquad (2.24)$$

Another means of description of the Laplacian is by regarding it as the two-dimensional convolution of the primary picture with the 5-point grid function defined in Fig. 2.12.

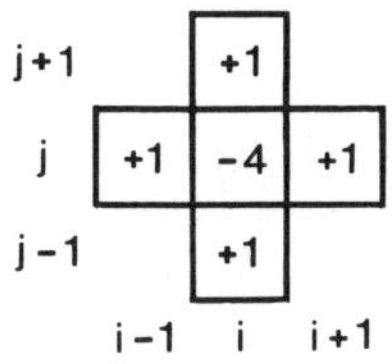

Fig. 2.12 Grid function

A good indication of the orthogonality of preprocessed patterns can be obtained in the Gram-Schmidt orthogonalization process: when the relative norms of the "novelty components" $\tilde{x}_k$ are plotted vs. the ordinal number of the patterns k, the value of this entity decreases the slower with k the more orthogonal the patterns are inherently. An experiment with 100 optical images, each one consisting of 3024 elements, shows the effect of different preprocessing methods. It is discernible that the Laplacian is superior to the other methods studied (Fig. 2.13).

Results obtained from experiments in which images were recognized from their fragments are listed in Table 2.4. As the preprocessing method, the *Laplacian* was used. The recognition was based upon comparison of the coefficients γ_k in (2.22). As a criterion for correct recognition, the ratio of γ_r, corresponding to the correct image, to the next largest γ_k was used (cf. Table 2.3).

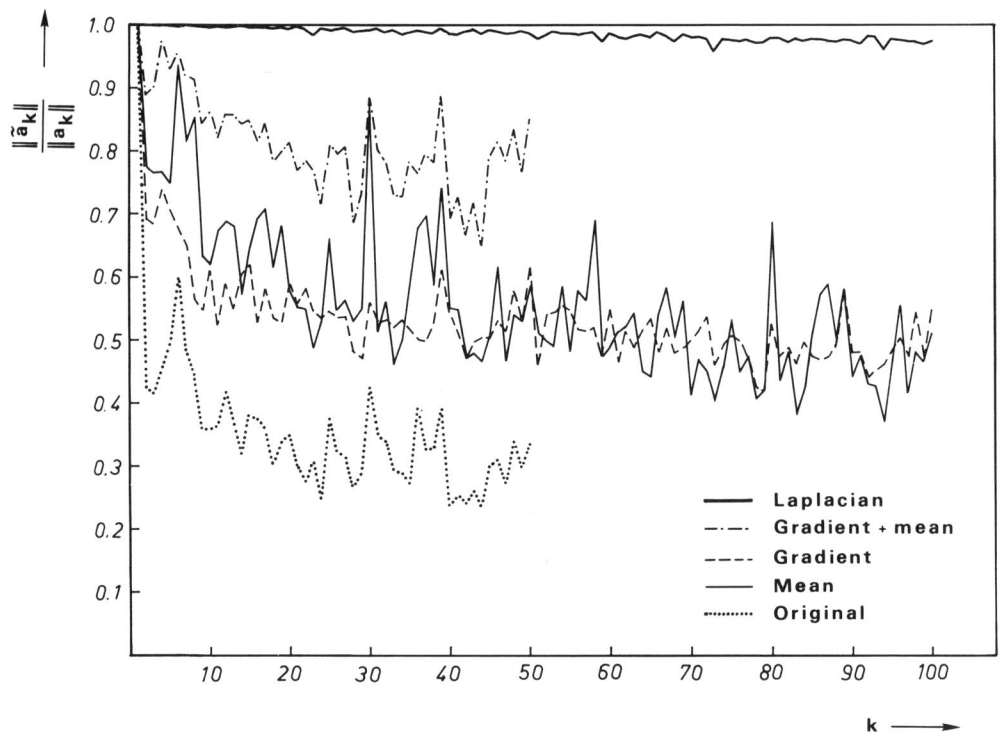

Fig. 2.13 Norms of successive basis vectors obtained in the Gram-Schmidt orthogonalization of photographic images. Original = images were orthogonalized as such. Mean = the mean of the picture elements was subtracted before orthogonalization. Gradient = the absolute value of the gradient was taken. Gradient + mean = after taking the gradient, the mean of it was subtracted. Laplacian = the images were preprocessed by the Laplacian before orthogonalization

Table 2.4 Average ratio of the largest element γ_r in the recollection to the next largest γ_k. Preprocessing operator: Laplacian (cf. Table 2.3)

10 reference patterns		100 reference patterns	
Key 50%	Key 10%	Key 50%	Key 10%
34.86	13.45	17.08	5.65

2.3.6 Optimal Nonlinear Associative Mappings

Linear associative mappings may be regarded as the lowest-order approach to the problem of associative transformations, in an attempt to find a mathematical operator by which arbitrary output patterns can be obtained from arbitrary input patterns. In view of the results of Subsection 1.3.4 it may be clear that the question about the existence of such a transformation is equivalent to the problem concerning the existence of a solution to the corresponding matrix equation. If the output responses are arbitrary, a necessary condition for an exact solution to exist is the linear independence of the columns of X, or of the patterns x_k. At least when the number of patterns is greater than their dimensionality, the vectors must be linearly dependent and no exact solution exists. For this reason there arises a need to generalize the class of associative mappings. Using nonlinear transformations it is possible to implement selective associative mappings for patterns which on account of their linear dependence would not be distinguishable in a linear transformation. The problem again can be formulated as follows: Between a set of column vectors $\{x_k\}$ which represents a set of input patterns, and another set of column vectors $\{y_k\}$ which corresponds to the set of output patterns associated with the x_k by pairs, there is to be found a transformation T by which every y_k is obtained from the corresponding x_k, either exactly, or approximately in the sense of least squares, as $y_k = T(x_k)$. It should be noted that in a special case, the y_k can be identified with the unit vectors.

Because there are infinitely many classes of nonlinear mappings, it may not be proper to speak of nonlinear transformations which are optimal in an absolute sense. The expression "optimal nonlinear associative mapping" used here only refers to a case in which a certain nonlinear functional form is assumed for the relation between the input and output vectors, and there is a finite number of parameters in this form which have to be optimized. Consider, for instance, polynomial transforms [47]

$$P_r(X) = L_0 + L_1(X) + L_2(X,X) + \ldots + L_r(X,\ldots,X) \; , \tag{2.25}$$

in which X is a matrix with the x_j as its columns, and L_q, $q = 0 \ldots r$ is a product form of degree q. The expression $P_r(X)$ is written explicitly as

$$(P_r(X))_{ik} = (L_0)_{ik} + \sum_{\alpha_1} (L_1)_{i\alpha_1} \xi_{\alpha_1 k}$$

$$+ \ldots + \sum_{\alpha_1 \ldots \alpha_r} (L_r)_{i,\alpha_1 \ldots \alpha_r} \xi_{\alpha_1 k} \ldots \xi_{\alpha_r k} \qquad (2.26)$$

where
$$x_k = [\xi_{1k}, \xi_{2k}, \ldots, \xi_{nk}]^T \; .$$

Denoting by Y a matrix with the y_k as its columns, the scalar coefficients

$$(L_j)_{i,\alpha_1 \ldots \alpha_j}$$

are to be determined in such a way that $P_r(X)$ approximates Y in the sense of least squares.

The above case belongs to a class of regression problems which are linear in the parameters although nonlinear with respect to the input vectors. It is demonstrable that the polynomial case can be discussed in a more general setting. Assume an arbitrary preprocessing transformation for the primary input patterns x_k such that every $x_k \in R^n$ is transformed into a new column vector $f_k \in R^q$. A matrix F is now defined which has the f_k as its columns. In the above example,

$$f_k = [1, \xi_{1k}, \xi_{2k}, \ldots, \xi_{nk}, \xi^2_{1k}, \xi^2_{2k}, \ldots, \xi^2_{nk}, \xi_{1k} \xi_{2k}, \ldots]^T \; . \qquad (2.27)$$

The problem is to find a linear form LF which approximates the matrix Y of the output vectors y_k in the sense of least squares, or possibly equals it. Here L is a matrix for which the least-square solution by the previous formalism reads as $\hat{L} = Y F^+$. The most important result achievable by the nonlinear preprocessing transformation is that the dimensionality of the vector $f_k \in R^q$ is increased; the probability for the transformed vectors becoming linearly independent thereby respectively increases.

A Numerical Example

The nonlinear preprocessing mapping is particularly effective if the primary pattern vector is of low dimensionality. In the following example, the primary patterns consisted of acoustic spectra taken with a commercial spectrum analyzer; the frequency scale was divided into 100 channels between 0 and 2 kHz, and the intensities of the channel outputs, integrated in each channel with a certain time constant, were chosen as the pattern elements. Fig. 2.14 shows one typical example of the spectra studied in the experiment [49].

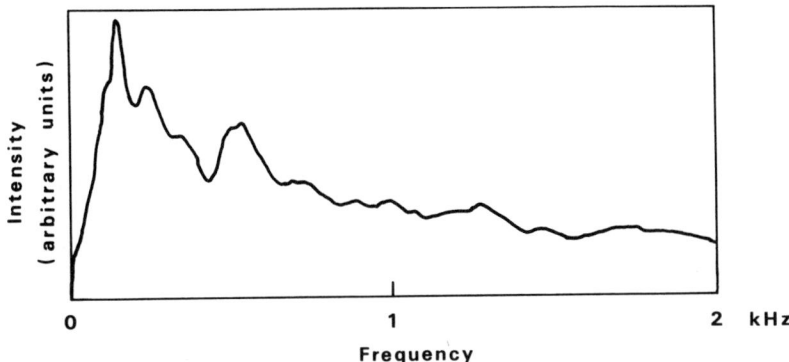

Fig. 2.14 A sample of acoustic spectra used in the identification experiment

If the preprocessing function is a homogeneous polynomial of the ξ_{ik}, then it is easy to see that multiplication of the original vector by a scalar results in a new f_k which is multiplied by another scalar; in other words, the relative magnitudes of the elements of f_k are not changed. This is an advantageous property in identification. In this particular example, the following form for the preprocessing function was selected:

$$f_k = [\xi_{1k}\xi_{2k}, \xi_{1k}\xi_{3k}, \ldots, \xi_{n-1,k}\xi_{n,k}]^T \tag{2.28}$$

This vector had $n(n-1)/2 = 4950$ elements, a dimensionality that is quite manageable by the above optimal mappings.

The primary purpose of this example was to demonstrate the following effect. It was pointed out in Subsections 2.3.2 and 2.3.5 that random noise is attenuated in an associative mapping by a factor $\sqrt{m/n}$ where m is the number of reference patterns and n their dimensionality. If n could artificially be enlarged, for instance, by the above nonlinear mapping where it was increased from 100 to 4950, one might expect that the noise-attenuation factor would be improved correspondingly. The theoretical analysis of Subsection 2.3.2 is not directly transferable to the present case since the elements of f_k depend on each other; nonetheless, numerical experiments have shown that the basic idea was valid. Fig. 2.15 shows results from an identification experiment with original and preprocessed vectors.

There were 45 spectra used as reference patterns, and the key patterns were formed by superimposing artificial white noise with different intensities on the original spectra. The reliability of the recognition was measured in terms of the

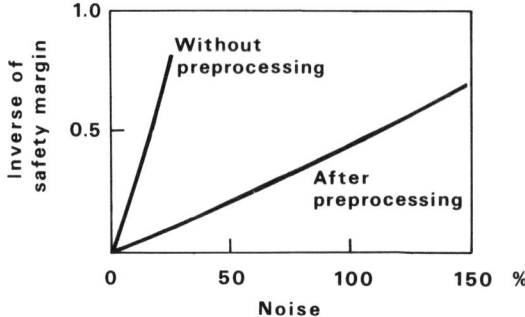

Fig. 2.15 Demonstration of improved identification when nonlinear preprocessing was used

relative magnitudes of elements in the output vector $\hat{u}$. As the ratio of the two largest elements is roughly inversely proportional to noise intensity, its inverse value was shown as the ordinate in the diagram.

The above results show that the reliability of identification of a noisy spectrum was improved by a factor of 6.2 to 6.9. Although this number theoretically is not quite the same as the inverse of the noise-attenuation factor, it may be interesting to compare that these two numbers were demonstrated to be close to each other: $\sqrt{4950/100} \approx 7$.

2.3.7 The Problem of Invariant Recognition

There is a question which frequently turns up in connection with new theories of associative memory, and which for long has constituted one of the central problems in pattern recognition, too. Based perhaps on subjective experiences, it is often maintained that an associative or recognitive scheme is not genuine unless it has the ability of identifying an object from its transformed versions; for instance, a visual object ought to be identifiable regardless of its position or location, or the size of an image projected from it on the retina of the eye. In psychology, a related phenomenon is called stimulus equivalence; if different stimulus patterns represent the same object or have the same meaning, they are experienced similar.

In an attempt to develop recognition schemes which tolerate various kinds of transformations of the patterns, it has been found that analytical identification schemes can easily be made insensitive to a single transformation group, for instance, translation of the patterns in the image plane, whereas simultaneous invariance to translation, rotation, changes in size, etc., has not succeeded. It seems that the requirement of invariance thereby may have been understood as too categorical. On the other hand, it ought to be known that even the biological systems are not perfectly ideal in this respect; for instance, recognition of an object becomes much more difficult if the latter is rotated by more than 45 degrees.

It would perhaps be more expedient to ask whether there exist recognition schemes which are able to extrapolate or interpolate patterned information with respect to a few reference patterns that represent the objects in different variations. This author holds the opinion that linear mappings in general have a remarkable interpolating and extrapolating ability if the patterns are rather "smooth" and several variations of them are used as reference patterns. This view has been validated in some voice identification experiments in which several (say, five or more) slightly different versions from each pattern were used as a set of reference patterns. With optical images, the recognition scheme can similarly be made to interpolate and extrapolate with respect to reference patterns with random translational, rotational, and other variations.

Nonetheless, frequently there occur tasks in practice whereby at least a high degree of translational invariance is needed. Below, a couple of such schemes are given. But before that, a typical organization of a recognition and identification scheme for patterns is introduced.

Organization of a Recognition System

A couple of previous examples, viz. the operation of the two-dimensional images by the Laplacian, and the transformation of spectra by polynomial mappings already gave hints for that there often exists special information in the patterns which can be extracted and enhanced by proper analysis, above named *preprocessing*. This may give us an idea that, in general, there exists with every recognition problem a particular type of preprocessing which is most suitable for it; the best method may be found heuristically, or by trial and error. Sometimes the necessary preprocessing operation is obvious from the given requirements, for instance, when the recognition must be invariant with respect to a group of transformations applied to the primary patterns.

A usual organization of a pattern-recognition system is shown in Fig. 2.16
It may not always be necessary that the preprocessing transformation is describable by a simple analytical algorithm. For instance, it seems that in the sensory systems of biological organisms there are many types of independent feature analyzers based

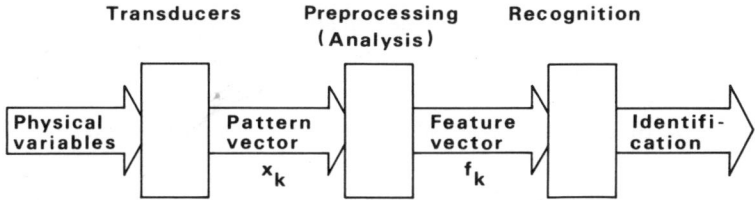

Fig. 2.16 Organization of a pattern recognition system

on different functional principles, and they all contribute to the feature vector f_k which accordingly may be of a very high dimensionality.

Preprocessing by Frequency Analysis

If a pattern is defined as a time series, for instance, as a set of subsequent samples taken from an acoustic signal, an often occurring requirement in its recognition is invariance with respect to an arbitrary shift of the pattern in time. Similarly, recognition of two-dimensional images may have to be invariant with respect to an arbitrary displacement of the objects in the image plane. Familiar types of preprocessing function with this property are the frequency spectra of the primary patterns: temporal frequency spectra of acoustic signals, and two-dimensional spatial frequency spectra of optic patterns.

The well-known Fourier transform from which frequency spectra can be derived has a computational implementation, named discrete Fourier transform (DFT) which for the time series $\{x_k\}_{k=0}^{N-1}$ has been defined as

$$f(p) = \frac{1}{N} \sum_{k=0}^{N-1} x_k w^{-pk},$$

with
$$w = e^{2\pi i/N}, \quad i = \sqrt{-1}.$$
(2.29)

The discrete amplitude spectrum of the DFT, namely, $|f(p)|$, and the discrete power spectrum of the DFT, or $|f(p)|^2$, are preprocessing functions of the $\{x_k\}$ which, for sufficiently long time series, have the required translational invariance.

The DFT can also be expressed in two dimensions. There exist extremely fast algorithms, named Fast Fourier Transform (FFT), for the computation of the DFT in one or more dimensions [41].

Analysis of Local Features

One possibility for the implementation of translationally invariant recognition is to analyze what "local features" there occur in the images. The feature vector f_k may be defined in such a way that each of its elements indicates the statistical frequency with which a certain local feature is present in the picture. As the positions of such local features are not specified in any way, the vector f_k obtained is invariant with respect to an arbitrary shift of the original pattern in the image plane, and even with respect to an interchange of some of its fragments [42].

The above idea is illustrated by a simple example in Fig. 2.17 in which the original patterns are defined in a square lattice, and the picture elements are assumed binary. The signal values surrounding any picture element may be regarded as a local feature, equivalent to a binary code. With eight neighbouring points there

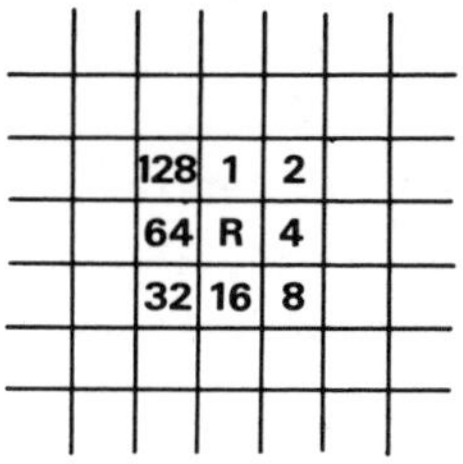

	128	1	2	
	64	R	4	
	32	16	8	

Fig. 2.17 Binary weights assigned to the neighbouring elements in a local feature. R: picture element under consideration

are 256 different local features or codes which can be regarded as binary numbers (cf. the binary weights assigned in Fig. 2.17 where the picture element under consideration is denoted by "R"). The frequencies with which the various features occur in the picture are then counted, and a histogram is formed. These histograms may as such be useful as the feature vectors f_k. It is also possible to consider other types of local features, for instance, value combinations in larger sets of neighbouring points. This method also has a bearing on the so-called Golay surroundings [40] defined in hexagonal lattices.

Utilization of Linear Dependence

Linear mappings have a property that generally has not been considered in pattern recognition. If, for instance, two patterns produce the same response in a linear associative mapping, then a similar response is produced by a linear combination of these patterns Similarity means here that the relative magnitudes of the pattern elements are not changed. So, if x_1 and x_2 are two patterns both of which produce an output pattern y when multiplied by the matrix M, and α_1 and α_2 are two scalars, then

$$M(\alpha_1 x_1 + \alpha_2 x_2) = (\alpha_1 + \alpha_2) y \ . \tag{2.30}$$

This property may be utilized in the case that the patterns have a spectral decomposition which is rather peaked, i.e., the patterns consist of a few strong frequency components.

For the demonstration of translational invariance, a one-dimensional pattern is first discussed. Assume the existence of a hypothetical signal axis defining a coordinate ζ. A one-dimensional function $f(\zeta)$ is defined on this axis. A pattern is derived from this function in the following way: for the pattern elements, a set of samples from the ζ-axis is taken. The samples need not be located equidistantly, but with random spacings. Other patterns are derived from $f(\zeta)$ by taking the samples from different locations of the ζ-axis, preserving the mutual distances of the sampling points unaltered. Let us first assume that $f(\zeta)$ is a sinusoidal function. A sinusoidal

function of any phase is obtainable from two fundamental waves with the same
frequency but different phases, as a linear combination. If now function $f(\zeta)$ is
composed of a finite number m of frequency components, and at least 2 m reference
patterns are derived from $f(\zeta)$ taken at different locations of the ζ-axis, then a
linear associative mapping based on these reference patterns becomes insensitive
to an arbitrary displacement of this pattern on the ζ-axis; this property is due
to the fact that the displaced pattern is a linear combination of the 2m reference
patterns.

Example

As the above principle works with two-dimensional spatial frequencies, too, an original
pattern was formed of five spatial frequencies, the wave vectors of which are shown
in Fig. 2.18 [50].

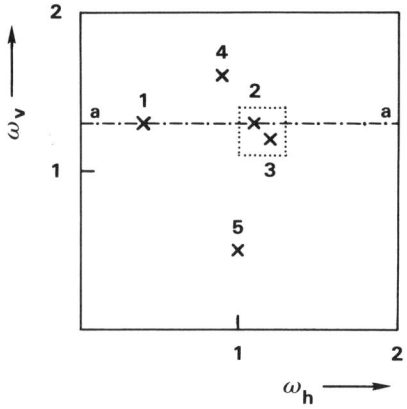

Fig. 2.18 Two-dimensional wave vectors
(with end points indicated by numbers 1
through 5) that define a spatial pattern.
Dotted lines: see Figs. 2.19 and 2.20

This pattern was stored in ten randomly displaced positions of the image plane and
each of such displaced patterns was mapped on a zero element. After this, it was
expected that when the original pattern was shown in an arbitrary position of the
image plane, its mapping result was zero. In order to check this, a frequency analysis
was performed. The output of the linear mapping was plotted in a logarithmic scale
versus a monochromatic test signal, the wave vector of which was varied over the
(ω_h, ω_v)-plane (h = horizontal, v = vertical). Fig. 2.19 shows the phase-averaged
output along the section a-a of Fig. 2.18 (ω_v = 1.3), and Fig. 2.20 an enlarged portion
of the (ω_h, ω_v)-plane indicated by the dotted line in Fig. 2.18.

It ought to be noticed that the decomposition of a pattern into a finite number
of frequency components is a special case of approximation of the patterns by functions generated by finite-order differential systems [41], and this is a standard
approach in linear system theory.

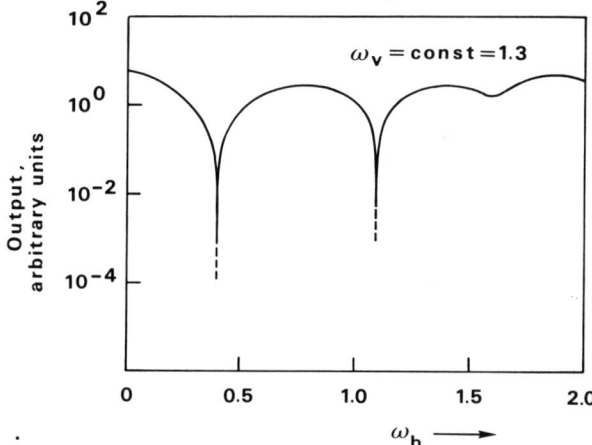

Fig. 2.19 Output of the linear associative mapping for input wave vectors corresponding to the points along the line a-a in Fig. 2.18

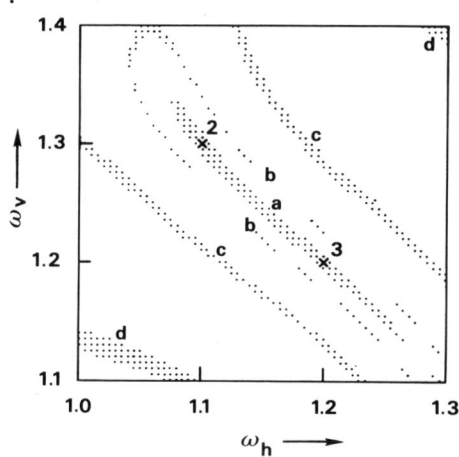

Fig. 2.20 Output of the linear associative mapping for input wave vectors corresponding to the dotted region in Fig. 2.18. The output has been given as a relief map where the contours indicated by a,b,c, and d correspond to the following (logarithmic) output levels:

a: -10   to -1.0
b: - 0.50   to -0.45
c: 0   to 0.05
d: 0.50   to 0.55

Linguistic Approach to Invariant Recognition

Because of difficulties in the implementation of invariant mappings, another line of research has recently been chosen in pattern recognition. This approach starts with an assumption that the recognitive scheme must actively take part in the analysis of patterns. One method thereby applied is called scene analysis, or perhaps representation of knowledge in vision, which tries to solve the recognition problem in this most complete form by linguistic analysis. This approach is probably based on a view that a natural (visual) recognition process is similar to a thought process, operating on elements which are related in a semantic way. Although this finding may be quite correct, it does not detract importance from the theories of basic associative mappings, beause one ought to realize that complex information processes may be composed of successive associative mappings along the same lines as the complex programs of digital computers can be derived from elementary logic.

Although it would be natural to think that associative mappings can be combined into very complex processes, the value of this approach has not yet been fully realized since no large-scale artificial computing facilities for such analog computations have been available; the digital computers, on account of their nature, are not very effective for the extensive parallel computations thereby needed.

2.3.8 Relationship Between Associative Mapping, Linear Regression, and Linear Estimation

Consider again the linear mapping $y_k = M x_k$, $k = 1, 2, \ldots, m$, where $x_k \in R^n$, $y_k \in R^p$. The case in which m was smaller than n was discussed above in detail; an exact solution for M was obtained at least in the case that the x_k were linearly independent. Let alone this restriction, it is necessary to point out that the x_k and y_k could be selected *completely independently*.

The associative mapping has a superficial resemblance to certain statistical regression problems in which a linear dependence between stochastic vectorial variables x and y is assumed. Notice carefully, however, that a linear statistical model *a priori* assumes y *dependent* on x, for instance, by $y = \Omega x$ where Ω is a matrix that may describe a physical, economical, or other process. Any deviations from this dependence are solely assumed to be due to stochastic errors or noise, and if (x_k, y_k) is a pair of realizations of x and y, respectively, then $y_k = \Omega x_k + v_k$ where v_k is the residual which has a certain statistical distribution. Hence x_k and y_k cannot be selected independently. The mathematical regression problem is to find the best value of Ω for which the average of v_k over a large number of observed realizations x_k and y_k is minimized in the sense of some statistical measure; in the simplest case, the sum of the $\|v_k\|^2$ is used. The number of pairs (x_k, y_k) may now be much greater than the dimensionality of x_k. Formally, however, the problem can be set as before: denoting

$$X = [x_1, x_2, \ldots, x_m] \;,\; Y = [y_1, y_2, \ldots, y_m] \tag{2.31}$$

the problem is to minimize the norm of the matrix expression $Y - \Omega X$.

Because the Penrose formalism was applicable to matrix equations of any dimensionality, the best approximate solution to the above problem can formally be written

$$\hat{\Omega} = Y X^+ \;. \tag{2.32}$$

Notice, however, that the columns of X are now linearly dependent. If the x_k are stochastic variables with, say, a normal distribution, the *rows* of X, however, can then be assumed linearly independent. For this reason, the regression solution for the matrix $\hat{\Omega}$ reads

$$\hat{\Omega} = Y X^T (XX^T)^{-1} \;. \tag{2.33}$$

For comparison, let us recall that a matrix of the form BA^+, with the *columns* of A linearly independent, can be written $B(A^T A)^{-1} A^T$.

The difference between these two cases shall yet be subjected to closer inspection in Section 3.3 where recursive computational solutions to matrix equation are derived.

Relationship of the Regression Solution to the Linear Estimator

The least-squares optimal solution to the matrix equation $Y = \Omega X$ has a close relationship to the so-called best linear unbiased estimator (BLUE). If, namely, a linear statistical dependence between the stochastic vectors x and y is assumed, and x is regarded as a measurement from which y is to be estimated, the problem is to construct an operator Ω (called estimator) by which the best approximation $\hat{y}$ of y in the sense of least squares is obtained as $\hat{y} = \Omega x$. In estimation problems, the a priori statistical information about the vectoral variables x and y may be expressed in terms of the theoretical correlation matrices

$$E(xx^T) = C_{xx} \quad \text{and} \quad E(yx^T) = C_{yx} \tag{2.34}$$

which are assumed to be known. The BLUE of y, given an observation x, is then

$$\hat{y} = C_{yx} C_{xx}^{-1} x = \Omega x \;. \tag{2.35}$$

It is assumed that the inverse of C_{xx} exists which holds true if x is a stochastic variable for which the rank of C_{xx} is full.

On the other hand, the regression solution for $\hat{\Omega}$ from (2.34) can be written, after expanding by m^{-1},

$$\hat{\Omega} = YX^T(XX^T)^{-1} = (\frac{1}{m} \sum_{k=1}^{m} y_k x_k^T)(\frac{1}{m} \sum_{k=1}^{m} x_k x_k^T)^{-1} = \hat{C}_{yx}\hat{C}_{xx}^{-1} \;. \quad (2.36)$$

It is now directly discernible that $\hat{\Omega}$ corresponds to the operator $\Omega = C_{yx}C_{xx}^{-1}$ with the only difference that the theoretical correlation matrices C_{xx} and C_{yx} have been replaced by their approximations $\hat{C}_{xx}$ and $\hat{C}_{yx}$, respectively, computed from a finite series of observations; thus there is a simple correspondence between regression and the BLUE.

2.4 Relationship of Associative Mappings to Pattern Classification

Pattern recognition may be regarded as a special case of associative mappings, namely, as a process in which classes of patterns are directly mapped on a set of discrete elements. Most pattern recognition methods work as pattern identification schemes, too; however, the problem is largely that of mathematical statistics and does not necessarily presuppose physical realizability. Because a thorough discussion of pattern recognition principles can be found in many excellent textbooks (cf. [51] through [64]), it is felt that presentation of such methods can be abandoned here. Instead, only a few topics are reviewed which may be relevant in the connection of system-theoretical models of associative memory.

2.4.1 Discriminant Functions

Let us consider patterns which are represented as vectors in the multidimensional Euclidean space R^n. One of the most fundamental approaches in pattern recognition is the classification of patterns by means of *discriminant functions*. Assume that the representation vectors (or their end points in R^n) are grouped into a finite number of clusters, each of them corresponding to a particular class. The problem is then to mathematically define the equations of those hypersurfaces which optimally separate all clusters from each other. To the first, it should be noticed that there are infinitely many alternatives for mathematical forms; one possibility is to try the simplest ones. The lowest-degree surface is linear (hyperplane); if the clusters are not linearly separable, it is then possible to take polynomial forms of successively higher degree. Of course, expansions in other elementary or special functions can be tried for the separating surfaces if there are good reasons to assume that the data are distributed accordingly. But it ought to be noticed, too, that the separation of points can be optimal only with respect to some criterion which, for instance, takes into account the distances of all points from the separating surfaces. One frequently used criterion is the sum of squares of the Euclidean distances.

The separating surface between two classes can be defined in terms of *discriminant functions* $\delta_k(x)$, $k = 1,2,\ldots,m$ which are continuous, scalar-valued functions of the pattern vector x. The separating surface between classes S_i and S_j is then defined by the equation

$$\delta_i(x) - \delta_j(x) = 0 \quad . \tag{2.37}$$

If $x \in S_i$, then for all $j \neq i$ there must hold $\delta_i(x) > \delta_j(x)$, or

$$\delta_i(x) = \max_k \{\delta_k(x)\} \quad . \tag{2.38}$$

The Linear Classifier

As an example of the application of discriminant functions, the linear classifier may be mentioned. The discriminant functions take the form

$$\delta_k(x) = w_k^T x + \kappa_k \tag{2.39}$$

where w_k is the kth *weight vector*, and κ_k is a scalar. A hyperplane which separates the classes S_i and S_j has the equation

$$w'^T x = \kappa'$$

where

$$w' = w_i - w_j \text{ and } \kappa' = \kappa_j - \kappa_i \quad . \tag{2.40}$$

If κ' can be set equal to zero, in other words, if only the relative magnitudes of the pattern elements are considered to be significant, or if the mean of the elements is always subtracted from all patterns, then the discriminant functions of the linear classifier have a relationship to the optimal linear associative mapping. In that formulation, the problem is to find a matrix M by which pattern x is to be multiplied to obtain a set of linear discriminant functions,

$$M x = [\delta_1(x), \delta_2(x), \ldots, \delta_m(x)]^T \tag{2.41}$$

the latter performing the separation of the given patterns in the sense of least squares. This problem is solved by assuming that for all reference patterns belonging to the kth class, the $\delta_j(x)$ must be of the form δ_{jk} (the Kronecker delta). Eq.(2.41) is obviously equivalent to the matrix equation

$$MX = U, \text{ with } X = [x_1, x_2, \ldots, x_m]^T, \ U = [u_1, u_2, \ldots, u_m]^T, \tag{2.42}$$

the u_j being unit vectors having a 1 at their kth position if x_j belongs to class S_k. The familiar solution reads

$$M = UX^+ . \tag{2.43}$$

2.4.2 Comparison Methods

The most trivial of all classification methods is to compare the unknown pattern with all known reference patterns on the basis of some criterion for "degree of similarity", in order to decide to which class the pattern belongs. One criterion of similarity between two patterns x and x_k is their mutual distance $d(x,x_k)$ in some metric. For instance, Euclidean metric is often quite useful. It is obvious that for the final resolution plenty of computations are needed, unless a small representative set of reference patterns from each class can be used for comparison. In the *Nearest-Neighbour (NN) Method*, $d(x,x_k)$ is computed for all reference patterns and pattern x is classified according to the smallest value. In order to increase reliability, a majority decision over a number of nearest neighbours is sometimes taken for the basis of classification [52]. The nearest-neighbour methods usually yield separating surfaces which are piecewise linear, i.e., they consist of segments of hyperplanes.

If the Euclidean distance measure is applied, and one reference pattern from each class (or the average of each class) is used for comparison, then the nearest-neighbour method is simply equivalent with the correlation matrix formalism mentioned in Subsection 1.2.5.

Identification of Patterns by the Angles

One nearest-neighbour strategy for the search of information from files uses the following simple similarity criterion. Because the patterned representations may have different norms, and the norm of a key pattern too depends on the number of data elements employed in it, it is often reasonable to define as the degree of matching of the key with stored patterns the *angle* between these vectors: in the n-dimensional space, the angle between vectors x and x_k is defined as

$$\theta_k = \arccos \frac{(x,x_k)}{\|x\| \|x_k\|} . \tag{2.44}$$

The above heuristically founded strategy is in general not optimal, but practical experience has shown that it performs rather well even with a large number of patterns if these are sufficiently orthogonal. Then, namely, the inner product (x, x_k) is much larger for a pattern with which the key has a higher correlation than for any other. Because inherent orthogonality of the stored patterns cannot be presupposed, it may be necessary to improve the orthogonality by preprocessing. With two-dimensional patterns such an effective and simple preprocessing method is spatial differentation, already mentioned in Subsection 2.3.5. Operation of the patterns by higher-order spatial differential operators, e.g., by the two-dimensional Laplacian $\partial^2/\partial \zeta_h^2 + \partial^2/\partial \zeta_v^2$, or perhaps by $\partial^2/\partial \zeta_h \partial \zeta_v$, where ζ_h and ζ_v are the horizontal and vertical coordinates in the image plane, respectively, has proven effective for the identification of, say, photographic images. The effect of differential operators is to suppress lower spatial frequencies with the result that the orthogonality of any arbitrarily selected portion of a pattern with respect to the same portion in all other patterns is increased.

A comparison of the optimal associative mapping with the identification method by the angles was performed. The purpose was to demonstrate associative recall, and so a fragment of 50% of the images (left half) was used as the key pattern. In the optimal associative mapping, the ratio of the two largest elements of the output vector $\hat{u}$ was used as an indicator of selectivity. In the identification by the angles, the respective measure was the ratio of the two largest values of $\cos \theta_k$. The results with 10 and 100 reference patterns, respectively, were compared. The values in Table 2.4 are averages taken over the ten first patterns. Results with 1000 reference patterns were computable by the identification by the angles method; computational resources were not sufficient to perform the comparison with the optimal method. With both methods, the patterns were preprocessed by $\partial^2/\partial \zeta_h \partial \zeta_v$.

Table 2.5 Comparison of the results in optimal identification and in the identification by the angles, respectively (Dimensionality = 3240)

Method	Number of patterns		
	10	100	1000
Optimal	28.8	15.8	-
Identification by the angles	24.5	9.6	7.9

The Correlation Matrix Memory

Especially in the modelling of adaptive physical associative networks, the correlation matrix formalism (cf. Secs. 1.2 and 4.2) is often obtained as a solution to system equations. For instance, the memory matrix may be

$$M = \sum_{k=1}^{m} y_k x_k^T = Y X^T , \qquad (2.45)$$

with X and Y two rectangular matrices having the key vectors x_k and some associated data y_k as their columns, respectively. The recollection y is the product of M with a key pattern x:

$$y = M x = \sum_{k=1}^{m} (x, x_k) y_k \qquad (2.46)$$

so that y is a linear mixture of the patterns y_k, with relative intensities proportional to the inner products (x, x_k). If the patterns x_k and the key x have equal norms, this method agrees with the method of the angles.

It may be stated that the correlation matrix is equivalent to the optimal linear associative operator if the stored vectors x_k are orthonormal; in this case, the correlation matrix mapping has the same error-correcting properties as the optimal operators. The optimality condition can be shown, for instance, by the following direct derivation: since the x_k are orthonormal, there follows that $X^T X = I$. The optimal solution for M is then

$$Y X^+ = Y (X^T X)^{-1} X^T = Y X^T .$$

The above considerations give us an idea that physical models of associative memory which are described by the correlation matrix may be useful if the input patterns x_k can be orthogonalized by a proper preprocessing. This idea is applied in some modelling approaches of distributed biological memory (cf. Sec. 4.2).

2.4.3 Statistical Formulation of Pattern Classification

In the previous examples, the discriminant functions were completely defined by the reference data. The efficiency of classification might significantly be improved, however, if all available a priori knowledge is utilized. In many cases there are good reasons to assume on the basis of physical or other properties of observations that their distribution has some familiar theoretical form; it is then sufficient to determine a few parameters in the distributions for optimal design of the classification algorithm. This method is called *parametric classification*.

Pattern classification is a process that is related to decision-making, detection-theory, etc., and may be discussed in these settings. The only motive for the following discussion is to point out that certain forms of separating surfaces, for instance, the linear and quadratic ones, may have a statistical justification.

A Note on Probabilistic Notations

If a process is assumed in which only a finite number of distinct events $X_1, X_2, \ldots, X_s$ may occur, the relative frequencies of their occurrences are denoted by $P(X_k)$, $k = 1, 2, \ldots, s$ where $P(.)$ may be identified with the usual *probability* function. On the other hand, if x is a continuous-valued stochastic variable with a *distribution* $p(x)$, then $p(.)$ has the property of a density function and is often called *probability density*. If the domain of x, being a subset of Euclidean space R^n, is divided into contiguous volume differentials dV_x, then, obviously, $p(x) \, dV_x$ is the probability for the occurrence of a value x within this differential volume. In the following, probabilities for discrete events are denoted by capital letter $P(.)$, and the probability for X on the condition that Y occurs is $P(X|Y)$. The probability densities are denoted by lower-case letters $p(.)$, and the probability density of variable x on the condition that Y occurs is $p(x|Y)$. It should be noted that quite consistently in this convention $P(Y|x)$ is the probability for Y on the condition that the continuous variable x attains a certain value.

Statistical Definition of the Discriminant Functions

When the prototype data are replaced by conditional distributions of the patterns, the a priori probability density for the occurrence of an observation of a continuous-valued vector x is denoted by $p(x)$. The probability for any observed pattern really belonging to class S_k is abbreviated $P(S_k)$. The distribution of those pattern vectors which belong to class S_k is $p(x|S_k)$. This expression is the usual conditional probability of x, or its a priori probability on a condition abbreviated as S_k. In many cases, the theoretical form of $p(x|S_k)$ can be assumed, or can be approximately found out from samples in preliminary studies.

The theories of decision processes are centrally based on the concept of a *loss function* (cost function) the value of which depends on external factors, for instance, the importance of detection of a particular occurrence, or of a miss to detect it. Let $C(S_i, S_k)$ be the unit cost of one decision which indicates the reward or punishment of classification of a pattern to S_i when it was actually from S_k. If all patterns were considered equally important and the cost of a correct classification were denoted by 0, then all false classifications may cause a unit cost. (In classification, only relative costs are significant.) Therefore, one simple case of unit cost function might be $C(S_i, S_k) = 1 - \delta_{ik}$. Now the *conditional average loss*, or the cost of classifying patterns into class S_k their actually being statistically distributed into classes S_i, $i = 1, 2, \ldots, m$ is

$$L(x, S_k) = \sum_{i=1}^{m} P(S_i|x) \, C(S_k, S_i) \tag{2.47}$$

where $P(S_i|x)$ is the probability of pattern with value x belonging to class S_i. This conditional probability is related to $p(x|S_i)$ and it may be thought to result from the fact that the distributions $p(x|S_i)$ may overlap in R^n, whereby there is a definite probability for x belonging to any class. There is a fundamental identity in the theory of probability which states that if $P(X,Y)$ is the joint probability for the events X and Y to occur, then

$$P(X,Y) = P(X|Y) \, P(Y) = P(Y|X) \, P(X) \,. \tag{2.48}$$

This is the foundation of the so-called Bayesian philosophy of probability which deals with probabilities that are dependent on new observations. When applied to the present case, the above formula yields

$$-L(x, S_k) = \max_i \{-L(x, S_i)\} \,. \tag{2.49}$$

It will now be seen that the negative of the loss function satisfies the requirements set on the discriminant functions; since the cost of classifying x into S_i any other than S_k is higher, $-L(x, S_k) = \max \{-L(x, S_i)\}$. On the other hand, when considering candidates for discriminant functions, any factors or additive terms in this expression which are common to all classes can be dropped. It may now be a good strategy to select the discriminant functions as

$$\delta_k(x) = - \sum_{i=1}^{m} p(x|S_i) \, P(S_i) \, C(S_k, S_i) \,. \tag{2.50}$$

One basic case of discriminant functions is obtained by taking $C(S_k, S_i) = 1 - \delta_{ki}$, whereby

$$\delta_k(x) = - \sum_{i=1}^{m} p(x|S_i) \, P(S_i) + p(x|S_k) \, P(S_k) \,. \tag{2.51}$$

Since now all possible classes occur among the S_i, $i = 1, 2, \ldots, m$, then an identity holds that

$$\sum_{i=1}^{m} p(x|S_i) \, P(S_i) = p(x)$$

and being constant with k, this term can be dropped. For a new discriminant function it is possible to redefine

$$\delta_k(x) = p(x|S_k) \, P(S_k) \quad . \tag{2.52}$$

It should be realized that according to the definition of discriminant functions, the form of the separating surface is not changed if any monotonically increasing function of $p(x|S_k) \, P(S_k)$ is selected for $\delta_k(x)$.

An Example of Parametric Classification

Assume that the patterns of every class have normal distributions with different statistics:

$$p(x|S_k) = \lambda_k \exp\{-\tfrac{1}{2}(x-\mu_k)^T C_k^{-1}(x-\mu_k)\} \tag{2.53}$$

where λ_k is a normalizing constant that depends on C_k. For the discriminant function, $\log\{p(x|S_k) \, P(S_k)\}$ is selected:

$$\delta_k(x) = \log \lambda_k - \tfrac{1}{2}(x-\mu_k)^T C_k^{-1}(x-\mu_k) + \log P(S_k) \tag{2.54}$$

which is a quadratic function of x. Consequently, the separating surfaces are *second-degree surfaces*.

As a special case, distributions which have equal covariance matrices $C_k = C$ may be studied, whereby $\lambda_k = \lambda$. This may be the case, e.g., with patterns derived from univariate time series. All terms independent of k are now dropped. Moreover, the symmetry of covariance matrices is utilized for simplification, whereby

$$\delta_k(x) = \mu_k^T C^{-1} x - \tfrac{1}{2} \mu_k^T C^{-1} \mu_k + \log P(S_k) \quad . \tag{2.55}$$

Surprisingly, this is *linear* in x even for arbitrary a priori probabilities of the classes, and with arbitrary class means.

Chapter 3
Adaptive Formation of Optimal Associative Mappings

3.1 On the Implementation of Conditioned Responses in Simple Physical Systems

The idea of machine learning was originally based on the application of variable elements which change their parametric values by the signals they transmit; later, learning processes have been discussed on a more abstract algorithmic level, and mathematical statistics has become the general setting of these problems. Nevertheless, in its genuine form machine learning is a physical process.

The adaptive networks devised for learning machines almost without exception have been constructed of elements which have a discrimination threshold, i.e., which perform elementary classification operations. It seems, however, that the generation of optimal linear or nonlinear associative mappings in adaptive processes has not been subject to much investigation. This section therefore first reviews the basic adaptive process in its simplest form. After that, new mathematical formalisms are reported in Section 3.2 which allow the application of almost similar physical principles to the implementation of optimal associative memory. Chapter 3 ends up with the mathematically ideal recursive algorithms for the generation of optimal associative mappings by computational techniques.

3.1.1 A Simple Adaptive Linear System

There exist several adaptive systems which at least partly make use of linear operations: the adaptive linear unit discussed below is the basic paradigm of them [142]. In a simple physical implementation (Fig. 3.1) this device comprises a set of variable resistors connected to a circuit which can sum up the currents caused by the input voltage signals.

Although the physical implementation of an adaptive process is here exemplified in a case when there is only one output, it may be clear that a system with many parallel outputs is directly implementable by multiple units of the above kind.

If the input conductances are denoted by μ_i, $i = 0,1,2,\ldots,n$, and the input and output signals by ξ_i and η, respectively, then the system transfer equation reads:

$$\eta = \sum_{i=1}^{n} \mu_i \xi_i + \mu_0 \quad . \tag{3.1}$$

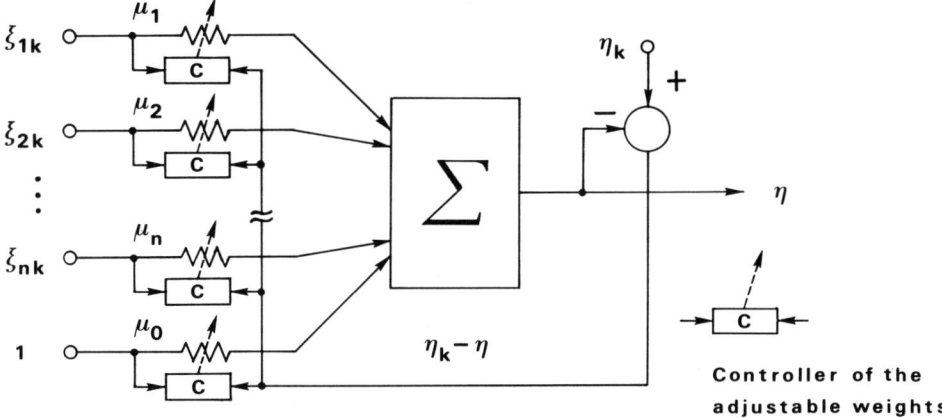

Fig. 3.1 An adaptive linear unit

The purpose of this device is to yield a given value η_k at its output when the set of values $\{\xi_{ik}\}$, $i = 0,1,\ldots,n$, is applied at the inputs. The problem is to determine the coefficients μ_i, $i = 0,1,\ldots,n$ in such a way that the input-output-response is correct for a large number of arbitrarily chosen signal sets. Apparently this is the problem of associative mapping in the case of a single output. If an accurate mapping is not possible, η has to approximate the η_k, for instance, in the sense of least squares. An adaptive operation means that there exists a mechanism by which the μ_i can be adjusted, usually iteratively, to attain the correct values. Systems with this ability are sometimes named learning machines [66, 67].

One problem, postponed to the next section, is connected with the representation of *negative* values of the μ_i. A solution for it with fixed linear networks was mentioned in Subsection 1.2.5; here adaptation causes extra problems.

The adaptive changes of the μ_i may be discussed as a so-called discrete-time process. If the signals and parameters are examined at a series of instances of time $\{t_k\}$, $k = 1, 2, \ldots$ and the same subscript k is used for variables, it is assumed that the parametric changes can be defined by the recursion

$$\mu_{i,k+1} = \mu_{ik} + \alpha_k(\eta_k - \eta)\xi_{ik} \tag{3.2}$$

with α_k a sufficiently small positive constant. In a simpler case, especially if the t_k are equidistant, α_k may be taken constant, equal to α. This is clearly a *corrective* process in which, if the response η was wrong, the values of μ_i are adjusted in a direction in which the error $\eta - \eta_k$ is apparently diminished.

As mentioned above, adaptive systems frequently include nonlinear (discrimination) operations, usually in the form of a threshold-logic unit (TLU) [67]. Another class of adaptive units, named perceptrons, combines several threshold-logic units into a single system which is then used to implement an adaptive pattern classifier. These devices, although fundamental in simple pattern classification problems, will be omitted here.

Description of Adaptation by the Stochastic Approximation

Below, adaptation of a linear system is described by a formalism which has been developed for regression problems. Let it be recalled that the linear regression solution is explicitly expressed in (2.33) and (2.36) of Section 2.3.8, although computation of inverse matrices may be tedious if the dimensionality is high. Solution methods called stochastic approximation as exemplified here are especially useful in more complicated regression problems when other means do not apply, for instance, when nonlinearities are present in the model, or the stochastic processes have complicated or unknown statistics. A rigorous discussion of stochastic approximation and nonlinear regression can be found elsewhere [65,68-70].

Without loss of generality, μ_0 may now be omitted since the corresponding input (=1) is equivalent to a constant pattern element. Let us denote the set of input signals by a vector $x = [\xi_1, \xi_2, \ldots, \xi_n]^T$ and let $m^T = [\mu_1, \mu_2, \ldots, \mu_n]$. If $x \in R^n$ and $\eta \in R$ are stochastic variables, and a linear dependence is assumed between them, $\eta = m^T x + \varepsilon$, with ε a stochastic error with zero expectation value, a quadratic error criterion is defined by a functional

$$J = E\{(\eta - m^T x)^2\} \qquad (3.3)$$

where $E\{\cdot\}$ is the mathematical expectation. The problem is to find a value m^* for m which minimizes the functional J; the condition of extremality is

$$\nabla_m J \Big|_{m=m^*} = \left[\frac{\partial J}{\partial \mu_1}, \frac{\partial J}{\partial \mu_2}, \ldots, \frac{\partial J}{\partial \mu_n}\right]^T \Big|_{m=m^*} = 0 \quad . \qquad (3.4)$$

The local extremum of functional J can be found by the gradient method; starting with an arbitrary initial value for m denoted by m_0, a sequence of discrete values $\{m_k^T\}$ is defined by

$$m_k^T = m_{k-1}^T - G_k \nabla_m J \Big|_{m=m_{k-1}} \qquad (3.5)$$

where G_k is a gain matrix. It has been shown that a condition for the convergence of m_k is that matrix G_k be positive definite. The norm of G_k has some bounds, too. One important choice is $G_k = \alpha_k I$ (this complies with the method of steepest descent when α_k is suitably chosen).

If it is not a priori assumed that the statistics of the linear model are known, the least-square optimal value must be computed from a series of realizations of x and η. The idea followed in stochastic approximation is to replace $\nabla_m J$ by its approximate value, or the gradient of the integrand $(\eta - m^T x)^2$ which is then a stochastic vector, its value depending on the realizations $x = x_k$ and $\eta = \eta_k$. Now it is obtained, when a new value for m_k is computed every time when a pair (x_k, η_k) is observed,

$$m_k^T = m_{k-1}^T + \alpha_k (\eta_k - m_{k-1}^T x_k) x_k^T \quad . \tag{3.6}$$

This is apparently identical with the reinforcement rule (3.2) written in vector notation. It has been shown that this sequence converges (with probability one) towards the optimal value $(m*)^T$ for which J is minimum, if the following conditions are valid for the sequence $\{\alpha_k\}$:

$$\sum_{k=1}^{\infty} \alpha_k = \infty \; , \; \sum_{k=1}^{\infty} \alpha_k^2 < \infty \quad . \tag{3.7}$$

For instance, $\alpha_k = k^{-1}$ satisfies these conditions. The following choice for the gain [70] has been found to yield a rather fast convergence in many applications:

$$\alpha_k = (\sum_{p=1}^{k} \|x_p\|^2)^{-1} \quad . \tag{3.8}$$

The results derived from stochastic approximation are not directly applicable to simple physical systems in which the constancy of the α_k would be a desirable feature. A new result, discussed in this book, is the possibility for having a large constant value α_k and still achieving optimal asymptotic properties under the constraint that the patterns x_k are mutually linearly independent. This analysis will be given in Subsection 3.2.2.

3.1.2 On the Physical Realizability of Adaptive Elements

There are three basic problems to be solved before the implementation of simple and cheap adaptive units by analog methods becomes feasible. One is the representation of negative weights by physical elements such as resistors which have parameter values that are always positive; the second problem concerns the simplest mechanism which would form the product of two signals. To the third, permanent parametric changes ought to be caused in circuit elements.

Although adaptive devices have been implemented for a small number of variable elements, their real breakthrough is still subject to technological development which would make the automatic production of adaptive networks feasible. In this book it has been preferred to discuss the mathematical conditions of adaptation and to omit the appraisal of technological implementations.

Representation of Negative Weights

One might think that a straightforward method for the implementation of negative parameters is the shift of the parameter scale whereby a positive value $\bar{\mu}$ of a parameter corresponds to a numerical value zero; a value of the parameter which is less than $\bar{\mu}$ would then be regarded negative. A drawback of this method is that the implementation of the multiplication operation becomes more difficult. For this reason, the antagonistic encoding of negative signals as shown in Fig. 1.9 ought to be preferred. Another possibility is to apply the input signal together with its negative at the opposite ends of a potentiometer, and to take the output from its slide; a continuous adjustment from the positive to the negative range of parameters then becomes possible. Although potentiometers have been used in adaptive systems with a few parameters, they certainly comprise too expensive a solution in an adaptive associative memory with a very great number of variable elements.

A further method for the representation of negative weights will be considered below with the capacitor memory.

Computation of Signal Products

Assume now that the problem of negative weights has in some way been solved, and the task is to implement a multiplier in which one of the multiplicands may have an arbitrary sign.

A particularly simple solution is possible if the output of the unit is followed by a threshold device which makes the output η binary, discretized to the values 0 and 1. Although the adaptive process is then no more the same as above, it can be shown to converge, too. If now η_k and the ξ_{ik} similarly attain only binary values, then one of the multiplicands in (3.2) has the value 0 or 1, and the other, one of the values -1, 0, and 1. It is a simple task to implement a multiplication circuit for such operands, using electronic logic gates.

A variant of the previous method for continuous signal values might make use of pulse-frequency modulation. Assume that all signal values can be represented by trains of impulses, and the signal intensity is represented by the frequency of the impulses. If two incoherent (asynchronous) trains of impulses converge upon a simple logic circuit which forms the logic product or conjunction of them, an output impulse train is obtained, the rate of which is obviously proportional to the product of the input frequencies.

Finally it may be mentioned that it is always possible to use digital representation for signal values and to apply digitally operating processor circuits for the execution of multiplications. Although this seems an expensive solution, it ought to be realized that extra-large-scale integrated circuits (with tens of thousands of elementary digital circuits on a silicon chip) are already technologically feasible. Implementation of a highly parallel digital processor for the adaptive system might therefore be developed.

Adaptive Resistors

A simple variable resistor can be implemented by the electroplating process. The thickness of a conductive film on the cathode of a plating cell can be increased or decreased by controlling the direction and intensity of the plating current (Fig. 3.2). The conductance of the film is directly proportional to its thickness. Sensing of the conductance, without interference from the plating process, can be made using ac signals.

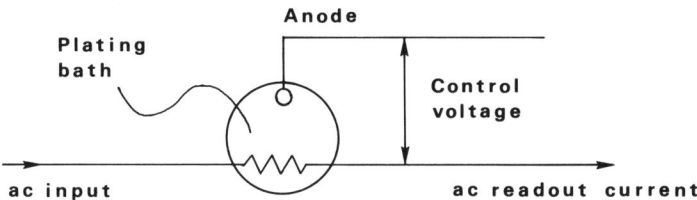

Fig. 3.2 Plating cell for an adaptive resistor

Electroplated resistors have a drawback of losing their stability during many reversible changes. Although they have been used for adaptive devices, they may not satisfy the demands of continuous use.

Capacitor Memory

The following system has adaptive weights which are represented by electrical charges in a set of capacitances. A high degree of linearity is thereby achieved. A minor drawback of this principle is that the stored information is volatile whereby the time constants characterizing the leakage of charge ought to be high. There exist some promises for that so-called charge-coupled devices might be applied, and they are amenable to mass-production by integrated circuit technology. To date, a memory system using a similar principle has been built of discrete electronic components (Fig. 3.3).

The following scheme shows the principle in major features. It is simplest to assume that the ξ-signals are binary, while η can attain arbitrary positive or negative values.

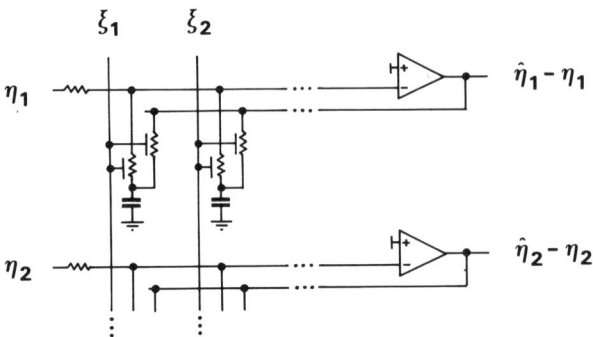

Fig. 3.3 Capacitor memory

The voltage-controllable resistances, here represented by field-effect transistors, are controlled between the cut-off and conductive states by the ξ-signals. The gain of the output amplifier is much greater than unity, whereby negative feedback drives the capacitor voltages to stationary values for any persistent values of the ξ_{ik} and η_k. The voltages of the capacitors can be shown to be built up approximately according to (3.6). During readout the left input η-signal is zero, whereby the associated value η_k is obtained at the output.

3.2 Adaptive Filters Which Compute Orthogonal Projections

It was shown in Section 2.3 that two basic types of orthogonal projection operations, characterized as the autoassociative mapping and the Novelty Filter, respectively, could be used to reconstruct missing parts in key patterns. Random noise components superimposed on the input information were thereby optimally attenuated. These particular mappings thus have the property of restoration of information which is optimal in the sense of least squares. The autoassociative mapping is that paradigm which theoretically implements the optimal autoassociative recall. On the other hand, it seems that the optimal Novelty Filter is more readily implementable by adaptive physical systems. The purpose of this section is to demonstrate the adaptive generation of such orthogonalizing filters in physical systems.

3.2.1 The Novelty Detector Paradigm

In order to gain a view about the basic adaptive filter functions, it may be expedient to start the discussion with the mathematically simplest paradigm, here named the Novelty Detector. This is a system unit with several inputs and one output, depicted in Fig. 3.4. An application of this system may be to monitor spatial input patterns formed of simultaneous signal values. As long as these patterns are *familiar* in the sense of having occurred frequently enough, the output remains at a value zero. If, however, the present input is "new", the output signal deviates from zero. The following system is shown to have this property.

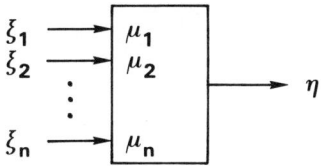

Fig. 3.4 Novelty Detector

All inputs are coupled to the output through channels with varying weights and summed up. The input weights μ_i, $i=1,2,\ldots n$, can be positive or negative, and so are the input and output signal values, denoted by ξ_i, $i=1,2,\ldots n$ and η, respectively. The physical realizability of the system equations with arbitrary signs of the signals and parameters are subject to similar discussions as carried out with the adaptive linear unit in Section 3.1. The system equations are now assumed to read

$$\eta = \sum_{i=1}^{n} \mu_i \xi_i \,, \tag{3.9}$$

$$d\mu_i/dt = -\alpha \xi_i \eta \,. \tag{3.10}$$

Using the earlier introduced vector notations, (3.9) and (3.10) can be written in the form

$$\eta = m^T x \,, \tag{3.11}$$

$$dm^T/dt = -\alpha x^T \eta = -\alpha m^T x x^T \,. \tag{3.12}$$

The adaptive behaviour of the above system can easily be analyzed in the case of stationary input patterns. Assume first that the input vector x is constant with time for $t \geq t_0$; then, by substitution, the following expression can be found to constitute the solution of (3.12):

$$m^T(t) = m^T(t_0) [I - \omega(t) x x^T]$$

where $\tag{3.13}$

$$\omega(t) = \|x\|^{-2} (1 - e^{-\alpha \|x\|^2 (t - t_0)}) \,.$$

Notice that $0 \leq \omega(t) \leq \|x\|^{-2}$.

Consider now a finite set of patterns $S = \{x_1, x_2, \ldots, x_m\}$ which are made to appear at the system input as an infinite sequence

$$\{x_{i_k}\}_{k=1}^{\infty}, \; i_k \in \{1, 2, \ldots, m\} \,,$$

with an arbitrary frequency and in an arbitrary order. Consider further a series of instants of time $\{t_k\}_{k=1}^{\infty}$ between which the input patterns are assumed to be stationary. In other words, the input signal patterns are constant in time during arbitrarily long half-open intervals $[t_{k-1}, t_k)$ but otherwise their appearance is almost arbitrary. When the above system equations are integrated over the intervals $[t_{k-1}, t_k)$, always replacing t_0 by t_{k-1}, there follows

$$m^T(t_k) = m^T(t_{k-1}) \left[I - \alpha_k x_{i_k} x_{i_k}^T \right]$$
$$= m^T(t_{k-1}) Q_k \qquad (3.14)$$

where the scalars α_k have a close bearing on the $\omega(t)$ in (3.13), and the Q_k are matrices which have the form of an *elementary matrix* (Subsec. 1.3.3). Recursive application of (3.14) yields

$$m^T(t_k) = m^T(t_0) \prod_{i=1}^{k} Q_i = m^T(t_0) T_k \quad . \qquad (3.15)$$

The central mathematical problem is now to study the convergence conditions of the product matrix T_k as k tends to infinity. It will be shown that if, in general, the α_k are scalars within certain limits and each of the vectors of S occurs infinitely often in T_k, then T_k will converge to a projection matrix P such that $m^T(t_0)P$ is orthogonal to all vectors of S. In other words, if one of these pattern vectors or their arbitrary linear combination is shown as input to the converged system, the corresponding output will be zero. On the other hand, if an arbitrary new pattern not belonging to the subspace $\mathcal{L}$ spanned by the vectors of S is chosen for input, the output in general will be nonzero unless, in a highly improbable case, the new pattern happens to be orthogonal to the weighting vector of the converged system.

The following results have been analyzed in detail in [74] and [75].

A Limit Theorem for a Product of Elementary Matrices

Let $S = \{x_1, \ldots, x_m\}$ be a set of arbitrary (not necessarily linearly independent) vectors in R^n. Consider the product matrix T_k of (3.15) in which the scalar sequence $\{\alpha_k\}$ and the index sequence $\{i_k\}$ satisfy the following assumptions:

A1) $\delta \leq \alpha_k \leq 2\|x_{i_k}\|^{-2} - \delta$

where δ is an arbitrarily small fixed number satisfying

$$0 < \delta < 2(\max_j \|x_j\|^2)^{-1} \quad .$$

A2) For every fixed r ∈ {1,...m} and every p∈N (N is the set of natural numbers) there exists an index k ≥ p such that i_k = r.

In fact, the first assumption guarantees that the norms of the elementary matrices

$$\left[I - \alpha_k x_{i_k} x_{i_k}^T \right]$$

do not exceed unity and $\{\alpha_k\}$ does not converge to zero, while the second assumption expresses the fact that each vector x_k appears in the product infinitely often. The following result [75] is here given without proof.

Theorem: Let A1 and A2 hold. Then the sequence $\{T_k\}$ converges (in any matrix norm) to the projection matrix on the subspace $\mathscr{L}^\perp(x_1,...,x_m)$.

If the set $S = \{x_1,...,x_m\}$ spans R^n, then the projection matrix on $\mathscr{L}^\perp(x_1,...,x_m)$ is the zero matrix and the following corollary holds true.

Corollary: Let the assumptions of the theorem hold and let $\mathscr{L}(x_1,...,x_m) = R^n$. Then $\lim_{k \to \infty} T_k$ is the zero matrix.

Numerical Example

In order to obtain a concrete conception about the speed of convergence in the above process, the following result is reported. Ten 35-component binary patterns, earlier depicted in Fig. 2.9, comprised the set S, and they were cyclically applied at the input. Denoting $m^* = \lim_{k \to \infty} m_k$, then, as the measure of convergence $\|m_k - m^*\| / \|m^*\|$ was selected. The scalar α_k was selected constant, with a value from the middle of its allowed range which provided the fastest convergence.

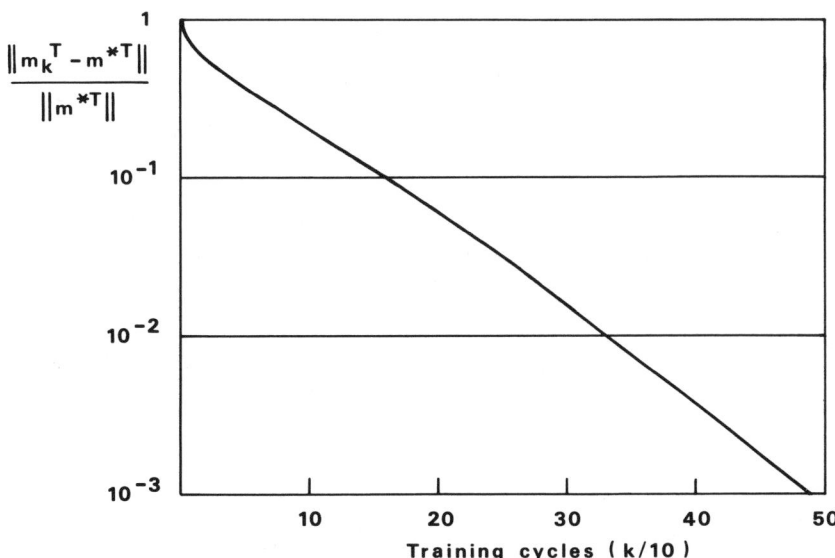

Fig. 3.5 Speed of convergence in a Novelty Detector-process

The diagram in Fig. 3.5 shows that the convergence was almost exponential. Other results, not shown here, have indicated that in general the speed of convergence in this process is roughly inversely proportional to the dimensionality of the patterns n. The speed of convergence in general depends strongly on the ratio m/n with radical slowdown when m → n.

3.2.2 Analysis of the Adaptive Linear Unit by Means of Matrix Products

In the previous example the input patterns were assumed arbitrary, i.e., linearly dependent or independent. This section discusses an iterative process related to the stochastic approximation with the difference that the input patterns in S are assumed linearly independent; otherwise their order of occurrence and the lengths of the intervals $[t_{k-1}, t_k)$ are as arbitrary as above. With the above restriction, the gain sequence $\{\alpha_k\}$ of (3.14) need not converge to zero, and the α_k can even be chosen constant which is a desirable feature in simple physical systems.

After association of the input vectors x_{i_k} with arbitrary scalars η_{i_k} by pairs, the system equations in continuous time may be written in vector form as follows:

$$\eta = m^T x_{i_k}, \qquad (3.16)$$

$$dm^T/dt = \alpha(\eta_{i_k} - \eta) x_{i_k}^T, \qquad (3.17)$$

or, since the signals x_{i_k} and η_{i_k} are constant over the intervals $[t_{k-1}, t_k)$, the discrete-time formalism (difference equations) can be applied. In this case the system equations read

$$\begin{aligned} m_k^T &= m_{k-1}^T + \alpha_k(\eta_{i_k} - m_{k-1}^T x_{i_k}) x_{i_k}^T \\ &= m_{k-1}^T (I - \alpha_k x_{i_k} x_{i_k}^T) + \alpha_k \eta_{i_k} x_{i_k}^T . \end{aligned} \qquad (3.18)$$

Again each i_k, k=1,2,... is one of the numbers 1,2,...,m. First of all, by recursive application of (3.18), the following form for the solution can be constructed:

$$\begin{aligned} m_k^T &= m_0^T \prod_{r=1}^{k} (I - \alpha_r x_{i_r} x_{i_r}^T) \\ &+ \sum_{r=1}^{k} \alpha_r \eta_{i_r} x_{i_r}^T \prod_{j=r+1}^{k} (I - \alpha_j x_{i_j} x_{i_j}^T) \end{aligned} \qquad (3.19)$$

where only the first term depends on m_0^T whereas the second term is independent of it, and to start the recursion right it is defined

$$\prod_{j=k+1}^{k} (I - \alpha_j x_{i_j} x_{i_j}^T) = I \; .$$

Under the above assumptions

$$\prod_{r=1}^{k} (I - \alpha_r x_{i_r} x_{i_r}^T)$$

converges to the *orthogonal projection operator* P of Subsection 1.3.5. Because of the assumed linear independence of the vectors x_{i_r}, the form

$$P = I - X(X^T X)^{-1} X^T \tag{3.20}$$

can be used in which X has the vectors $x_1, x_2, \ldots, x_m$ as its columns in this order or in any permutation of it.

For the determination of $\lim_{k \to \infty} m_k^T$, the following shortcut method is used. Consider the matrix $X = [x_1, x_2, \ldots, x_m]$ and the vector $y^T = [\eta_1, \eta_2, \ldots, \eta_m]$. Since the vectors $x_1, \ldots, x_m$ are assumed linearly independent, X has rank m and $X^T X$ is nonsingular. Then there exists a vector $m*^T = y^T (X^T X)^{-1} X^T$ satisfying $m*^T X = y^T$. Choose $m*^T$ as the initial vector m_0^T in the process. Then

$$m_1^T = m*^T + \alpha_1 (\eta_{i_1} - m*^T x_{i_1}) x_{i_1}^T = m*^T \quad \text{since } m*^T x_{i_1} = \eta_{i_1} \; .$$

Similarly it can be trivially concluded that $m_k^T = m*^T$ for every k. Thus also $\lim m_k^T = m*^T$. Now the first term in m_k^T of (3.19) yields

$$\lim_{k \to \infty} m*^T \prod_{r=1}^{k} (I - \alpha_r x_{i_r} x_{i_r}^T) = m*^T P = 0 \; , \tag{3.21}$$

and, hence, for the second part of (3.19) there holds

$$\lim_{k \to \infty} \sum_{r=1}^{k} \alpha_r \eta_{i_r} x_{i_r}^T \prod_{j=r+1}^{k} (I - \alpha_j x_{i_j} x_{i_j}^T)$$
$$= \lim_{k \to \infty} m_k^T = m*^T \; . \tag{3.22}$$

Notice that this part does not include initial vector m_0^T, so (3.22) holds generally, for arbitrary m_0^T. After these considerations, for arbitrary initial conditions, it is obtained by collecting the above results,

$$\lim_{k \to \infty} m_k^T = m_0^T [I - X(X^TX)^{-1}X^T] + y^T(X^TX)^{-1}X^T \quad . \tag{3.23}$$

It may be interesting to recall that a matrix-vector-equation of the form $z^TA=b^T$ has a solution for z with arbitrary b if and only if the columns of A are linearly independent, in which case the general solution reads

$$z^T = b^T(A^TA)^{-1}A^T + h^T[I - A(A^TA)^{-1}A^T] \tag{3.24}$$

where h is an arbitrary vector of the same dimension as z.

Notice that the convergence in the adaptive linear unit to an exact associative mapping was here proven with a rather mild condition imposed on the gain sequence, namely, α_k satisfying the assumption A1 of the limit theorem in Subsection 3.2.1.

3.2.3 An Extremely Fast Adaptive Process Which Generates the Novelty Filter

From the example given in Subsection 3.3.1 it can be deduced that convergence in a Novelty Detector-type process is rather slow. It is therefore believed that physical processes with accelerated adaptation as discussed here might be of considerable interest in machine learning. Acceleration of convergence is achieved by the inclusion of negative feedback in the system. There have been presented several adaptive models with different types of feedback connection (Subsec. 3.3.6) which, accordingly, have varying degrees of convergence. In this section it is pointed out that there exists one particular type of feedback which guarantees extremely prompt convergence: the asymptotic state of the optimal Novelty Filter can be achieved in one single cycle of application of the input patterns.

The System Model of the Novelty Filter

Instead of taking a set of independent Novelty Detectors, an adaptive filter is here constructed assuming mutual interactions between the units, i.e., this model is based on collective phenomena. A theoretically simplified model which generates orthogonal projections is discussed first; after that, a more realistic variant is discussed in which the process involves the effect of forgetting.

Consider the system model of Fig. 3.6 with $x \in R^n$ its input pattern vector, and $\tilde{x} \in R^n$ the vector of output signals. A feedback taken from the output is again assumed to recurrently affect the output through variable weights. In the simplest case the feedback is assumed direct. However, the dynamics is not significantly changed if feedback is taken through low-pass filters; it can be shown that the asymptotic properties are not affected.

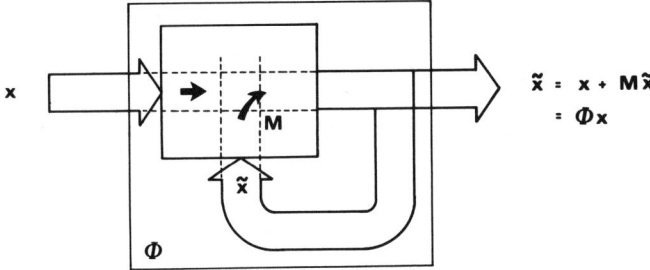

Fig. 3.6 System model of the Novelty Filter

Every element of the output vector $\tilde{x}$, denoted by $\tilde{\xi}_i$, is thus assumed to receive a feedback from the other elements $\tilde{\xi}_j$ through variable weights μ_{ij}. The output signals $\tilde{\xi}_i$ are assumed to be linear combinations of the input signals ξ_i and the feedback signals as

$$\tilde{\xi}_i = \xi_i + \sum_j \mu_{ij}\tilde{\xi}_j \ . \tag{3.25}$$

The feedback connections μ_{ij} are assumed adaptive. In pursuance of the system principles discussed with the linear adaptive unit and the Novelty Detector, these weights are discussed in the case where they change as

$$d\mu_{ij}/dt = -\alpha\tilde{\xi}_i\tilde{\xi}_j \ . \tag{3.26}$$

In matrix notation, the feedback "gain" may be denoted by a time-variable matrix M. On the other hand, the *overall* transfer operator for the input patterns is described by a square matrix ϕ that can be solved from the implicit feedback equations:

$$\tilde{x} = x + M\tilde{x} = (I-M)^{-1} x = \phi x \ . \tag{3.27}$$

It is tentatively assumed that $(I-M)^{-1}$ always exists. As long as the process is physically realizable, this is the case.

The feedback matrix $M = (\mu_{ij})$ has a state equation

$$dM/dt = -\alpha\tilde{x}\tilde{x}^T \ . \tag{3.28}$$

The differential equation for ϕ is obtained as follows:

$$\frac{d\phi^{-1}}{dt} = -\phi^{-1}\frac{d\phi}{dt}\phi^{-1} = -\frac{dM}{dt} \ ; \tag{3.29}$$

$$d\phi/dt = -\alpha\phi^2 xx^T\phi^T\phi \ . \tag{3.30}$$

This is a *matrix Bernoulli equation*. It will be shown that it has stable asymptotic solutions if $\alpha \geq 0$.

Extensive study of all matrix Bernoulli equations has been confined to the Riccati differential equations, in which the right-hand side is of second degree in ϕ, and which naturally originate in various applications of control and systems theory (cf. [77]). Bernoulli equations of higher degree in ϕ do not seem to have been treated in literature, although the asymptotic solutions of some of them have proved to be extremely interesting.

The solution of (3.30) seems difficult if $x = x(t)$ is an arbitrary function of time. However, if x is constant, or piecewise constant in time, it is then readily observable that (3.30) becomes autonomous (globally or piecewise), and a solution in the form of a series expansion is demonstrable, say, by the Picard-Lindelöf method [73]. Since it is desirable to have at least some basic results in closed form, it is hereafter assumed that the initial condition of ϕ is *symmetric* (for instance, if M was initially a zero matrix, then $\phi(0) = I$). If this is the case, then ϕ can be seen to remain symmetric at all times, and the differential equation is written

$$d\phi/dt = - \alpha \phi^2 xx^T \phi^2 . \tag{3.31}$$

Although the general solution is not needed in the rest of this discussion, it is outlined as follows. The successive approximations of the Picard-Lindelöf method yield an expression for $\phi(t)$ which is a series containing rising powers of $\phi(0)$. Because all vectors $\phi(0)^j x$, with $j > 0$, can be expressed as linear combinations of the vectors $\phi(0)x, \phi(0)^2 x,...,\phi(0)^r x$ where r is less than or equal to the degree of the so-called minimum polynomial of $\phi(0)$ (cf., e.g., [72], pp. 60-61), only a finite number of terms is retained in the series expansion which is then of the general form

$$\phi(t) = \phi(0) + \sum_{i=1}^{r} \sum_{j=1}^{r} \phi(0)^i xx^T \phi(0)^j f_{ij}(t) , \tag{3.32}$$

on an interval where x is constant. The sequence $f_{ij}(t)$ is a symmetrical double sequence of continuous scalar-valued functions which could, in principle at least, be solved by the substitution of $\phi(t)$ from (3.32) into (3.31).

The lack of further knowledge in regard to the functions f_{ij} means that the asymptotic properties of $\phi(t)$ are not obvious. However, in one important class of initial matrices $\phi(0)$ the solution is enormously simplified, i.e., that of projection matrices (see Subsec. 1.3.5). In particular, $\phi(0) = I$ constitutes a special case of them. *This corresponds to the case in which the memory was originally empty*, $M(0) = 0$, as mentioned above. If x is now constant everywhere, then (3.32) is reduced to

$$\phi(t) = \phi(0) + \phi(0)xx^T\phi(0)f(t) \tag{3.33}$$

which by substitution into (3.31) yields

$$f(t) = \alpha h^{-1}\left[(3ht + 1)^{-1/3} - 1\right], \text{ if } \phi(0)x \neq 0 ,$$
$$h = \alpha x^T\phi(0)x ; \tag{3.34}$$
$$f(t) = 0, \text{ if } \phi(0)x = 0 .$$

Unfortunately, if x is only piecewise constant, then this simple method no longer applies; it can be seen that $\phi(t)$, $t > 0$, is not generally idempotent; consequently, on successive intervals of constant x, resort has to be made to the more general solution.

Successive Adaptations

It can now be shown that if the input vector x is constant for a sufficiently long time, the system output $\tilde{x}$ approaches the zero vector, although ϕ does not approach the zero matrix. If a set of input patterns $\{x_k\}$ is successively applied at the input, and each one is displayed for an adequate time, it is demonstrable that this system will then be adapted to each one *in one cycle of presentation*.

There is another characteristic mathematical difficulty associated with the above matrix Bernoulli equation (in which $d\phi/dt$ is of rank 1). Even in the simplest case when $\phi(0) = I$, the asymptotic solution $\phi(\infty)$ will be *singular* which also implies that $M(\infty)$, or some of its elements, do not remain finite. In practice the integration times are always finite whereby ϕ remains nonsingular and M finite. Certain saturation limits can also be set on the elements of M. Then, however, the successive "asymptotic" solutions discussed below are only more or less good approximations.

The adaptation process can now be studied in greater detail, with the result of considerable simplification of the solution of (3.31). Define a series of successive instances of time $\{t_k\}_{k=0}^{S}$. During each half-open interval $[t_{k-1}, t_k)$, a new constant pattern is applied at the input, and the state matrix ϕ is allowed to approximately converge towards the asymptotic value during each interval. The accuracy with which ϕ converges towards the asymptotic value can be made arbitrarily good by the selection of intervals that are sufficiently long. An approximate recursive expression for the successive state changes is then derivable in the following way. We are primarily interested in the asymptotic solution of (3.31), which for idempotent $\phi(0)$ reads

$$\phi(\infty) = \phi(0) - \frac{\phi(0)x_1 x_1^T \phi(0)}{x_1^T \phi(0) x_1} \text{ if } \phi(0)x_1 \neq 0 ,$$
$$\phi(\infty) = \phi(0) \text{ if } \phi(0)x_1 = 0 . \tag{3.35}$$

If the interval $[0,t_1)$ is long, then $t = \infty$ is approximately replaceable by $t = t_1$. Next, use is made of the fact which is easily proven by squaring both sides of (3.35), viz., that $\phi(\infty)$ is idempotent, too.

Since $\phi(0)$ is idempotent, then $\phi(t_1)$ is also approximately idempotent. It can now be shown that (3.33) and (3.35) remain valid if t_1 is taken for the time of initialization: it is sufficient to assume that $\phi(t_1)$ is idempotent. Continuation of the induction results in a recursive expression being obtained for successive state changes, with use being made of the fact that all of the $\phi(t_k)$ remain approximately idempotent:

$$\phi(t_k) \approx \phi(t_{k-1}) - \frac{\phi(t_{k-1})x_k x_k^T \phi(t_{k-1})}{x_k^T \phi(t_{k-1}) x_k}$$

$$\text{if} \quad \phi(t_{k-1}) x_k \neq 0 \quad , \tag{3.36}$$

$$\phi(t_k) = \phi(t_{k-1}) \quad \text{if} \quad \phi(t_{k-1}) x_k = 0 \quad .$$

$$(k = 2, 3, \ldots)$$

This set of equations resembles a very important mathematical expression: it has the same structure as the recursive formulas for the *orthogonal projection operator* (cf. Subsec. 1.3.5). Thus the $\phi(t_k)$ are approximately projection matrices.

Iterative Convergence in the Fast Adaptive Process

The above approximative treatment can be replaced by a mathematically more strict discussion. In discrete-time formalism the matrix Bernoulli equation is written

$$\phi_p = \phi_{p-1} - \alpha_p \phi_{p-1}^2 x x^T \phi_{p-1}^2 \quad , \quad p > 0 \quad . \tag{3.37}$$

If, for each p, $\alpha_p = \alpha \cdot \Delta t$, and we interpret the ϕ_p-matrices as $\phi_p = \phi(p \cdot \Delta t)$, then (3.37) yields (3.31) as $\Delta t \to 0$, $p \cdot \Delta t \to t$. In this manner, (3.37) can be regarded as a one-step (Euler) numerical quadrature of (3.31). However, as (3.37) has some value in its own right, the results are discussed with the more general gain sequence $\{\alpha_p\}$.

As a complete discussion [44] is too lengthy to be reviewed here, only the results are given in the form of three lemmas, a theorem, and a corollary.

Let x be constant during each step. Let us define an integer sequence $\{i_p\}_{p=1}^{\infty}$, where each i_p belongs to the discrete set $\{1, 2, \ldots, m\}$. With the help of i_p, the input vector is expressible as $x = x_{i_p}$; it is then understood that x is one of the vectors $x_1, \ldots x_m$, with no specification of which one.

In Lemma 2, a restriction will be imposed on $\{i_p\}$, telling something about the frequency with which each vector of S is used as input.

With this convention, (3.37) becomes

$$\phi_p = \phi_{p-1} - \alpha_p \phi_{p-1}^2 x_{i_p} x_{i_p}^T \phi_{p-1}^2 \qquad (3.38)$$

The aim of this section is that of showing that the matrix ϕ_p, starting from a *projection matrix* ϕ_0, will converge to another projection matrix under fairly general conditions on $\{i_p\}$ and the gain sequence $\{\alpha_p\}$. (Note that $\phi_0 = I$ is also a projection matrix.) These conditions will now be presented in two lemmas followed by a theorem.

Lemma 1: Let ϕ_0 be a symmetric positive semidefinite (psd) matrix, and for every p

$$\varepsilon \le \alpha_p \le \lambda_p - \varepsilon$$

with

$$\lambda_p = (x_{i_p}^T \phi_{p-1}^3 x_{i_p}) (x_{i_p}^T \phi_{p-1}^2 x_{i_p})^{-1} \cdot (x_{i_p}^T \phi_{p-1}^4 x_{i_p})^{-1}$$

and

$$0 < \varepsilon < \lambda_p \; ;$$

then every ϕ_p is symmetric and psd.

Lemma 2: Let ϕ_p be symmetric psd for every p. Let the sequence $\{i_p\}$ be such that every integer $1, 2, \ldots, m$ appears in it infinitely often. Then all the vector sequences $\phi_p x_1, \phi_p x_2, \ldots, \phi_p x_m$ converge to zero as $p \to \infty$.

Theorem: Let ϕ_0 be a projection matrix, and $\{\alpha_p\}$ and $\{i_p\}$ satisfy the conditions imposed by Lemma 1 and Lemma 2. The sequence of matrices $\{\phi_p\}$ then converges to the unique projection matrix $\bar{\phi}$ on the subspace $\mathcal{M} = \mathcal{R}(\phi_0) \cap \mathcal{L}^\perp$, where $\mathcal{R}(\phi_0)$ is the range space of ϕ_0, and $\mathcal{L}^\perp$ is the orthogonal complement of the subspace $\mathcal{L}$ spanned by the vectors $x_1, \ldots, x_m$.

By employment of the concept of matrix pseudoinverse an explicit form can be given to the limit matrix $\bar{\phi}$. Let X denote, as before, the (n × m) matrix with columns $x_1, x_2, \ldots x_m$. It is then easy to confirm that

$$\bar{\phi} = \phi_0 - \phi_0 X (X^T \phi_0 X)^+ X^T \phi_0 \qquad (3.39)$$

is the unique projection matrix on the subspace $\mathcal{M} = \mathcal{R}(\phi_0) \cap \mathcal{L}^\perp$.

If, in particular, we have $\phi_0 = I$, then (3.39) yields (by application of the well-known identity $(X^T X)^+ X^T = X^+$):

Corollary: If the assumptions of Lemma 1 and Lemma 2 hold, and ϕ_0 is the unit matrix, then ϕ_p converges to $\bar{\phi} = I - XX^+$ which is the projection operator on the subspace $\mathcal{R}(I) \cap \mathcal{L}^\perp = \mathcal{L}^\perp$.

So far, no reference has been made to the nature and the speed of convergence of ϕ_p. The concluding lemma of this section is the following.

Lemma 3: If α_p remains within the bounds defined in Lemma 1, and the input vector is held constant, then the norm of the output vector is monotonically decreasing. The larger α_p is, the faster is the convergence.

The assumptions of the above theorem may not be immediately clear in terms of the original feedback system. The main purpose of introducing the index sequence $\{i_p\}$ was that of elimination of any suggestions concerning the order in which the different input vectors are employed in the course of training. Thus many possible processes are covered, for example a cyclic training in which the vectors of S are used repeatedly, and particularly the process where they are used one at a time for long periods. In the latter process the index sequence might be the following: $\{i_p\} = \{1,1,\ldots,1,2,2,\ldots,2,3,\ldots,m,\ldots\}$ where it is understood that each interval of constant i_p is arbitrarily long. Then convergence is guaranteed if α_p is sufficiently small. By letting the step size which is now proportional to α_p become infinitesimal (which is allowed by Lemma 1), the discrete process is an arbitrarily close approximation of the continuous one. This question is intrinsically connected with the stability and convergence properties of one-step discretization formulas, as the step size becomes very small.

If the learning process of a pattern is interrupted, as is always the case when each input vector is used in the training for a limited period only, then an iterative improvement by repetitive use of the input vector is due in the above process. Lemma 3 then guarantees that the error must always decrease in a monotonous fashion.

3.2.4 Adaptation With Forgetting

Memory effects in physical systems are usually volatile. For this reason it is desirable to study adaptation equations when the memory traces are allowed to decay. The discussion of this type of process with "forgetting" is yet amenable to the matrix equation formalism if, in the case that the external signals are zero, every memory element is assumed to decay at a rate which is directly proportional to its value. This is the simplest law of "leakage" in most physical processes, and the equation for M is then written

$$dM/dt = -\alpha \tilde{x}\tilde{x}^T - \beta M \tag{3.40}$$

with α and β constant positive scalars. In discrete-time formalism, this equation would read

$$M_p = \gamma_p M_{p-1} - \alpha_p x_{i_p} x_{i_p}^T \qquad (3.41)$$

with γ_p and α_p certain scalar-valued parameters and the subscripts p and i_p as explained in Subsection 3.2.3.

In place of the matrix Bernoulli equation, the following more general differential equation is now obtained, with ϕ the overall transfer matrix as before:

$$d\phi/dt = -\alpha\phi^2 x x^T \phi^T \phi + \beta(\phi - \phi^2) \quad . \qquad (3.42)$$

Again, a mathematical discussion becomes possible if the initial value $\phi(0) = \phi_0$ is assumed symmetrical and idempotent and x is taken constant from the time $t = 0$ on.

The following discussion is due to OJA [75]. A conjecture about the solution being of the form

$$\phi = \phi_0 + f(t) \phi_0 x x^T \phi_0 \qquad (3.43)$$

is now made, where $f(t)$ is a time function to be determined. Using the fact that ϕ_0 is idempotent, the following scalar differential equation for $f(t)$ is obtained:

$$df/dt = -\alpha[1 + \lambda f(t)]^4 - \beta f(t)[1 + \lambda f(t)] ,$$

$$f(0) = 0 , \qquad (3.44)$$

with $\lambda = x^T \phi_0 x$ (a scalar) .

In order that the above trial solution be applicable, it is necessary that $f(t)$ remain bounded. For convenience, the function

$$s(t) = 1 + \lambda f(t) \qquad (3.45)$$

is introduced. The differential equation for it reads

$$ds/dt = -\alpha\lambda s^4 - \beta(s^2 - s), \quad s(0) = 1 \quad . \qquad (3.46)$$

To the first it is shown that $s(t) > 0$ for $0 \leq t < \infty$. This follows from the fact that the right-hand side of (3.46) is continuous and continuously differentiable in s. The solution for $s(t)$ is then unique. On the other hand, because $s(t) \equiv 0$ is the solution for the initial value $s(0) = 0$, there follows that the solution for $s(0) = 1$ cannot become zero with finite t without contradiction of uniqueness. Therefore, with $s(0) = 1$, $s(t)$ remains positive.

The asymptotic properties of $s(t)$ can now be determined. Especially in the case that β can be selected arbitrarily small, all real roots of the equation $ds/dt = 0$

are also small, and it can be deduced (although a formal proof is omitted here) that the solution of s(t) monotonically tends to a small positive number ε. Thereby

$$\lim_{t \to \infty} \phi(t) = \phi_0 + \frac{\varepsilon - 1}{x^T \phi_0 x} \phi_0 x x^T \phi_0 . \qquad (3.47)$$

This is an approximation of the recursive formula (3.35). It is to be noted that the asymptotic solution with forgetting has the same form as a solution of the original matrix Bernoulli equation (without forgetting) when it was integrated over a finite interval of time.

3.3 Recursive Generation of the Optimal Associative Mapping

The purpose of this section is to point out what the theoretically fastest adaptive processes are by which a new value for the operator describing the optimal associative mapping can be determined. This kind of computation is based on a mapping which is optimal with respect to a set of pairs of earlier input-output vectors (x_i, y_i), and on a new pair of input-output vectors that shall be taken into account, too. As this is a mathematical problem, in the first place it is not stipulated that it must have a physically realizable implementation. The mathematical discussion yields an upper limit for the system performance against which various physical realizations can be compared. The recursive formulas that result may as such be useful as computational algorithms when the associative mappings are implemented in digital computers.

3.3.1 Linear Corrective Algorithms

Consider the optimal linear associative memory that transforms input patterns x_k into output patterns y_k by a linear operation $y_k = M x_k$. The best value of M was determined by the matrix equation method in Subsection 2.3.5. A new problem that is central to the present chapter is the following: if it is assumed that the transfer matrix M is optimal for a series of observations ending up with the pair (x_{k-1}, y_{k-1}), then what is the *correction* to M if its new value shall be optimal with respect to all of the previous patterns and the new pair (x_k, y_k), too? This is a so-called *recursive* problem. The new optimal value M_k is a function of the previous optimal value M_{k-1} and of the new observations x_k and y_k. All the cases of recursive processes discussed in this context obey the following difference equation

$$M_k = M_{k-1} + (y_k - M_{k-1} x_k) c_k^T \qquad (3.48)$$

where c_k^T is a *gain vector* that defines the correction. It may be noted that $M_{k-1} x_k$ is a *prediction* of y_k, denoted by $\hat{y}_k$; the correction is always directly proportional to the prediction error $y_k - \hat{y}_k$. Expressions for the gain vector for various choices of data shall be derived. It will be interesting to notice that simpler adaptive systems too are governed by adaption equations which very much resemble (3.48), with the principal difference that another value for the gain vector is used. Accordingly, the correction is then not optimal but suboptimal; the optimal value of M can be achieved only if the presentation of the pairs (x_k, y_k) is repeated iteratively.

3.3.2 The General Setting for the Computation of $M = YX^+$

If exact solutions to the matrix equation $Y = MX$ exist, $M = YX^+$ is that particular solution which yields the associative mapping with the best error-tolerance. If exact solutions do not exist, $M = YX^+$ is the best approximative solution in the sense of least squares. Hereupon YX^+ is called the "best" solution. Evaluation of YX^+ follows the same lines as the computation of the pseudoinverse X^+ for an arbitrary matrix X. For this purpose, consider matrix X which has the input vectors $x_1, x_2, \ldots, x_k$ as its columns. This matrix is partitioned as $[X_{k-1} \vdots x_k]$ and, with k columns, denoted by X_k. Similarly matrix Y formed of $y_1, y_2, \ldots, y_k$ is also partitioned and, with k columns, denoted as $Y_k = [Y_{k-1} \vdots y_k]$. If matrix M, when computed from X_k and Y_k, is denoted by $M_k = Y_k X_k^+$, it obtains the recursive form (cf. Subsec. 1.3.4)

$$M_k = Y_k X_k^+ = [Y_{k-1} \vdots y_k] \begin{bmatrix} X_{k-1}^+ (I - x_k p_k^T) \\ \hdashline p_k^T \end{bmatrix}$$

(3.49)

$$= Y_{k-1} X_{k-1}^+ + (y_k - Y_{k-1} X_{k-1}^+ x_k) p_k^T$$

$$= M_{k-1} + (y_k - M_{k-1} x_k) p_k^T$$

where the "gain vector" p_k^T has the value given in (1.49). It should be noticed that M_k is always immediately the "best" solution when a pair of new observations (x_k, y_k) has been taken into account; the recursion is started with $M_0 = 0$.

3.3.3 Recursive Evaluation of the Best Exact Solution
      (Gradient Projection Method)

The expression p_k of (1.49) is simplified if exact solutions to $Y = MX$ exist. This is the case which normally occurs in the design of optimal associative mappings. If x_k is now linearly independent of the previous columns, then $(I - X_{k-1} X_{k-1}^+) x_k$ is a nonzero vector and the upper expression for p_k in (1.49) is applied. In the case that x_k is a linear combination of the previous columns, the lower expression of p_k yields

$$M_k = M_{k-1} + (y_k - M_{k-1}x_k)x_k^T (X_{k-1}^+)^T X_{k-1}^+ (1 + \| X_{k-1}^+ x_k \|^2)^{-1} . \qquad (3.50)$$

Multiplication of both sides by x_k and rearrangement results in

$$y_k = M_k x_k = M_{k-1} x_k + (y_k - M_{k-1}x_k) \| X_{k-1}^+ x_k \|^2 (1 + \| X_{k-1}^+ x_k \|^2)^{-1} . \qquad (3.51)$$

Since $\| X_{k-1}^+ x_k \|^2 \geq 0$, the above equation cannot be satisfied unless $y_k - M_{k-1}x_k = 0$. Substitution of this result into (3.49) then yields $M_k = M_{k-1}$. If it is now denoted

$$(I - X_{k-1}X_{k-1}^+) x_k = \phi_{k-1}x_k = \tilde{x}_k , \qquad (3.52)$$

and it is realized that the condition $\tilde{x}_k = 0$ is equivalent to the linear dependence of the columns $x_1, x_2, \ldots, x_k$, then the expression for M_k can be put into the form [79]

$$M_k = \begin{cases} M_{k-1} + (y_k - M_{k-1}x_k) \dfrac{\tilde{x}_k^T}{\|\tilde{x}_k\|^2} & \text{for } \tilde{x}_k \neq 0 , \\ M_{k-1} & \text{otherwise,} \end{cases}$$

$$\tilde{x}_k = \phi_{k-1}x_k ,$$

$$\phi_k = \phi_{k-1} - \dfrac{\tilde{x}_k \tilde{x}_k^T}{\|\tilde{x}_k\|^2} , \quad \text{with } \phi_0 = I, \; \tilde{x}_1 = x_1 .$$

(3.53)

Instead of using the last two equations, a computationally easier method is to determine the $\tilde{x}_i$, $i = 1, 2, \ldots, k$ using the Gram-Schmidt orthogonalization process:

$$\tilde{x}_i = x_i - \sum_{j=1}^{i-1} \frac{(x_i, \tilde{x}_j)\tilde{x}_j}{\|\tilde{x}_j\|^2} \qquad (3.54)$$

where the summation over j must be taken for nonzero $\tilde{x}_j$ only.

The derivation of (3.53) also follows directly from a method for the solution of vector equations of the type $Ax = b$, as discussed by PYLE [80]. Accordingly, the name *gradient projection method* is used for the above method, generalized for matrix equations.

A Computational Scheme

If the objective is to find out the optimal output $\hat{y}$ in response to a key pattern x, computation of matrix operator M may not be necessary. If the estimate of y_i at the ith step is denoted $\hat{y}_i = M_{i-1}x_i$, and its error is $\tilde{y}_i = y_i - \hat{y}_i$, multiplication of M_k of (3.53) by x_k, change of index, and exchange of terms yields [49]

$$\tilde{y}_i = y_i - \sum_{j=1}^{i-1} \frac{(x_i, \tilde{x}_j)}{\|\tilde{x}_j\|^2} \tilde{y}_j \tag{3.55}$$

where use is made of the existence of exact solutions, whence there must hold $M_i x_i = y_i$, $M_{i-1} x_i = \hat{y}_i$. In the computational scheme, recursive evaluation of the $\tilde{y}_i$ proceeds in parallel with the Gram-Schmidt process used for the calculation of the $\tilde{x}_i$, and only the $\tilde{y}_i$, i=1,2,...,k are stored. Application of (3.55) one step further yields

$$\hat{y} = \sum_{i=1}^{k} \frac{(x, \tilde{x}_i)}{\|\tilde{x}_i\|^2} \tilde{y}_i . \tag{3.56}$$

3.3.4 Recursive Evaluation of the Best Approximate Solution
(Regression Solution)

If the number of columns in X and Y is greater than the dimension of the x_k, the latter are then linearly dependent. This is the case in which the best approximate solution in the sense of least squares to Y = MX is called *linear regression*. The recursive expressions derived from the algorithm of Greville can now be applied, when for the "gain vectors" p_k the lower alternatives from (1.49) are selected. It should be carefully noticed that the recursive expressions do not yield correct solutions unless they are correctly initiated, and in order to be sure that the lower alternative for p_k from (1.49) is always applicable, the new column x_k must be a linear combination of the columns of X_{k-1}. Obviously a sufficient condition for this occurrence is that there are n linearly independent columns among the $x_1,...,x_{k-1}$. If the x_k are stochastic variables and k-1 ≥ n, it is known from elementary statistics that this is normally the case. In order to guarantee numerical stability in practical computations, it is advantageous to have in X_{k-1} columns in excess to n. Now the recursion can be initiated by computing X_{k-1}^+ as

$$X_{k-1}^+ = X_{k-1}^T (X_{k-1} X_{k-1}^T)^{-1} . \tag{3.57}$$

For the matrix inversion, for instance, a method derived from the familiar Gauss-Jordan elimination procedure can be used; the inverse of a square matrix C of full rank can be computed by solving the matrix equation CX = I, partitioned as C · $[x_1, x_2, \ldots, x_n]$ = $[u_1, u_2, \ldots, u_n]$, with u_i, i = 1,2,... n the unit vectors. The vector equations $Cx_i = u_i$ are then solved independently by the Gauss-Jordan algorithm, whereby $X = C^{-1}$ is obtained. Another possibility, although a little heavier computationally, is to apply the gradient projection method until n linearly independent vectors x_k are found, and then to switch over to the present method (cf. also Subsec. 3.2.6).

Under the assumption that $(X_{k-1} X_{k-1}^T)^{-1}$ exists, $(X_k X_k^T)^{-1}$ can be derived from the matrix inversion lemma (Subsec. 1.3.4). Denoting

$$\psi_k = (X_k X_k^T)^{-1} = (X_{k-1} X_{k-1}^T + x_k x_k^T)^{-1}, \qquad (3.58)$$

there follows

$$\psi_k = \psi_{k-1} - \frac{\psi_{k-1} x_k x_k^T \psi_{k-1}}{1 + x_k^T \psi_{k-1} x_k}. \qquad (3.59)$$

This recursion for the square matrix ψ_k, with its initial condition computed, for instance, by the matrix inversion method, is applied together with the formula for M_k obtained as follows. Based on the general properties of pseudoinverses, p_k^T is written

$$p_k^T = \frac{x_k^T (X_{k-1} X_{k-1}^T)^+}{1 + x_k^T (X_{k-1} X_{k-1}^T)^+ x_k} = \frac{x_k^T \psi_{k-1}}{1 + x_k^T \psi_{k-1} x_k} \qquad (3.60)$$

where use is made of the fact that $(X_{k-1} X_{k-1}^T)^+ = (X_{k-1} X_{k-1}^T)^{-1}$ if the inverse exists. Then, according to (3.49),

$$M_k = M_{k-1} + (y_k - M_{k-1} x_k) \frac{x_k^T \psi_{k-1}}{1 + x_k^T \psi_{k-1} x_k} \qquad (3.61)$$

3.3.5 Recursive Solution in the General Case

It shall now be demonstrated that the recursive solutions for the general equation Y = MX can be unified. The following formulas [75] are presented here without derivation (their proof is in fact computational and follows from the algorithm of Greville and general properties of the pseudoinverse matrices). Two sequences of square matrices $\{\phi_k\}$ and $\{\psi_k\}$ are defined by

$$\phi_k = I - X_k X_k^+ \, , \ \psi_k = (X_k X_k^T)^+ = (X_k^+)^T X_k^+ \, , \tag{3.62}$$

their initial conditions being $\phi_0 = I$ and $\psi_0 = 0$. Two sequences of vectors h_k and g_k are defined by

$$h_k = \phi_{k-1} x_k \, , \ g_k = \psi_{k-1} x_k \, . \tag{3.63}$$

If now $h_k = 0$, then the following formulas are applied:

$$p_k = g_k (1 + g_k^T x_k)^{-1} \, ,$$

$$\phi_k = \phi_{k-1} \, ,$$

$$\psi_k = \psi_{k-1} - g_k p_k^T \, . \tag{2.64}$$

If, on the other hand, $h_k \neq 0$, then

$$p_k = h_k (h_k^T h_k)^{-1} \, ,$$

$$\phi_k = \phi_{k-1} - h_k p_k^T \, , \tag{3.65}$$

$$\psi_k = \psi_{k-1} + (1 + x_k^T g_k) p_k p_k^T - g_k p_k^T - p_k g_k^T \, .$$

With the sequence $\{p_k\}$ so defined,

$$M_k = M_{k-1} + (y_k - M_{k-1} x_k) p_k^T, \ \text{with} \ M_0 = 0 \, . \tag{3.66}$$

The main significance of these equations may not lie on the computational side, because the practical applications are normally either of the type of associative mapping or of linear regression; it may also be difficult to decide in computation whether $h_k = 0$ or $h_k \neq 0$, due to numerical instabilities. Nonetheless, these expressions make it possible to obtain an answer to the theoretical question what happens if there are terms in the sequence $\{x_k\}$ which are irregularly either linearly dependent or independent with respect to the previous terms.

Chapter 4
On Biological Associative Memory

4.1 Physiological Foundations of Memory

4.1.1 On the Mechanisms of Memory in Biological Systems

Apparently the memory functions of biological organisms have been implemented in the neural realms; but in spite of extensive experimental research pursued on biological memory, it seems that many central questions concerning its functional and organizational principles have remained unanswered. In view of the theoretical knowledge recently acquired about the information processing principles of adaptive networks, it seems that the experimental results need a new theory to which they can be related.

An intriguing experimental fact about biological memory is that it does not seem to apply principles known from computers. First of all, there is plenty of experimental evidence, starting with the classical results of LASHLEY [98], that information is stored in the brain tissue as some sort of collective effect. When lesions were made in various parts of the cortex, the level of performance sustained in various behavioural tasks in the first place seemed to depend on the amount of damage and to much lesser extent on the exact location of the lesion. Thus every fragment of the tissue seemed to carry information relating to similar learned behaviour. Although the original experimental techniques have been criticized, subsequent research (of which a review can be found in [111]) has validated the essential ideas. It can be stated that the memory in the cortex is of the distributed and not of the local type.

A particular notice about the biological memory is due. The role of the complex and apparently specific anatomical organization of the central nervous system should not be ignored. As the biological organisms have been formed in a very long course of phylogenesis, adaptation that has occurred in the evolution means that complex structural forms, the purposes of which are not completely clear to us, have been produced. In the macroscopic scale, different neural areas have been specialized for signals of different sensory modalities, for information processing operations at different levels, as well as for the animal and vegetative functions of the organism. Consequently, memory traces from different kinds and levels of experience may be left in different areas, although they were locally distributed.

On the Chemical and Neural Theories of Memory

In brain research there are two opposed faculties which hold different views of the embodiment of memory. The largest discrepancy in opinions concerns the principle of encoding of "memories". In the neurochemical branch of research it is thought that the stored information is represented as permutations of molecular components, perhaps mononucleotides, which form long chain-like macromolecules in a similar way as the genetic information is expressed in the DNA and messenger RNA molecules. The "memory molecules" in this theory are assumed to reside in the intracellular cytoplasm of the neural cells [96,112].

The second faculty of research identifies the memory traces with functional and partly structural changes of the neural networks; the collective transmission properties of the network are changed by the signals. The neural network is thereby regarded as an adaptive filter. Reading of information is equivalent to an action in which new features are added to the primary input (key) signals when they are transmitted through the network. The adaptive associative memory networks discussed in the previous chapters may thereby constitute one paradigm.

Since it is self-evident that macromolecule reactions may play a role with any complex activity in living organisms, and the experimentally observed changes in intracellular macromolecule concentrations during specific learning tasks are therefore easily explained by the fact that strong specific neural activity has been present, the problem that is left concerns the question whether the neural signals are directly translated into molecular codes, or the representation of information is more indirect, expressed in the microanatomical and microphysiological features of the neural network. In the latter case, the molecular changes may be thought to belong as an integral part to the complex process in which the neural tissue is modified. In the present work the latter view is preferred, especially since it becomes possible to demonstrate that adaptive networks can have a sufficiently high memory capacity. For samples of proposed memory mechanisms, see [85,86,88,99,101,108,111].

One of the most severe objections to the code theory concerns the representation of associations. If, as it is apparent, information is not stored as isolated items but the encoding of every item by the other items is necessary for their later retrieval, then the storage of a large number of signals must be made in parallel, at the same time preserving their interrelations. This is not possible unless the cells are able to interact, for instance, through neural communication. A view about direct translation of cell activity into a code which then would be stored in it does not take into account this requirement. Accordingly, reconstruction of a simultaneous, highly coherent, patterned activity in thousands of cells during recall is not possible if the only storage of information were intracellular, i.e., isolated from the other cells.

It should also be noticed that our experiences are seldom quite unique and distinct, and if direct coding were used, there would be a different specific code for each experience. How can then, for instance, stereotypic representation be formed of many almost similar but incomplete versions? Even if it were supposed that information could be averaged by some sort of collation mechanisms, a particular difficulty arises when trying to explain the reading of information: as the code on a macromolecule is a linear array, it must be scanned (by ribosomes) since no address decoder mechanism is known to exist. But where should the reading be started and where to be stopped? Assume that this problem were solved in some way. The ribosome, however, only produces another protein, and this should be translated into neural signals. Although the neurochemists might claim that this still can be rendered possible, in view of the degree and number of assumptions involved, the code theory does not quite comply with Newton's Rule: "We are to admit no more causes of natural things, than such as are both true and sufficient to explain their appearances".

Suppose now that the neural memory can be regarded as a filter function. There yet remain different opinions about the type of adaptive processes involved.

Holographic vs. Nonholographic Neural Memory

It has been suggested, although never demonstrated by any simulation, that distributed memory in the neural systems might be based on holography [83,84,87,90,100,105,114]. However, there seem to arise plenty of difficulties in the application of this principle to the neural realms; for instance, there would be a need of optic-quality media, coherent wave fronts, and reference waves by which the stored information should be encoded. It seems that the hypothesis about holography as the principle of biological memory was originally introduced in lack of knowledge about the existence of other principles which also allow spatial distributedness of information; for instance, the adaptive network model is an alternative principle which has a high selectivity in the associative recall of information from it. The holographic explanations of biological memory have one particular advantage, namely, it is possible to recall information from them although the key pattern were translated from its due position. The responses and perceptions of human beings and animals are similarly known to have a limited invariance with respect to size, rotation, and form of the stimulus patterns. But it should be realized that only translational invariance is taken into account by the holographic mapping. The linear filter models used in this book to exemplify selective recall from simple physical systems, on the other hand, also have a limited ability to interpolate and extrapolate patterns that have been shown in a few reference versions; this ability is not restricted to translation but other types of variation, too (cf. Subsec. 2.3.7).

A further possibility for achievement of stimulus-equivalence ought to be mentioned. Since all sensory information that enters the memory is preprocessed by peripheral systems, a significant degree of standardization of the patterns can be performed before memorization. Examples of effective and simple standardizing devices are the oculomotor systems of biological organisms which by regulatory control keep the optic images fixed on the retina for short intervals of time. The saccadic movements of the eyes tend to direct the gaze at important details of the patterns, irrespective of their mutual distances.

If it is supposed that the adaptive associative network models may serve as a basic paradigm of biological memory functions, one can proceed to the details of neural systems that may implement it.

4.1.2 Structural Features of Some Neural Networks

Laminated Structures in Neural Networks

There are many types of neural cells and structures in the nervous system. A high degree of specialization is found in the sensory organs and in the older parts of the brain, whereas within the cerebral cortex which incorporates the newest and highest functions, the variety of cells does not greatly differ between the various areas. If consideration is restricted to the highest levels of the central nervous system where memory and higher information processing operations probably are located, the neurons are found to form laminated structures (the various types of cortices, the grey substance).

The main body of the neural cell, called *soma*, contains those intracellular components that are common to most cells: the nucleus and different kinds of particles necessary for the metabolism and protein synthesis. The intracellular liquid, the cytoplasm, together with some particles fills all parts of the cell.

As it is necessary for a neuron to make signal contacts with many other neurons, the outer cell membrane is usually shaped into many extensive branches called *dendrites*. There are cells in which the dendrites almost form a star. A very important cell type is the pyramidal cell (Fig. 4.1) in which there are two sets of dendrites; those which are most distant from the soma are the apical dendrites, and they are connected to the soma through a shaft-like formation of the membrane. At the base of the pyramidal soma, there is another set of branches called the basal or basilar dendrites.

In Fig. 4.1, a section of the cerebral neocortex that forms the main part of the brain in man is shown. The majority of the cells are of the pyramidal cell type which transmit neural signals mainly in the top-down direction. A neuron sends signals to other neurons through its output fibre, the *axon*. The external signal input to the cortex comes through the output axons of the other cells which ascend the cortex either directly or through small intervening cells, the interneurons. Details of these connections are temporarily left unspecified and denoted by dashed lines in Fig. 4.1. The pyramidal cells, again, make connections with other neurons through their axons, and part of these cells are output cells which send signals to the muscles, glands, etc. The pyramidal cells are interconnected in the lateral direction

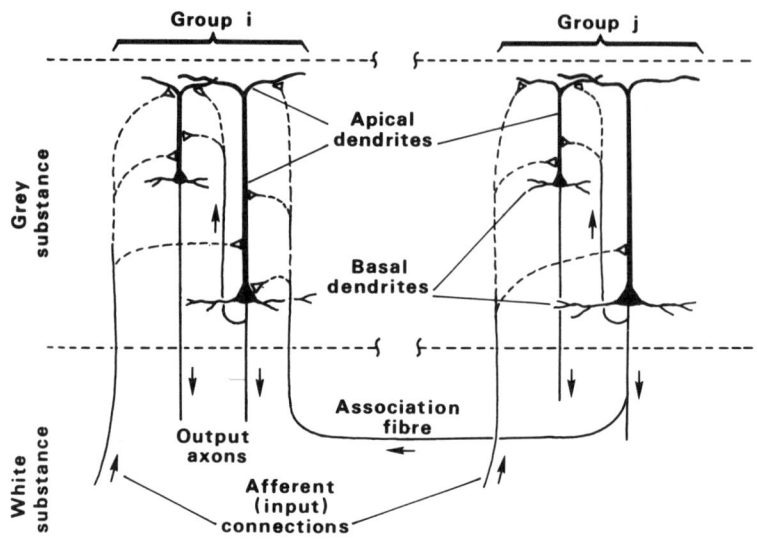

Fig. 4.1 Simplified diagram of the cerebral neocortex showing tightly interconnected "groups" of neurons, and distant connections between the "groups" via the white substance. The "groups", however, need not have any sharp borders and they may even overlap (cf. Subsec. 4.1.5 and [110]). Only pyramidal cells are shown since there are many types of intervening connections at short distance. These are often made through interneurons, roughly corresponding to the dashed portions of the lines

in different ways. Within the cortex, this occurs through the so-called collateral branches of their output axons, either direct, or through interneurons. In man, these intracortical connections have a maximum range of 2 to 3 mm. Some recent studies strongly stress the possibility that short-range interactions may spread directly between the dendrites, too (cf. Subsec. 4.1.5 and 4.2.1). At longer distances, reaching over centimeters, the mutual interconnections are exclusively made by the output axons of the pyramidal cells which then form the well-known white substance. These connections are called subcortical. Very roughly speaking it is possible to distinguish in the cortex between the top-down parallel lines, and the transversal connections.

The cerebellum, the organ which takes care of the coordination of movements, has neural structures that are slightly different (Fig. 4.2). The most important cells in it are the Purkinje cells which have a great number of dendritic input branches that are confined in thin sheets, spatially separated from each other by other, nonneural cells. Input to the Purkinje cells mainly comes in two ways: first, there is usually one special input to each cell called the climbing fibre. These fibres emerge from the cerebrum and apparently they transfer some important information to the cerebellum. Another input comes through the so-called parallel fibres which pierce the sheets in perpendicular direction. This picture has been simplified on

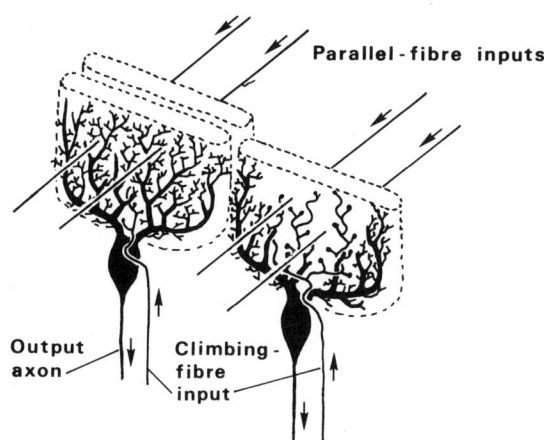

Fig. 4.2 An array of Purkinje cells in the cerebellum with their inputs and outputs

purpose, in order to avoid loading the discussion with other functions which may not be central from the point of view of memory.

There are many other parts in the brain in addition to the cerebral and cerebellar cortices which cannot be touched here. This introduction was solely intended to show that there may be network structures in the brain in which, possibly, adaptive network principles might be implemented. Whether this is true, depends on the functional properties of the network elements discussed below.

Coupling of Signals Between Neurons

It seems safe to state that one of the main purposes of a neural cell is to function as a signal-amplifying element, in the similar way as amplification is implemented by transistors in electronic circuits. But in addition a neuron performs information processing in it. Usually there is a very great number of input signals converging upon a neuron, for instance, some thousands in pyramidal cells, but as many as 10^5 in Purkinje cells. There also exist small neurons with only a few hundred inputs. Each cell has one output which, however, may branch to many places by the collateral branches mentioned above. It is not quite clear, however, whether a neural cell with many inputs and one output from a system-theoretical point of view should be regarded as a logic gate, as sometimes believed, or whether it is more like an analog computing device. The view held in this work is biased in the latter direction.

The neural signals are transmitted as series or volleys of electrical impulses that travel along the output fibres, the axons, as propagatory waveforms. It is not possible to discuss in detail within this context how this phenomenon is generated; let it be mentioned that the cell membrane is biophysically active. By selective ionic diffusion, an electrical resting potential of about 70 mV is built up between the outside and the inside of the tubular membrane. It is possible to increase the permeability of the membrane to ions by the application of certain chemicals, or by electric excitation. An increased diffusion of ions depolarizes the membrane. This again increases the permeability. Thus there is a positive (regenerative) biophysical feedback action on account of which the membrane potential and the diffusion of sodium, potassium, and chlorine ions through the membrane undergo a dynamic triggering cycle which generates the neural impulses about 100 mV high and 0.5 to 2 ms wide. The triggering of the impulses is initiated at the junction of the axon and the cell body, called the axon hillock. The travelling speed of the impulses down the axon varies from 0.5 m/s to about 100 m/s, depending on the diameter of the axon, and the tissue covering it.

The signals are connected from the axons of the neurons to the dendrites or to the soma of other neurons via special formations called *synapses* (Fig. 4.3). Every axon

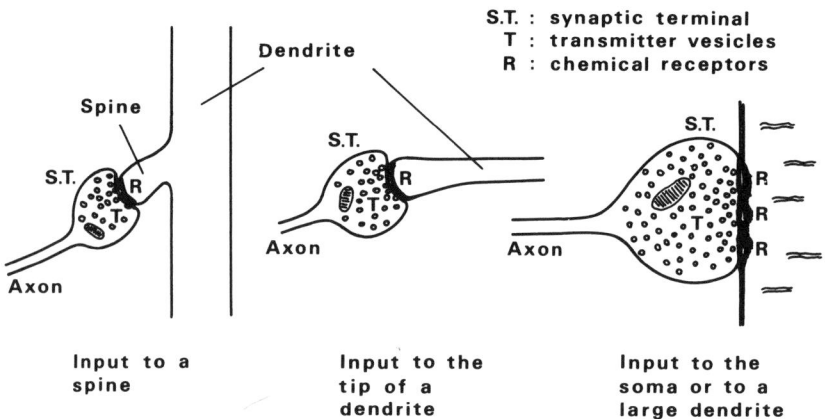

Fig. 4.3 Various types of synaptic connections, briefly named synapses

has a synaptic ending or terminal which is able to release chemicals called transmitters. There are many different types of them, but one neuron usually has only one type of transmitter. A small amount of transmitter is released from the terminal at every neural impulse, and after passing a narrow cleft, it arrives at the membrane of the receiving (postsynaptic) cell. The transmitter substances are as such able to excite the membrane, but the coupling is made far more efficient by special proteins called chemical receptors, or briefly, receptors, located at the postsynaptic membrane. By a combined action of transmitters and receptors, hereupon called transmission, the electrical potential over the postsynaptic membrane is changed by a small amount at every input impulse. As there is a large number of inputs, the potential of the membrane is gradually changed until its value (at the axon hillock) reaches a threshold; an output pulse is thereby initiated. If the input transmission is continuous and high enough, the neuron generates a continuous series of output impulses which, again, are able to excite other neurons.

Signal transmission and amplification are thus electrochemical and partly more complicated biophysical processes. There are some additional details associated with the synapses and the transmission which cannot be discussed here. From a functional point of view it would be most important to know what the mathematical law is that describes the dependence of the output impulses on the input transmission. Two facts can be mentioned: with reasonable accuracy, the effects of the different synapses on the membrane potential are summed up linearly. This is called spatial summation. Individual synapses, however, may have different weights or efficacies in signal coupling which depend on their sizes and perhaps even more on the amount of their receptors. Two main types of synapses are now distinguished: the *excitatory* ones which increase the postsynaptic depolarization, or bring the neuron closer to triggering, and the *inhibitory* ones which work in the opposite direction. Both types are necessary in order to achieve a stable operation, as will be seen below. The type of the synapse is determined by the chemical receptors.

In time, the cell integrates the small changes in the membrane potential caused by the inputs, but this does not occur linearly with the time integral of transmission; the potential tends to level off. If transmission is constant, the levelling occurs approximately according to an exponential law as will be shown in connection with Fig. 4.4. This effect is named temporal summation. Actually even the exponential law is not quite accurate; in reality, the levelling occurs a bit more quickly.

4.1.3 Functional Features of Neurons

On the Analytical Modelling of the Transfer Function

In spite of the indisputable fact that rather little of information has been gathered about the exact functional laws of signal transmission in different neural cells, with the exception of the motoneuron (the output neuron in the spinal cord which relays signals from the brain to the muscles) that has been studied extensively, certain simplified models for general neurons are continuously circulated in cybernetic literature and rather far-reaching conclusions are made concerning the possible organizations and computational algorithms of the neural units. One frequently referred model for a neural cell is the so-called *formal neuron* as suggested by McCULLOCH and PITTS [102]; there a neuron is imagined as a triggering device which has a threshold. When the sum of the input signals exceeds this threshold, an output with a value, say, "1" is obtained. Otherwise the output is "0". In this way it is possible to identify a formal neuron with a logic gate which may implement arbitrary Boolean functions depending on the input weights and the threshold. Because a computer of any complexity can be built of such logic gates, it has thereby frequently been concluded that the brain is a computer, perhaps not quite numerically-oriented, but anyway using functional principles as they occur in digital computer technology. It now becomes necessary to have a deeper look at the neuron models in light of the present knowledge.

Let us start with the basic assumptions of the formal neurons [102]:

"1) The activity of the neuron is an 'all-or-none' process.

2) A certain fixed number of synapses must be excited within the period of latent addition in order to excite a neuron at any time, and this number is independent of previous activity and position of the neuron.

3) The only significant delay within the nervous system is synaptic delay.

4) The activity of any inhibitory synapse absolutely prevents excitation of the neuron at that time.

5) The structure of the net does not change with time."

The most fatal misinterpretation of these assumptions now concerns the "all-or-none"-principle. It ought to be generally known that, on the highest levels of the central nervous system at least, neurons are firing continuously and their firing rate can be raised by excitatory inputs and lowered by the inhibitory ones. It cannot be said that an inhibitory input always absolutely blocks the activity, but the efficacy of an inhibitory synapse is normally much higher than that of the excitatory one. There is another generally accepted principle that the signal intensities, at least in the peripheral nerves, are coded by their impulse frequency, i.e., in a continuous scale of values. Why should the flow of information in higher-level neurons be interrupted when the first output impulse is triggered? The transfer function of a neuron is more akin to that of a *pulse-frequency modulator*. Referring to Fig.4.4 and Eqs.(4.1) to (4.3), the operation of a neuron is first illustrated by a coarse but clearly comprehensible electrical model, consisting of passive electrical components and an active triggering device. If all input to a neuron resulting from excitatory and inhibitory presynaptic transmitter actions is simply represented by a generator of electrical current I(t), the transmission has an electrical analogy in which the generator charges up a capacitor C, representing the membrane capacitance, shunted by a leakage resistance R. When the voltage of the capacitance exceeds a critical

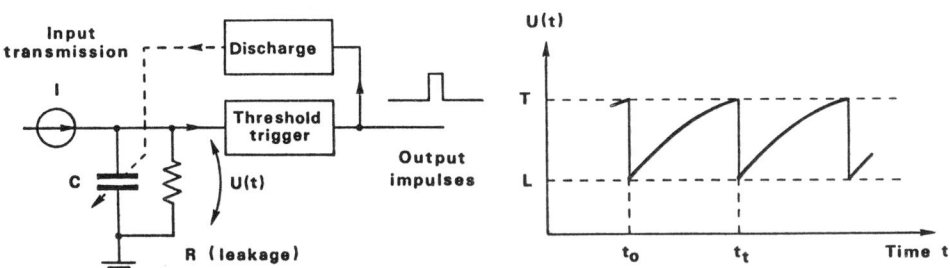

Fig. 4.4 Pulse-frequency modulator model of a neuron

value, the triggering threshold T, an output impulse with high energy is obtained and the capacitance is simultaneously discharged to a value L. In real neurons the triggering threshold is time-variable after the firing [113], and the discharge might not be as ideal as assumed here; these refinements, however, do not change the qualitative fact accentuated here, namely, that in a continuous operation the *rate* of the output impulses continuously follows the input transmission, as soon as this is sufficiently high.

In the simplified electrical model of temporal summation shown in Fig. 4.4 the charging and discharging phenomena of the membrane capacitance, here represented by C, are isolated from the generation of the output impulses. Accordingly, the voltage waveform U(t) which is built up at the capacitance is not quite the same as that recorded from a real cell, mainly because the triggering of the neuron is not superimposed on it.

Suppose now that the input transmission is a constant I, and after discharge, the voltage U(t) begins to rise from a level L at time t_0. A simple dynamical analysis shows that the voltage is the following function of time (before the next triggering):

$$U(t) = RI + \left(\frac{L}{RC} - \frac{I}{C}\right) \exp\left(-\frac{t-t_0}{RC}\right) \qquad (4.1)$$

The instant at which U(t) reaches the threshold value T is denoted by t_t, whereby, after normalization of the time constant RC as unity,

$$t_t - t_0 = \ln(I - L/R) - \ln(I - T/R) \quad . \qquad (4.2)$$

After discharge, the same waveform is repeated. The triggering rate, denoted by f, is

$$f = \frac{1}{t_t - t_0} \quad . \qquad (4.3)$$

A graph describing function f(I) in relative coordinates is shown in Fig. 4.5. It is found that there exists a "threshold" for the input transmission, not the same as T, before the system becomes active. Notice, however, that if the state of normal operation is biased at a higher value by superimposing a constant background transmission on the input, the operation of the element becomes continuous and linear: variations in I are then reflected in directly proportional variations in f. This is the so-called *linearization assumption* which is very central to the present theory.

Simulations of the transfer function of a real neuron (the second-order neuron from the dorsal spino-cerebellar tract) have been carried out by WALLØE et al. [113], using more realistic models of the cell membrane, as well as of the statistical

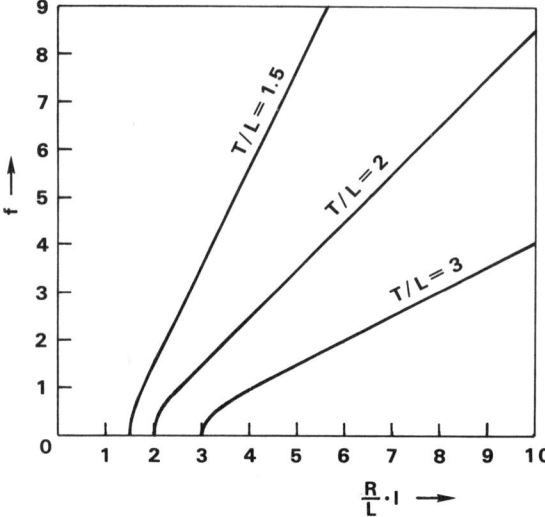

Fig. 4.5 Output frequency vs. input current of the model of Fig. 4.4

distribution of the neural impulses. The simulation results, shown in Fig. 4.6 were also compared with physiological recordings. It ought to be noticed that a normalized background activity is implicit in the curves whereby at zero input there is assumed a spontaneous-like output activity, 20 impulses/s. Deviations from linearity are not great whereby the linearization assumption may be regarded valid in the continuation, in the first approximation at least.

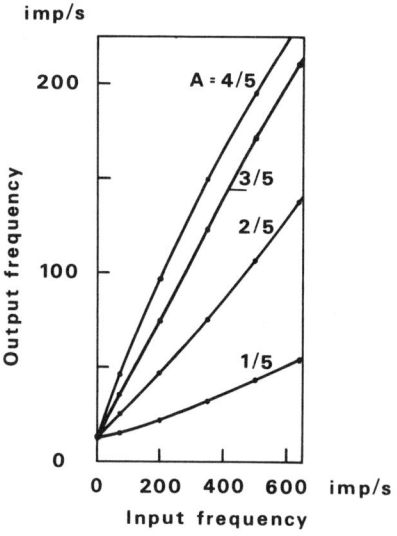

Fig. 4.6 Output frequency vs. input frequency in a simulation with a Poisson-distributed input impulse train. The value of A corresponds to the size of the so-called excitatory postsynaptic potentials (EPSP's), i.e., jumps in the membrane potential after each input pulse [113]

Summation of the Inputs

The total time-averaged input transmission I of the simplified model can now be expressed as a weighted sum of the impulse frequencies of the individual inputs, converging upon the neuron. If the output frequency is denoted by η, the background activity by η_b, and the presynaptic input frequencies by ξ_i, $i = 1,2,\ldots,n$, respectively, then a linearized frequency-to-frequency transfer function reads

$$\eta = \eta_b + \sum_{i=1}^{n} \mu_i \xi_i \qquad (4.4)$$

with parameters μ_i that describe the efficacies of the synapses. In Fig. 4.7, a neuron is represented by a circular symbol, and the signal values together with the input weights are shown.

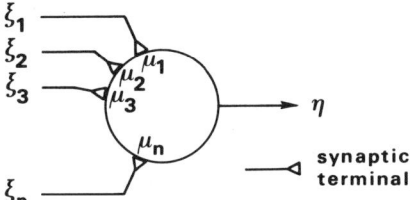

Fig. 4.7 Symbolic notation for a neuron

If a synapse is excitatory, the μ-coefficient is positive. For an inhibitory synapse, this coefficient is negative. It is assumed that the range of the linear operation is not exceeded, in other words, (4.4) is valid only within the so-called dynamic range of the neuron. Notice that there are no restrictions for η becoming *less* than the background activity, too. This is one feature owing to which the linearized model deviates from many other neuron models, for instance, the formal neurons.

4.1.4 Modelling of the Synaptic Plasticity

The signal transfer properties of a neural network may be changed in many different ways, and two categories of changes can be distinguished: *structural changes*, for instance, the sprouting of new axon collaterals, and *functional changes* in the already existing connections, first of all changes in the efficacies of the synapses. The latter can be changed by growth or regression of the terminals, or by alteration in the synaptic transmission which again may be due to transmitters or postsynaptic receptors. It seems that structural changes mostly occur at an early age [85,91], whereas chemical changes may be predominant in adults. Sprouting of new axon collaterals, following lesions made at the presynaptic terminals, have been observed in adults, though ([111], pp. 488-489). Primarily we hold the view that the most important memory effects in adults under normal conditions are due to changes in the number of active chemical receptors at the postsynaptic membrane [95,109], followed perhaps by structural changes of the membrane. It is also possible that these phenomena are escorted by other effects of different nature which makes accurate modelling rather difficult. Fortunately, it has turned out that many functional hypotheses yield almost similar results in simulations, so that an accurate description may not be mandatory.

Conjunction and Correlation Models for Synapses

A functional dependence which, in one form or another, is common to most modelling approaches of neural memory is the so-called *conjunction theory* of learning, independently introduced by several authors [86,89]. In order that the changes in the neural elements be specific enough, and in order that any information in memory could be encoded by other information, it must be supposed that changes in a memory element are not possible unless there is a simultaneous presence of several factors that depend on different signals. There are again several possibilities for such a synergism between various factors. If two signals converge on the membrane of a third neuron at a sufficiently close distance from each other, they may permanently facilitate each other through conformational changes of the membrane proteins, i.e., the sensitivity of the membrane is increased. Another possibility is that two signals make so-called presynaptic couplings (one terminal touching the other), and the strength of this coupling is proportional to both signals.

One of the most influential and frequently cited assumptions of synaptic modifiability, originally introduced by HEBB [89], is that the efficacy of a particular synapse changes if and only if there is a high triggering activity of the neuron in synchronism with a high input transmission at the synapse in question. The name "conjunction theory" used, e.g., by MARR and ECCLES [86] refers to a logic conjunction of "all-or-none" events of which one corresponds to the output activity, the other to the activity at a particular input terminal.

The presynaptic and postsynaptic activities, however, ought to be regarded as stochastic processes. Assume that an output activity exceeding a certain intensity level is a stochastic event Y with the probability of occurrence $p(Y)$, and a high activity at one input, exceeding a certain level, is another stochastic event X_i, with the probability of occurrence $p(X_i)$. The joint probability for the occurrence of both input and output events is $p(X_i,Y)$. Since the output Y depends upon many input events (there may be thousands of synapses at one neuron), it is reasonable to approximate the situation by regarding X_i and Y as being statistically independent, whereby $p(X_i,Y) = p(X_i)p(Y)$.

The conjunction hypothesis can now be formulated in statistical terms by assuming that the average or expectation value of the synaptic efficacy μ_i, denoted by $E(\mu_i)$, changes in time in proportion to $p(X_i,Y)$, and to a free parameter α_i':

$$\frac{d\,E(\mu_i)}{dt} = \alpha'_i p(X_i)p(Y) \quad . \tag{4.5}$$

Below, a simplified notation is employed. The input activity is denoted by ξ_i and the output activity by η, and μ_i is written for $E(\mu_i)$. In analogy with (4.5) we then have

$$d\mu_i/dt = \alpha_i \xi_i \eta \tag{4.6}$$

where α_i is named the plasticity coefficient of this synapse. It can be briefly stated that a synapse in this theory is assumed to change in proportion to the *correlation* of the input and output signals.

A Physiological Theory of Synaptic Modification

The hypothesis of HEBB [89] was originally introduced, without specification of its physiological mechanisms, in order to explain the formation of specific connections in neural networks; after more than 25 years, it has not yet been verified experimentally. In view of the memory principle maintained in this book, experimental validation of the law according to which specific changes in synapses occur may be difficult since the effects are distributed over a great number of cells, and the individual changes may be extremely small. As it is necessary, however, to have some model of synaptic modification in order to explain any memory effects in neural realms at all, the physiological foundations of this theory must be subjected to closer inspection.

There is one feature in the simple conjunction hypothesis which does not quite comply with general biological principles. If the synapses changed in one direction only, i.e., either growing or regressing monotonically in time, resources of the modifiable elements would soon be exhausted. In most biological processes, however, there occur reversible changes in state variables. If the synaptic efficacies ensued from the postsynaptic receptor molecules, reversibility would mean that their number can be increased or decreased. If, as it seems, the receptor molecules are complex proteins, it is plausible that the total number of receptors within a cell cannot be changed promptly; the proteins must be synthetized in slower reactions. Therefore the possibility sounds more reasonable that during a shorter span, the most important dynamic process is the *redistribution* of receptors between the synapses of the same cell according to demand; quick relative changes in the synaptic efficacies can thereby be effected. This view is in fact reflected in some explanations of synaptic plasticity of which the one of STENT [109] deserves to be reviewed here.

With a number of observable effects and a plausible physical model as basis, Stent formulates the law of modifiability for both excitatory and inhibitory synapses along the following lines. The triggering of the postsynaptic neuron attempts

to release the receptors from all the synaptic sites by polarity-reversal of the
membrane. (The receptors may be electrical dipoles which, at least before their
fixation into chemical complexes, are bound or released by strong electric field
gradients at the membrane.) Nevertheless, if the presynaptic terminal is active,
an increase in the local ionic diffusion clamps the membrane potential, so that
a polarity reversal at this synaptic site becomes impossible. Consequently the
receptors at the active synapse are guarded.

A Kinetic Description of the Synaptic Modification

The memory trace hypothesis based on the postsynaptic receptors was put forward by
Stent to support Hebb's theory, and it has recently drawn interest as the first
detailed physicochemical process by which specific changes at the synapses can be
explained. For a series of papers discussing it, see [106]. Although this hypothesis
has been accepted with reservations, the idea of rapid redistribution of the synaptic
resources contained in it deserves to be discussed in one form or another. Thus,
without explicitly committing oneself to all details of this hypothesis, an approach
with this theory as a basis is made in the following which shows what kind of quantitative changes there result in a kinetic process when the distribution of a chemical
factor, for instance, macromolecule concentration, is changed according to demand.

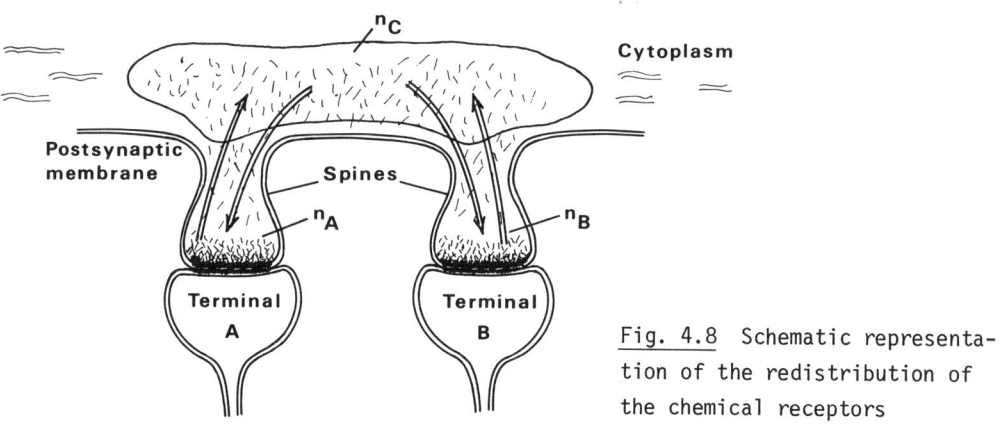

Fig. 4.8 Schematic representation of the redistribution of the chemical receptors

Fig. 4.8 depicts a part of the cell membrane on which adjacent synapses are shown. For
simplicity, many details like the intracellular membranes (the endoplasmic reticulum)
as well as the cytoplasmic organelles have been omitted, and the molecule distributions may not be such as imagined here; the density of the receptors in the cytoplasm
may have been exaggerated. If all such details should comply with reality, the dynamic
model of a synapse might become as complicated as that of an industrial process.

Nonetheless it is assumed that the efficacies of the synapses are directly proportional to the numbers of receptor molecules at the synaptic sites, here represented by pools of molecules. The synaptic site under consideration, denoted by index A, is surrounded by other sites. All of the nearby sites capable of interaction with A by the exchange of receptors are simply represented by another single synapse, denoted by index B. The total numbers of receptors at these sites are denoted by n_A and n_B, respectively. At the triggering of the neuron, a fraction of receptors is released to the liquid phase, here represented by an intermediate pool denoted by n_C. The sum of the receptors is assumed approximately constant during triggering, and a rapid redistribution of the receptors between the sites occurs thereafter. Before triggering, $n_C = 0$. The number of receptors Δn_C released at triggering is subsequently drawn back to the postsynaptic membrane, with p_A and p_B the redistribution probabilities which refer to the sites A and B, respectively ($p_A + p_B = 1$).

It seems rather safe to suppose that the release rates are directly proportional to the triggering rate η, and to the original populations n_A and n_B, respectively, whereas the strength of the electrical binding must be described by some unknown nonlinear, continuously differentiable function $f(\xi)$, with ξ the presynaptic transmission. This implies that the number of receptors transferred into the intermediate phase at triggering can be described as

$$\Delta n_C = [f(\xi_A) n_A + f(\xi_B) n_B]\eta \quad , \tag{4.7}$$

in which ξ_A is the presynaptic transmission at A, and ξ_B is a hypothetical transmission at B. After triggering, Δn_C is redistributed between the synapses, and the net changes therefore are:

$$\Delta n_A = [p_A \Delta n_C - f(\xi_A) n_A]\eta; \quad \Delta n_B = [p_B \Delta n_C - f(\xi_B) n_B]\eta \quad . \tag{4.8}$$

Let ξ_{A0} and ξ_{B0} be those values of input transmission at which no net changes occur: $\Delta n_A = -\Delta n_B = 0$. Now a differential expression is derived for the change Δn_A when the input transmission is $\xi_A = \xi_{A0} + \Delta\xi$. It is easy to obtain the expression

$$\Delta n_A = (p_A - 1) n_A \left. \frac{df(\xi)}{d\xi} \right|_{\xi = \xi_{A0}} \cdot \eta\Delta\xi = \alpha_A \eta (\xi_A - \xi_{A0}) \quad , \tag{4.9}$$

with α_A a factor dependent upon equilibrium values of the state variables. This factor may be regarded as the momentaneous plasticity coefficient of this synapse. Eq. (4.9) otherwise complies with (4.6) except for ξ_{A0}. Notice that if $\xi_A = \xi_{A0}$, the net change is zero.

A Comment on the State of the Receptors

As it might seem that the distribution of the postsynaptic receptors is not stable enough in order to serve as a basis of memory, two facts ought to be realized. One is that the memory traces in a linearly superpositive distributed memory as discussed in Section 4.2 will change whenever new information is accumulated, and therefore there is no need for the distribution to be stationary. The second fact is that in general, receptor molecules seem to be fixated onto the membrane before they can be regarded as completely activated for chemical transmission. The rate of this kind of "consolidation" can now be assumed directly proportional to the number of free receptors attached to the membrane by electrical fields, whereby the distribution of the free receptors corresponds to a medium-term memory, and the fixated receptors to a long-term memory. This consolidation may be followed by a growth process in which the thickness of the membrane, or the shape of the spine is permanently altered (cf. [108], pp. 326-327).

4.1.5 Can the Memory Capacity Ensue from Synaptic Changes?

There exist several parts in the nervous systems which exhibit memory effects. Consideration is here mainly restricted to the cerebral neocortex. It may be reasoned that since this part is very pronounced in man who among all beings also has the greatest capability to memorize, the most important memory capacity, especially for the associations, is provided by the cerebral cortex. (Although some clinical studies have shown that the ability to memorize is very sensitive to lesions made in deeper-lying parts of the brain, this effect can be explained by the fact that these parts have general importance in the control of mental functions.) The cerebral cortex is a pleated sheet about 2 to 3 mm thick and about two times 1000 cm^2 wide in man. There are a little more than 10^{10} neural cells in this tissue; the number of synapses, however, is a few thousands for every neuron on the average. If the neural memory capacity would ensue from the changes in the synapses, then there might be some 10^{13} to 10^{14} memory elements available in the cortex alone.

In all probability, the physiological memory relies on a large number of variable elements and a mechanism by which they can be made to change specifically in a great number of variations. If those elements are synapses, it then becomes possible to try to estimate the memory capacity thereby achievable.

The Columnar Organization of the Neocortex

In recent years, plenty of evidence has been collected which indicates that at least in the cerebral neocortex, the smallest operational unit is not a single neuron but the cell mass is organized into much larger units which act collectively [103]. In the neocortex there is a typical vertical dispersion in cell activity; all cells which lie along a line perpendicular to the cortex respond in an approximately similar way. This effect is most marked in the primary visual cortex where the signals from the eyes terminate: this area is known to be organized in "columns" of the order of 100 μm wide, the cells in one column responding, for instance, to line segments of a certain orientation in the visual field [92-94]. It is a common view that a similar columnar organization may be found anywhere in the cortex. The following facts support the assumption that the cortical neurons operate as large groups:

1) Anatomical studies have indicated that the pyramidal cells send their axon collaterals in definite directions. This structure is known up to a distance of 2 to 3 mm in man; the same types of connections seem to be found everywhere in the cortex. SZENTÁGOTHAI [110] has recently found in anatomical studies that the axon collaterals of the cortical pyramidal cells form circuits which make at least 30 neurons to operate as a tightly controlled group; the intracortical collaterals from one cell may actually contact as many as 700 cells.

2) In a cell mass with dimensions of about one column, all the different cell types that occur in a particular area are present.

3) The ascending (afferent) axons hit the cortex with an accuracy of the order of 1 mm, and their terminal arborization has a diameter of about 100 to 400 μm.

4) Electrophysiological recordings show that cells in the same column respond similarly. They have the same receptive fields, i.e., sensory regions where they originate.

5) Some newer findings show that neural signals are spread at short distance via interactions of different kinds, for instance, from one dendrite to another [108].

Comment. Although the neural circuits are very specific within a column, no information is available about similar specifity in the connections made by the association fibres which extend over centimeters. On the other hand, neurons from one area of the cortex have typical projections to other areas.

Information Capacity of a Distributed Memory

The capacities of memories are often expressed in information-theoretical units of elementary choices, i.e., in bits. As a view is held throughout this work that the practical limit for stored information in adaptive distributed networks is set by the *selectivity* achieved in associative mappings, the conventional information-theoretical estimates of the memory capacity of the brain are considered neither pertinent nor reliable. Furthermore it is not believed that the memory elements, for instance the synapses, take on binary values but they represent more or less continuous-valued couplings, at least statistically. A more reliable estimate for the practicable capacity of memory then depends on the number of independent patterns that can be stored in it without crosstalk in recall.

The central question is whether it is possible to modify the synapses individually, or only in groups or pools. Even if the latter would be the case, it is plausible that the activated pools are different from one case to another whereby the synaptic efficacies may be determined to a great extent individually.

In Section 4.2, models of neural networks will be set up which in effect are distributed, linear adaptive systems. From the previous discussions it may be obvious that the memory capacity of a linear system must be estimated in terms of the number of linearly independent patterns that can be represented in it. It is now crucial how the pattern elements are defined. Let us assume that a "column" about 100 μm wide is regarded as one pattern element whereby it contains about 500 neurons. If it is now assumed that each neuron has on the average some 2000 (modifiable) synaptic inputs, there would be a total of 10^6 inputs to such a "group" by which it can be encoded. This is then the parameter which roughly describes the number of linearly independent patterns by which the "group" can selectively be controlled. In other words, in a piece of network which consists of "groups" of this kind, it is possible to superimpose about 10^6 patterns in distributed form.

How Much Memory Does a Human Being Need?

The following analysis is based on an assumption that information is transferred into memory only under attentive concentration which accordingly fluctuates in time. At a high degree of attention, a great number of simultaneous or almost simultaneous signals, roughly corresponding to a pattern or a superpattern, are transferred into memory. If it were assumed that one sensory experience or other occurrence were stored every ten seconds on the average, a number which is apparently overestimated, there still would be no more than about 10^8 occurrences (or patterns) in the waking-state life of a human being to be stored.

The second important fact to notice is that signals of different sensory modalities (origin) use different cortical areas; if patterns caused by different experiences in general do not overlap very much, this means that one piece of the neural network needs a memory capacity which can be orders of magnitude smaller than the capacity of 10^8 patterns mentioned above. It will be pointed out below that there are yet other possibilities to lighten the burden of the neural memory.

Possibilities for Effective Utilization of the Memory Capacity

For explanation of the real capacity of biological memory, in particular the human memory, it seems necessary to incorporate further features in this model. If memory traces were collected from all the ongoing signals, a great deal of redundant information would be stored. The temporal differentiation of signals exerts an effect of

improvement, since the most relevant information is usually associated with changes
of state. It is known that neural systems enhance signal transients (phasic information); an equivalent effect is habituation, which in central systems may be of more
complex nature than just a fatigue effect. An extremely selective type of habituation
is exhibited by the Novelty Filter-type system which may be embodied in neural realms
as discussed in Subsection 4.2.2.

The experimentally demonstrated fact that memory traces are fixed only under
attentive concentration implies that the modifiability of the network depends upon
its macrostate; this state, or the modifiability of the synapses, might correspond
to the chemical state of the network or of the cells, controlled by activation systems.
The gating of the neural signals or their memory effects can also be implemented by
a known type of connections named presynaptic couplings where one synapse directly
contacts another one. It seems possible that such a control, whatever its mechanism
may be, can be exerted by the so-called arising reticular activation system existing
in the brain stem [107]; [111, pp. 436-448]. This control ensures that only those
signals which are of importance to the organism are stored in this way.

One advantage of the linear memory is that in a general way it responds to certain
classes of patterns. Linear combinations of the old input patterns need not be stored,
since the memory has already learned them and the activation control system recog-
nizes them as familiar. This ability to generalize may apply to many classes of
stored patterns, with the result that a great deal of memory space is saved by this
means.

Finally, emphasis is due that very probably primary signal patterns are not stored
as such. A great deal of experimental evidence exists that cells or cell units have
a fine structure which is specialized in the detection of various features. In
the primary sensory areas, these may be very simple; rather complex triggering conditions, however, may be due in the associative areas. Some discrepancy exists in
regard to the origin of these feature detectors; some researchers have claimed that
they are formed genetically [81,82], whereas other results relate to their post-natal
formation in slow adaptive processes [92-94]. Whatever the truth may be, such
detectors have a high selectivity to patterns, and thus effectively reduce the amount
of nonspecific signal activity. It is quite possible that such detectors are modifiable, and that memory traces are predominantly left at the higher processing steps.

4.2 Computerized Models of Associative Memory in Neural Networks

In view of the physiological argumentations of the previous section, the models
discussed here are transferable to the neural realms only to the extent that the
most crucial assumption, the law of synaptic modifiability, can be verified in the
central nervous system. Nonetheless, a modelling approach like this may be justified

in its own right because it predicts, for instance, the existence of collective effects that follow from simple mechanisms, as exemplified by (4.10) and (4.11).

There are two idealized paradigms of adaptive neural networks discussed in this section. The first of them is a memory network which has a few features from some earlier approaches, for instance, from the "learning matrix" of STEINBUCH [16], or the "associative net" of WILLSHAW et al. [146], except for internal feedback connections and different functional laws of adaptation, on account of which a high degree of distributed memory capacity can be achieved. The second paradigm, the "Novelty Filter", has been introduced in an attempt to devise a possibility for this function to exist in neural realms. It is believed that both paradigms are new.

4.2.1 The Associative Network Paradigm

The simplified network structure of this model (Fig. 4.9) might be sufficiently general for application to different parts of the central nervous system. The main

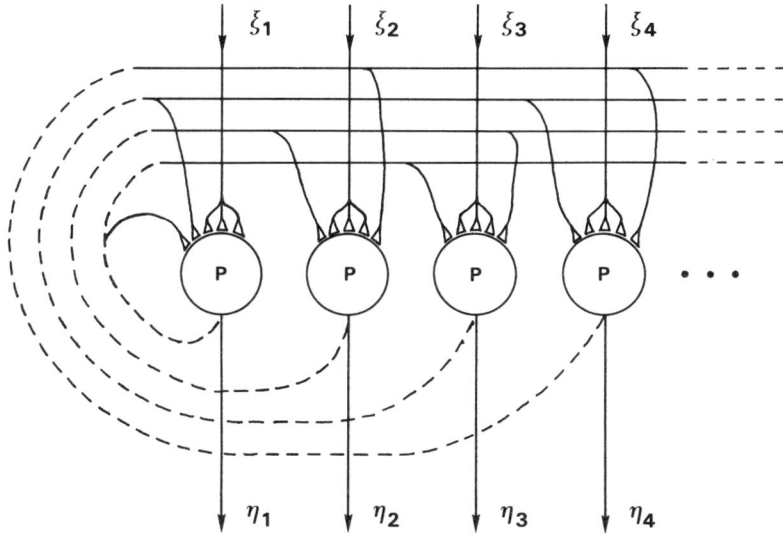

Fig. 4.9 A schematic structure for the discussion of associative memory in neural networks

network elements, the P-cells, stand, for instance, for the pyramidal neurons of the neocortex. All lateral interconnections are schematically shown by loops of lines, although in reality they may be made in the shortest way between the cells. The lateral connections between the P-cells in neocortex may be made by the pyramidal cell axons, the subcortical U-shaped association fibres which constitute the main bulk of the subcortical white substance. The P-cells, in addition to their long-range interconnections, also have short-distance interactions (lateral inhibition) of a slightly different nature as discussed later.

The input signals in this model are connected to each cell in a one-to-one fashion. In neocortex, the input axons may be unable to make contacts with such an accuracy, but there is a spread with an average diameter of the order of 1...2 mm in man. However, if every P-cell in Fig. 4.9 now stands for a set of neurons of about this dimension, then, again, this model may apply.

BRAITENBERG [118] has remarked that if the cells of the cortex are grouped into hypothetical "compartments", about 1 mm in width in man, it is possible to estimate on the basis of the volume of the white substance that on the average every compartment might be connected through the U-fibres with every other compartment. This might be true only within areas that are relatively small. It should be noted that such compartments need not have sharp boundaries, but may simply indicate the resolution ("point spread") by which spatial signal distribution is definable in the cortex. Each P-cell in Fig. 4.9 then represents cells of the same compartment.

The signal transmission properties of the network follow from the linearized frequency-to-frequency transfer function. In Fig. 4.9, ξ_i is used to denote the input impulse frequency to cell (or compartment) i, and n_i the output frequency of a cell, respectively. The linear transfer function may be formulated as

$$n_i = \xi_i + \sum_j \mu_{ij} n_j \qquad (4.10)$$

in which the parameters μ_{ij} describe the effective strengths of the interaction of cell j onto cell i, and the specific inputs ξ_i (assumed stronger than the intercouplings) are provided with unit weights. Notice that the domain of the summation index j is left open; this model thus allows an arbitrary distribution of the interconnections.

As has been presented earlier [97], we hold the opinion that memory traces are most directly identifiable with changes in synaptic connectivities between pairs of neurons. It is now assumed that the most important memory effects occur in the P-cells because they are supposed to have a much greater number of synaptic connections than the possible interneurons. The rate of change in the synaptic interconnections μ_{ij} is assumed to read (cf. (4.9))

$$d\mu_{ij}/dt = \alpha\, n_i (n_j - n_{jb}) \quad , \qquad (4.11)$$

in which the plasticity constants are replaced by an average value α, n_i is the postsynaptic triggering activity, n_j is the presynaptic impulse frequency coming from another cell, and n_{jb} is the corresponding value of n_j at which there do not occur any resultant changes in μ_{ij}. When this law is stated for inhibitory synapses for which μ_{ij} is defined negative, then α should be chosen negative; for excitatory synapses, α is positive. In this paradigm, for simplicity, α is chosen positive for every variable interconnection.

Assume that the μ_{ij} were initially zero, in other words, the memory was "empty" in the beginning. A set of simultaneous values of input signals at time t, $\{\xi_i(t)\}$ is now regarded as a *spatial input pattern*. The network is subsequently exposed to a set of input patterns each one being stationary for an interval of time Δt. By a direct substitution, the first approximation for the output from the network is then obtained:

$$\mu_{ij} = \alpha \Delta t \sum_{k=1}^{m} \eta_i(t_k) [\eta_j(t_k) - \eta_{jb}] \quad , \tag{4.12}$$

whereby the new outputs are

$$\eta_i(t) = \xi_i(t) + \sum_j \mu_{ij} \eta_j(t) = \xi_i(t) + \sum_{k=1}^{m} w(t,t_k) \eta_i(t_k) \quad , \tag{4.13}$$

with $w(t,t_k) = \alpha \Delta t \sum_j \eta_j(t) [\eta_j(t_k) - \eta_{jb}]$,

and the t_k are instants of time which relate to the different exposures. The last sum expression in $\eta_i(t)$ is a recollection of information from the memory. The recalled pattern is a linear mixture of all the previous output patterns with weighting factors $w(t,t_k)$ that express the similarity of the present output pattern to the respective earlier output patterns. If the key bears a higher correlation to one of the stored patterns than to any other one, then the respective output patterns also possess a strong correlation; it is then the corresponding stored pattern which is primarily recalled at the outputs.

A Preliminary Simulation of Associatively Reconstructed Images

Eq. (4.13) constitutes the basis of the simulation for associative recall and reconstruction of memorized images. Currently, it appears impossible to model any significantly more complex neuronal system in all its details. Use is now made of the hypothetical structure illustrated in Fig. 4.9. The P-cells of this system are assumed to form a single *two-dimensional* layer.

As no knowledge is possessed of the kinds of parallel patterns which are usually propagated in the cortex, artificial test patterns were employed for demonstration. In Fig. 4.10, a test pattern was formed of two-dimensional figures. Naturally, such pictorial patterns do not occur in the cortex, since the incoming signals are subjected to some form of preprocessing, feature extraction.

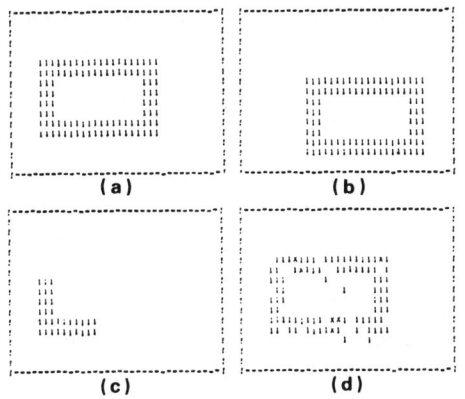

Fig. 4.10 Demonstration of associative recall from a randomly interconnected network model.
(a) First activity pattern.
(b) Second activity pattern.
(c) Key pattern.
(d) Recollection

There were 510 cells in this simulation, arranged in a rectangular array, corresponding to the display in Fig. 4.10. The signal lines which were drawn vertically in Fig. 4.9, must now be imagined as piercing this array perpendicularly to its plane at each cell. The rectangular array was chosen for line printer display, although in principle the cells could have been scattered at random. Signal values which were zero were shown by blanks, and other values that occurred were indicated by signs in a three-shade scale. However, the cells themselves located at these points were not shown. A total of 20.000 interconnections (corresponding to about 40 per each cell) was defined between randomly selected pairs of the cells. (In a real neural realm, the probability of interconnections should depend upon distance.) These interconnections correspond to the memory elements (synapses).

The first two of these illustrations, Figs. 4.10 a and b, depict patterns that were memorized. The third pattern shows a key in which were present a few signals from one of the stored patterns. The fourth picture indicates the recollection according to (4.13).

Since the key had a higher correlation with the first pattern, this is what predominates in the recollection. However, apparently the performance of this model is not yet of particularly high standard, as a consequence of some crosstalk from the second pattern. If the number of patterns were very large, the amount of crosstalk noise might become intolerable. A simple remedy, similar to that used in the introductory example of Subsection 1.2.5 is now the preprocessing of the patterns before they enter the memory network. This will be explained below.

Lateral Inhibition

The mechanism called lateral inhibition has been extensively documented in the sensory systems, particularly in vision [136], where it has usually been considered to enhance the contrast. This effect is very pronounced in the retina of the eye, but it occurs rather generally in other neural systems, too. Below, a similar preprocessing operation is found very effective in increasing the capacity and selectivity of a distributed network memory. CREUTZFELDT et al. [120] as well as HESS et al. [126] have shown that as a rule an excitatory input signal to the neocortex provokes a *decrease* of activity in the neighbouring cells. This effect attains its maximum at a radius of 100 to 200 microns from the point of excitation (in the cat); it is within the bounds of possibility that this effect might extend to a distance of 1 mm in man. Details of mechanisms underlying a similar effect are well-known in the retina, whereas in higher systems its origin is largely unknown. It is sometimes attributed to short-range inhibitory neural interconnections which are different from the long-distance connections; the latter are predominantly excitatory. But it is also possible that lateral inhibition is not mediated at a short distance by direct synaptic transmission, but through other couplings between the membranes, for instance, through electrical fields, or by nonsynaptic chemical effects. Whatever the origin of lateral inhibition is, the effect itself is reliably measurable. In Fig. 4.11,

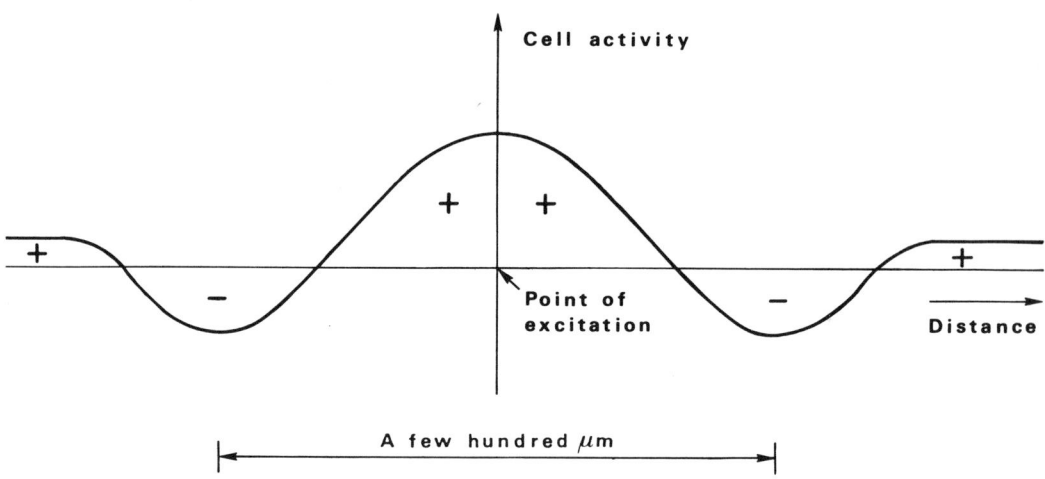

Fig. 4.11 Lateral spread of excitation (or inhibition) in a neural network

a frequently used diagram to illustrate the degree of activity (from which a constant background has been subtracted) as a function of distance from the point of application of excitation is used. Within about 100 microns the effect is excitatory. Outside this region, the effect is inhibitory, shown by negative value of "excitation". At still longer distances there ought to exist a small excitatory effect coming through the subcortical neural interconnections.

Simulation of an Associative Network with Lateral Inhibition

If the effect of lateral inhibition is included in the model, the transfer function of the neural network ought to be modified corresponding to the short-range interactions. The simplest method to take lateral inhibition into account, without loading the model by extra neuronal circuits that are to a great extent unknown, is to *preprocess* all patterns by a mathematical operation that would result from interactions, and then to use the preprocessed patterns and the above simpler network in the demonstration of memory. Mathematical operators almost equivalent to the effect of lateral interaction are the second-order spatial derivatives, of which the negative Laplace's differential operator $-\nabla^2$ was an example (cf. Subsec. 2.3.5). If a point, cell, or signal line in the input or output field is defined by two rectangular coordinates ζ_h and ζ_v, then $-\nabla^2 = -\partial^2/\partial\zeta_h^2 - \partial^2/\partial\zeta_v^2$. Another useful operator is $\partial^2/\partial\zeta_h\partial\zeta_v$. Experience has shown that these two have an approximately similar improving effect on the selectivity.

A computer simulation with preprocessed images is reported next. Picture material similar to that in previous sections was used. The adaptive neural network was then simulated by a computer program. The results obtained in this experiment are shown in a series of illustrations (Fig. 4.12); the memory network was first adapted to sets

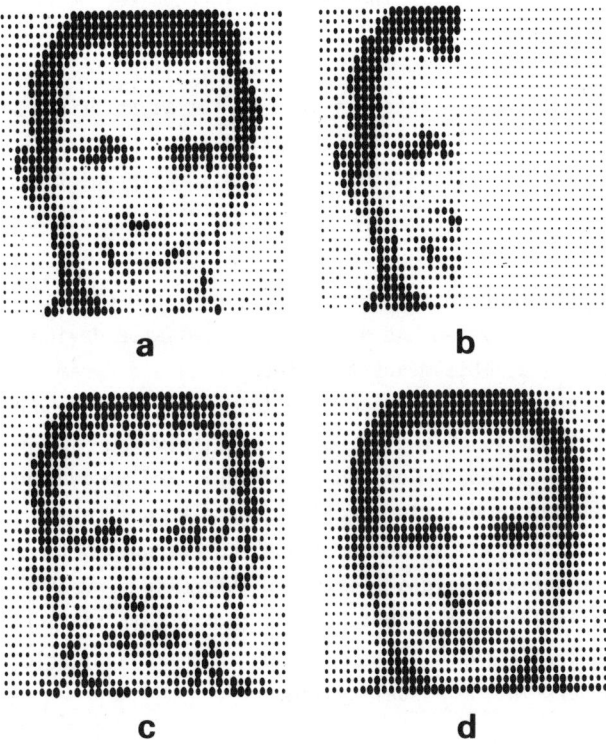

Fig. 4.12 Demonstration of associative recall in a network of the type of Fig. 4.9
(a) One of 500 stored images (cf. Fig. 1.11).
(b) Key excitation.
(c) Recollection from a randomly interconnected memory network with approximately 640 connections to every neuron.
(d) Recollection from a complete correlation matrix memory (cf. Fig. 1.11)

of patterns the number of which was 500. The left half of the patterns was then used as the key. In order to reconstruct the original appearance of the recollections, a computing process was used which had the same effect as application of the inverse transform of the preprocessing operation. Nevertheless, mention is due that the existence of the inverse transform is not necessary in natural memories, since the interpreting systems of the brain always operate on the transformed signals; the inverse transforms are "virtual images" of an equivalent primary excitation. A similar effect is that we do not experience optical images as being upside-down and distorted, as they are on the retina, since the exterior world is always experienced through the same intervening mappings.

4.2.2 The Novelty Filter Paradigm

There are known to exist functional units in the central nervous system which detect whether a signal pattern is "old" or "new"; the degree of familiarity or novelty of information is, of course, a relative concept. In an extreme case it may be said that every pattern that has occurred once is old, and only when a pattern occurs for the first time, it is regarded as new. However, familiarization to patterns may also be thought to require many iterative occurrences. If the patterns in repeated occurrences are subject to stochastic variations, then the familiarization occurs with respect to "stereotype" or average patterns.

A paradigm of hypothetical neuronal network which is able to act as an effective adaptive filter of this type is the Novelty Filter of Subsection 3.2.3. It may be regarded as an ideal case of many other models with more or less ideal properties.

Network Model for the Novelty Filter

In order to achieve the conditions under which an adaptive network can become an optimal filter, it is necessary that the system, as a signal-transmission device, operates in an approximately linear mode. This means that there exists a dynamic equilibrium from which the system can be deviated towards either side. There ought to be as wide a dynamic range on both sides of the state of equilibrium as possible. The operation of the neural cells themselves is very unsymmetrical, and to guarantee a symmetrical operation, some sort of antagonistic functions would be desirable whereby the signals occur in pairs, the activity of one signal corresponding to the negative of the other. Although antagonistic signals exist in autonomic nervous systems, no direct evidence is available about such functions existing in the information-processing networks of the central nervous system. A few hints are available about antagonistic encoding of colours in the visual system.

An assumption of a fully developed antagonistic encoding is not necessary since the same effect is implementable by lateral inhibition. A model for a Novelty Filter can easily be derived from the associative network paradigm. The most crucial modification of it is an assumption about the lateral interconnections being inhibitory, whereby the plasticity coefficient α of (4.11) becomes negative. There is some evidence for direct (so-called monosynaptic) lateral interconnections in the visual cortex that are inhibitory. An excitatory signal can also be converted to inhibitory by an interneuron.

In the schematic network representation of Fig. 4.13, the cells are grouped into "excited" and "inhibited" ones, denoted by superscripts E and I, respectively. This does not mean that they were permanently predestinated as such, but their role depends on the evoking conditions. It is assumed that a group of adjacent, excited cells is

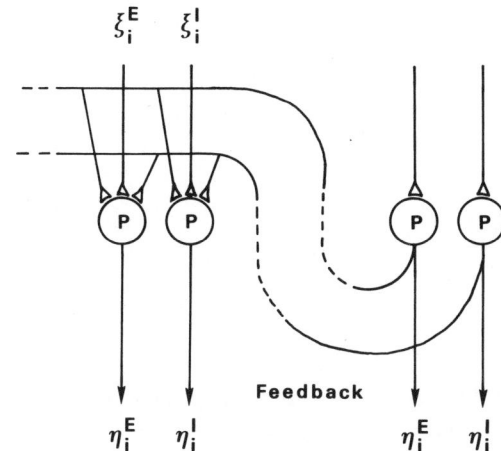

Fig. 4.13 Illustration of a paradigm for the differential encoding of the neural signals

represented by a single neuron, and the inhibited cells around it by another single cell. The geometrical arrangement of the excited and inhibited cells in the microscopic scale is not important, since these cells are assumed to be located at the same spatial position, within the limits of spatial resolution.

The P-cells are thus grouped into hypothetical *locations*. At a location denoted by the index i, the cells receive the presynaptic signals ξ_i^E and ξ_i^I. The output activities of these cells are denoted by η_i^E and η_i^I. At a location indexed by j, the output signals are denoted by η_j^E and η_j^I, respectively. If it is now assumed that lateral connections to location i stem from output axons of cells at locations j, then, according to the linearization assumption, the signal values are related by the equations

$$\eta_i^E = \xi_i^E + \sum_j (\mu_0 + \mu_{ij}^{EE}) \eta_j^E + \sum_j (\mu_0 + \mu_{ij}^{EI}) \eta_j^I + \eta_b$$

$$\eta_i^I = \xi_i^I + \sum_j (\mu_0 + \mu_{ij}^{IE}) \eta_j^E + \sum_j (\mu_0 + \mu_{ij}^{II}) \eta_j^I + \eta_b$$

(4.14)

where the index j runs over all cells which have connections with the location i. The background activities η_b as well as the initial lateral connectivities μ_0 have been taken into account and assumed constant with the location; this assumption is valid, statistically at least, if all cells in the network are identical and homogeneously distributed. The notations μ_{ij}^{EE}, μ_{ij}^{EI}, μ_{ij}^{IE}, μ_{ij}^{II}, corresponding to differential changes in the synaptic connections, may be self-explanatory from Fig. 4.13.

The next step in modelling is to apply the plasticity law of the inhibitory synapses analogous with (4.11). For each of the differential values μ_{ij}^{EE}, μ_{ij}^{EI}, μ_{ij}^{IE}, and μ_{ij}^{II}, respectively, there reads

$$d\mu_{ij}^{EE}/dt = -2\alpha \eta_i^E (\eta_j^E - \eta_0) ,$$

$$d\mu_{ij}^{EI}/dt = -2\alpha \eta_i^E (\eta_j^I - \eta_0) ,$$

$$d\mu_{ij}^{IE}/dt = -2\alpha \eta_i^I (\eta_j^E - \eta_0) ,$$

$$d\mu_{ij}^{II}/dt = -2\alpha \eta_i^I (\eta_j^I - \eta_0) .$$

(4.15)

A value of -2α has been written for the plasticity coefficient which is a free parameter, to simplify further formulas; now α itself is positive.

The above equations can be simplified into a more symmetrical form if the integral of the short-range lateral inhibition has a magnitude equal to that of excitation, in other words, if it can be assumed that

$$\eta_j^I - \eta_0 = -(\eta_j^E - \eta_0) ;$$

(4.16)

then $d\mu_{ij}^{EI}/dt$ is the negative of $d\mu_{ij}^{EE}/dt$, and $d\mu_{ij}^{II}/dt$ is the negative of $d\mu_{ij}^{IE}/dt$. Furthermore, if the initial values of the differential memory traces can be assumed zero, then also

$$-(\mu_{ij}^{EI} - \mu_{ij}^{II}) = (\mu_{ij}^{EE} - \mu_{ij}^{IE}) = \mu_{ij}$$

(4.17)

the latter notation μ_{ij} being introduced for convenience. If the spatial differences of the neighbouring excitatory and inhibitory signals are regarded as the effective "information", and denoted

$$\Delta\xi_i = \xi_i^E - \xi_i^I \ ,$$

$$\Delta n_i = n_i^E - n_i^I \ , \qquad (4.18)$$

$$\Delta n_j = n_j^E - n_j^I \ ,$$

subtraction of both sides of (4.14) from each other and substitution of the values of μ_{ij} from (4.17) yields

$$\Delta n_i = \Delta\xi_i + \sum_j \mu_{ij}\Delta n_j \ . \qquad (4.19)$$

A similar manipulation on the sides of (4.15), taking account of (4.16), and substitution of μ_{ij} results in

$$d\mu_{ij}/dt = -\alpha\Delta n_i \Delta n_j \ . \qquad (4.20)$$

Eqs. (4.19) and (4.20) together now have the same form as the system equations of the Novelty Filter written in component form and they hold true for all sign combinations of the $\Delta\xi_i$, Δn_i, and Δn_j.

The rather detailed discussion above was necessary in order to derive the equations into a form in which matrix analysis can be applied. In the case that every location i is interconnected with every location j, (4.19) and (4.20) can be expressed in vector-matrix form. A spatial input pattern is defined as a vector

$$x = [\Delta\xi_1, \Delta\xi_2, \ldots, \Delta\xi_n]^T \qquad (4.21)$$

the numbering of $\Delta\xi_i$ being made throughout the horizontal locations. The spatial output pattern is denoted (cf. Fig. 3.6)

$$\tilde{x} = [\Delta n_1, \Delta n_2, \ldots, \Delta n_n]^T \qquad (4.22)$$

and the array of the memory elements μ_{ij} is denoted by matrix M. The following equations are then obtained:

$$\tilde{x} = x + M\tilde{x} \qquad (4.23)$$

$$dM/dt = -\alpha\tilde{x}\tilde{x}^T \ . \qquad (4.24)$$

These are exactly identical with (3.27) and (3.28), and if the overall transfer matrix ϕ is defined by

$$\tilde{x} = \phi x \ , \qquad (4.25)$$

then the matrix Bernoulli equation for ϕ results:

$$d\phi/dt = -\alpha\phi^2 xx^T \phi^T \phi \qquad (4.26)$$

the asymptotic properties of which were treated earlier in Subsection 3.2.3.

4.2.3 Review of Related Approaches

The early investigations of "intelligent" functions in the neural realms, pursued around 1955-60 [16,121,137,138,142], were aimed at the demonstration of information-processing operations in networks, composed of elements which were then believed to be realistic models of physiological units. It seems that there was a firm view held of neurons as threshold-triggering devices, similar to certain computer-technological artifacts. It was apparently thought that the basic information processing operation performed by every neuron is classification of its input patterns, and that the main problem was to understand how such elementary classification decisions could be combined in multilevel or hierarchical processes in order to end up with higher information processing functions.

The early works were thus clearly biologically motivated, and they may be characterized as an attempt to implement self-organizing systems from simple components. When more experimental information accumulated which revealed that the threshold-logic view of the neurons was not accurate, and because the progress in the attempts to synthetize complex functions by elementary units was rather slow, many researchers who had started with the above problems soon became more interested in the utilization of digital computers, the breakthrough of which occurred during the 60's. Most of the research on artificial intelligence pursued since then can be characterized by a trend to widen the area of problems which are amenable to treatment by computers. At a panel discussion held at the Third International Joint Conference on Artificial Intelligence in 1973, this notion culminated in a definition of artificial intelligence as "anything that is at the head of computer science".

Nonetheless, psychophysiological research has revealed the existence of many interesting neural functions which can be characterized as selective filters for patterns; for instance, recordings of the activity from single neural cells shows responses to many kinds of stimulus patterns ranging from the simplest elementary features to rather complex sensory experiences.

Perhaps motivated by neurophysiological findings, a number of related works were started around 1970, dealing with the following problem: is it possible to explain the prompt formation of memory traces by filter models which are adaptive? These kinds of modelling approaches were primarily aimed at the explanation of distributed associative memory, whereby the purpose was to reconstruct signal patterns instead of their classification. Another fundamental difference with respect to the earlier adaptive threshold-logic approach was that the nonlinear threshold functions, if there was a need to consider them, were not regarded essential to the basic information processing operation, but their main purpose was understood as that of increasing stability by clipping away low-level signals or "noise", thereby also making the models to comply better with true neural cells.

Although in some models, adaptive filter functions were still implemented by threshold logic units, the latter were made to operate collectively [115]. But it seems that the explanation of the collective effects, especially in networks provided with feedback connections, is conveniently and even more accurately accomplished by a formalism which is based on a linear approximation of the signal transfer law, and on adaptive effects described by nonlinear equations for the parameters. In many independently introduced models, the adaptive effects were described by the correlation-matrix formalism [12,46,97,116,119,122,123,127-129,133,134,143-145]. The introduction of some type of nonlinear law for the adaptive effects, either for the synaptic modifiability or for any other effect which could be responsible for the adaptive signal transmission properties, was considered to be necessary in order to implement any *selective* memory functions at all. (Cf. also [124,125,130,132,140,141].)

There is one further known anatomical feature of the neural networks recently introduced in some models, namely, the internal feedback connections by which the signals can be made to act recurrently. Some alternative explanations for the role of these connections have been given: implementation of sequential or temporal recall [97,122,127], enhancement of selectivity by recycled processing [139,143,144], or the formation of certain orthogonalizing filters [46]. One aspect, discussed for the first time in [46] and this book (Subsec. 4.2.2) is how the signals thereby could be made to change their *signs* under adaptation. Some sort of "antagonistic" encoding of the signals seems to be necessary, although its details may be different from those imagined above.

It must be pointed out that some models discussed in this book are extremely idealized paradigms of processes which in reality may only partly reflect similar features; this concerns especially networks with feedback connections. But the formalism adopted here was found to have many advantages over the detailed network models, for instance, by having a close bearing on some basic mathematical disciplines as linear algebra, the theory of estimation, etc. Due to the compact mathematical expressions, the treatment of many special functions thereby became possible. As this text could not be made much longer, only the above mathematically oriented approach was presented in detail, and this is of course regrettable from the point of view of some related computer simulations of the adaptive processes that could not be presented here. For instance, the adaptive formation of special feature detectors [131,135] as well as self-organizing connections [147] would have deserved to be represented in this context, too.

In any case, it is hoped that this kind of discussions which are based on the methods of system theory and physics would stimulate further theoretical and experimental research on neural functions.

References

1. J.R. Anderson, C.H. Bower: *Human Associative Memory* (Winston & Sons, Washington, D.C. 1973)
2. D.G. Bobrow, A. Collins: *Representation and Understanding* (Academic Press, New York 1975)
3. J.A. Feldman, P.D. Rovner: Comm. ACM $\underline{12}$, 439 (1969)
4. M. Minsky: *Computation: Finite and Infinite Machines* (Prentice-Hall, Englewood Cliffs 1967)
5. D.E. Rumelhart, P.H. Lindsay, D.A. Norman: A Process Model for Long-Term Memory. In *Organization and Memory*, ed. by E. Tulving, W. Donaldson (Academic Press, New York 1972)
6. D.A. Savitt, H.H. Love, Jr., R.E. Troop: In *1967 Spring Joint Computer Conf., AFIPS Conf. Proc.* (AFIPS Press, Montvale 1967) p. 87
7. R.C. Schank, K.M. Colby: *Computer Models of Thought and Language* (W.H. Freeman & Co., San Francisco 1973)
8. H.A. Simon, A. Newell: Information-Processing in Computer and Man. In *Perspectives on the Computer Revolution*, ed. by Z.W. Pylyshyn (Prentice-Hall, Englewood Cliffs 1970)
9. R.J. Collier: IEEE Spectrum $\underline{3}$, 67 (1966)
10. A.G. Hanlon: IEEE Trans. EC-$\underline{15}$, 509 (1966)
11. P.J. van Heerden: Appl. Opt. $\underline{2}$, 393 (1963)
12. T. Kohonen: IEEE Trans. C-$\underline{21}$, 353 (1972)
13. G.R. Knight: Appl. Opt. $\underline{13}$, 904 (1974)
14. B. Parhami: Proc. IEEE $\underline{61}$, 722 (1973)
15. M. Sakaguchi, N. Nishida, T. Nemoto: IEEE Trans. C-$\underline{19}$, 1174 (1970)
16. K. Steinbuch: *Automat und Mensch* (Springer, Berlin, Heidelberg, New York 1963)
17. G.W. Stroke: *An Introduction to Coherent Optics and Holography* (Academic Press, New York 1966)
18. D.J. Willshaw, H.C. Longuet-Higgins: Associative Memory Models. In *Machine Intelligence*, vol.5, ed. by B. Meltzer and D. Michie (Edinburgh University Press, Edinburgh, 1970)
19. A. Albert: *Regression and the Moore-Penrose Pseudoinverse* (Academic Press, New York 1972)
20. A. Ben-Israel, T.N.E. Greville: *Generalized Inverses: Theory and Applications* (Wiley-Interscience, New York 1974)
21. T.L. Boullion, P.L. Odell: *Generalized Inverse Matrices* (Wiley-Interscience, New York 1971)
22. R.E. Cline: SIAM J. Appl. Math. $\underline{12}$, 588 (1964)
23. T.N.E. Greville: SIAM Rev. II, 15 (1960)
24. T. Kohonen, E. Reuhkala, K. Mäkisara, L. Vainio: Biol. Cyb. $\underline{22}$, 159 (1976)
25. T.O. Lewis, P.L. Odell: *Estimation in Linear Models* (Prentice-Hall, Englewood Cliffs 1971)
26. J.E. Mayer, M. Goeppert-Mayer: *Statistical Mechanics* (Wiley, New York 1940)
27. R. Penrose: Proc. Cambridge Philos. Soc. $\underline{51}$, 406 (1955)
28. R. Penrose: Proc. Cambridge Philos. Soc. $\underline{52}$, 17 (1956)
29. C.R. Rao, S.K. Mitra: *Generalized Inverse of Matrices and Its Applications* (Wiley-Interscience, New York 1971)
30. D. Bobrow, B. Raphael: ACM Comp. Surv. $\underline{6}$, 153 (1974)

31 F.R.A. Hopgood: *Compiling Techniques* (Elsevier Publishing Co., New York 1969)
32 L.R. Johnson: Comm. ACM **4**, 218 (1961)
33 M.D. McIlroy: Comm. ACM **6**, 101 (1963)
34 R. Morris: Comm. ACM **11**, 38 (1968)
35 W.W. Peterson: IBM J. Res. Dev. **1**, 130 (1957)
36 G. Schay, W.G. Spruth: Comm. ACM **5**, 459 (1962)
37 J.G. Williams: Comm. ACM **14**, 172 (1971)
38 C.C. Foster: IEEE Trans. C-**17**, 788 (1968)
39 J. Minker: Comput. Rev. **12**, 453 (1971)
40 M.J.E. Golay: IEEE Trans. C-**18**, 733 (1969)
41 B. Gold, C.M. Rader: *Digital Processing of Signals* (McGraw-Hill, New York 1969)
42 S.B. Gray: IEEE Trans. C-**20**, 551 (1971)
43 T. Kohonen: Tutkimus ja Tekniikka **9**, 7 (1972)
44 T. Kohonen, E. Oja: Biol. Cyb. **21**, 85 (1976)
45 T. Kohonen, M. Ruohonen: IEEE Trans. C-**22**, 701 (1973)
46 M.D. Levine: Proc. IEEE **57**, 1391 (1969)
47 T. Poggio: Biol. Cyb. **19**, 201 (1975)
48 E. Riihimäki, L.-E. Häll, T. Kohonen, P. Eistola, E. Tähti: "Application of Computerized Pattern Recognition Technique to Identification of Abnormal Brain Images". *IV Intern. Symp. Nuclear Medicine, May 20-23, 1975*, Karlovy Vary, Czechoslovakia
49 H. Riittinen: M.Sc. Thesis, Helsinki University of Technology, 1976
50 S. Ropponen: M.Sc. Thesis, Helsinki University of Technology, 1974
51 H. Andrews: *Introduction to Mathematical Techniques in Pattern Recognition* (Wiley, New York 1972)
52 R.O. Duda, P.E. Hart: *Pattern Classification and Scene Analysis* (Wiley, New York 1973)
53 K.S. Fu: *Sequential Methods in Pattern Recognition and Machine Learning* (Academic Press, New York 1968)
54 K.S. Fu: *Syntactic Methods in Pattern Recognition* (Academic Press, New York 1974)
55 Y.-C. Ho, A.K. Agrawala: Proc. IEEE **56**, 2101 (1968)
56 L. Kanal: IEEE Trans. IT-**20**, 697 (1974)
57 G. Nagy: Proc. IEEE **56**, 836 (1968)
58 J.J.O. Palgen: *International Bibliography of Pattern Recognition in Optical and Non-optical Imagery* (State University of New York 1969)
59 E.A. Patrick: *Fundamentals of Pattern Recognition* (Prentice-Hall, Englewood Cliffs 1972)
60 J.T. Tou, R.C. Gonzalez: *Pattern Recognition Principles* (Addison-Wesley, Reading 1974)
61 L. Uhr: *Pattern Recognition, Learning, and Thought* (Prentice-Hall, Englewood Cliffs 1973)
62 J.R. Ullman: *Pattern Recognition Techniques* (Butterworth, London 1973)
63 T.Y. Young, T.W. Calvert: *Classification, Estimation, and Pattern Recognition* (Elsevier, New York 1974)
64 S. Watanabe: *Knowing and Guessing* (Wiley, New York 1969)
65 A.E. Albert, L.A. Gardner, Jr.: *Stochastic Approximation and Nonlinear Regression* (MIT Press, Cambridge, MA 1967)
66 J.M. Mendel, K.S. Fu: *Adaptive, Learning, and Pattern Recognition Systems: Theory and Applications* (Academic Press, New York 1970)
67 N.J. Nilsson: *Learning Machines* (McGraw-Hill, New York 1965)
68 L. Schmetterer: Multidimensional Stochastic Approximation, In *Multivariate Analysis II*, ed. by P.R. Krishnaiah (Academic Press, New York 1969)
69 Ya.Z. Tsypkin: *Adaptation and Learning in Control Systems* (Academic Press, New York 1971)
70 Ya.Z. Tsypkin: *Foundations of the Theory of Learning Systems* (Academic Press, New York 1973)
71 M. Altman: Bull. Acad. Pol. Sci. V **4**, 365 (1957)
72 D.K. Faddeev, V.N. Faddeeva: *Computational Methods of Linear Algebra* (W.H. Freeman and Co., San Francisco 1963)
73 J.K. Hale: *Ordinary Differential Equations* (Wiley, New York 1969)
74 T. Kohonen, E. Oja, M. Ruohonen: *Adaptation of a Linear System to a Finite Set of Patterns Occurring in an Arbitrarily Varying Order*, Acta Polytechnica Scandinavica, Mathematics and Computer Science Series No. **25** (1974)

75 E. Oja: Lic. Techn. Thesis, Helsinki University of Technology, 1975
76 L. Pyle: Numer. Math. 10, 86 (1967)
77 W.T. Reid: *Riccati Differential Equations* (Academic Press, New York 1972)
78 T. Kohonen: IEEE Trans. C-23, 444 (1974)
79 T. Kohonen: *Proc. 1974 Intern. Symp. Multiple-Valued Logic, May 29-31* (West Virginia University) p. 493
80 L. Pyle: J. ACM 11, 422 (1964)
81 H.B. Barlow: Nature 258, 199 (1975)
82 C. Blakemore, D.E. Mitchell: Nature 241, 467 (1973)
83 J.P. Cavanagh: Ph.D. Thesis, Carnegie-Mellon University, 1972
84 P.T. Chopping: Nature 217, 781 (1968)
85 J.C. Eccles: *The Physiology of Synapses* (Springer, Berlin, Heidelberg, New York 1964)
86 J.C. Eccles: In *Brain and Human Behavior*, ed. by A.G. Karcmar, J.C. Eccles (Springer, Berlin, Heidelberg, New York 1972)
87 D. Gabor: IBM J. Res. Dev. 13, 156 (1969)
88 J.S. Griffith: Nature (Lond.) 211, 1160 (1966)
89 D. Hebb: *Organization of Behavior* (Wiley, New York 1949)
90 P.J. van Heerden: *The Foundation of Empirical Knowledge with a Theory of Artificial Intelligence* (Wistik, Wassenaar, Netherlands 1968)
91 G. Horn, S.P.R. Rose, P.P.G. Bateson: Science 181, 506 (1973)
92 D.H. Hubel, T.N. Wiesel: J. Comp. Neurol. 158, 307 (1974)
93 D.H. Hubel, T.N. Wiesel: J. Neurophysiol. 18, 229 (1965)
94 D.H. Hubel, T.N. Wiesel: J. Physiol. 160, 106 (1962)
95 M.O. Huttunen: Persp. Biol. Med. 17, 103 (1973)
96 H. Hyden, E. Egyhazi: Proc. Nat. Acad. Sci. 48, 1366 (1962)
97 T. Kohonen, P. Lehtiö, J. Rovamo: Ann. Acad. Sci. Fenn. A.V. Med. 167 (1974)
98 Y.S. Lashley: In *The Neurophysiology of Lashley; Selected Papers of K.S. Lashley*, ed. by F.A. Beach et al. (McGraw-Hill, New York 1960)
99 A.L. Leiman, C.N. Christian: "Electrophysiological Analysis of Learning and Memory", In *The Physiological Basis of Memory*, ed. by J.A. Deutsch (Academic Press, New York 1973)
100 H.C. Longuet-Higgins: Nature 217, 104 (1968)
101 R. Mark: *Memory and Nerve Cell Connections. Criticisms and Contributions from Developmental Neurophysiology* (Clarendon Press, Oxford 1974)
102 W.C. McCulloch, W.A. Pitts: Bull. Math. Biophysiol. 5, 115 (1943)
103 V.B. Mountcastle: J. Neurophysiol. 20, 408 (1957)
104 G.N. Polyakov: *Osnovyi sistematiki neironov novoi koryi bolchovo mozga čeloveka* (Medicina, Moscow 1973)
105 K. Pribram: *Languages of the Brain* (Prentice-Hall, Englewood Cliffs 1971)
106 M.R. Rosenzweig, E.L. Bennett (eds.): *Neural Mechanisms of Learning and Memory* (The MIT Press, Cambridge 1976)
107 J. Rovamo, J. Hyvärinen: *A Physiological Model of Associative Memory*, Experimental Brain Research (in press)
108 G.M. Shepherd: *The Synaptic Organization of the Brain* (Oxford University Press, New York 1974)
109 G.S. Stent: Proc. Nat. Acad. Sci. USA 70, 997 (1973)
110 J. Szentágothai: Brain Research 95, 475 (1975)
111 R.F. Thompson: *Introduction to Physiological Psychology* (Harper & Row, New York 1975)
112 G. Ungar: Int. J. Neurosci. 3, 193 (1972)
113 L. Walløe, J.K.S. Jansen, K. Nygaard: Kybernetik 6, 130 (1969)
114 P.R. Westlake: Kybernetik 7, 129 (1970)
115 S.I. Amari: IEEE Trans. C-21, 1197 (1972)
116 J.A. Anderson: Math. Biosci. 14, 197 (1972)
117 V. Braitenberg: In *Physics and Mathematics of the Nervous System*, ed. by M. Conrad, et al. (Springer, Berlin, Heidelberg, New York 1974)
118 V. Braitenberg: J. Theor. Biol. 46, 421 (1974)
119 L.N. Cooper: "A Possible Organization of Animal Memory and Learning", In *Proc. Nobel Symp. Collective Properties of Physical Systems*, ed. by B. Lundquist, S. Lundquist (Academic Press, New York 1974)

120 O.D. Creutzfeldt, U. Kuhnt, L.A. Benveneto: Exp. Brain Res. 21, 251 (1974)
121 B. Farley, W. Clark: IRE Trans. IT-4, 76 (1954)
122 K. Fukushima: Kybernetik 12, 58 (1973)
123 P.C. Gilbert: Brain Res. 70, 1 (1974)
124 P. Gilbert: Nature 254, 688 (1975)
125 S. Grossberg: Kybernetik 10, 49 (1972)
126 R. Hess, K. Negishi, O. Creutzfeldt: Exp. Brain Res. 22, 415 (1975)
127 T. Kohonen: *A Class of Randomly Organized Associative Memories*, Acta Polytechnica Scandinavica, Electrical Engineering Series No. El 25 (1971)
128 T. Kohonen: *Introduction of the Principle of Virtual Images in Associative Memories*, Acta Polytechnica Scandinavica, Electrical Engineering Series No. El 29 (1971)
129 T. Kohonen: Int. J. Neurosci. 5, 27 (1973)
130 H.C. Longuet-Higgins, D.J. Willshaw, O.P. Buneman: Quart. Rev. Biophys. 3, 223 (1970)
131 C. v. d. Malsburg: Kybernetik 14, 85 (1973)
132 D. Marr: J. Physiol, (Lond.) 202, 437 (1969)
133 K. Nakano, J. Nagumo: In *Advance Papers of the Conference, 2nd Intern. Joint Conf. Artificial Intelligence* (The British Computer Society, London 1971) p. 101
134 K. Nakano: IEEE Trans. SCM-2, 380 (1972)
135 M.M. Nass, L.N. Cooper: Biol. Cyb. 19, 1 (1975)
136 F. Ratliff: *Mach Bands* (Holden-Day, San Francisco 1965)
137 F. Rosenblatt: Psychol. Rev. 65, 386 (1958)
138 F. Rosenblatt: *Principles of Neurodynamics: Perceptrons and the Theory of Brain Mechanisms* (Spartan Books, Washington, D.C. 1961)
139 J.W. Silverstein: Biol. Cyb. 22, 73 (1976)
140 G.J. Simmons: In *1964 Spring Joint Computer Conf., AFIPS Conf. Proc.* (Spartan Books, Washington, D.C. 1964) Vol. 25, p. 493
141 A.M. Uttley: "Conditional Probability Computing in a Nervous System", In *Mechanization of Thought Processes* (H.M. Stationery Office, London 1950)
142 B. Widrow: "Generalization and Information Storage in Networks of Adaline Neurons", In *Self Organizing Systems 1962*, ed, by G.T. Yovits et al. (Spartan Books, Washington, d.c. 1962)
143 H. Wigström: Kybernetik 12, 204 (1973)
144 H. Wigström: Kybernetik 16, 103 (1974)
145 D. Willshaw: Ph.D. Thesis, University of Edinburgh, 1971
146 D.J. Willshaw, O.P. Buneman, H.C. Longuet-Higgins: Nature 222, 960 (1969)
147 D.J. Willshaw, C. v. d. Malsburg: Proc. Roy. Soc. (London) B 194, 431 (1976)

Author Index

Standard numbers refer to text pages and numbers in brackets indicate the Reference list numbers.

Agrawala, A.K. 94 [55]
Albert, A. 22, 38, 40, 42 [19], 104 [65]
Amari, S.I. 159 [115]
Anderson, J.A. 159 [116]
Anderson, J.R. 6, 9 [1]
Andrews, H. 94 [51]
Aristotle 1, 51

Barlow, H.B. 147 [81]
Bateson, P.P.G. 139 [91]
Ben-Israel, A. 40, 42 [20]
Bennett, E.L. 142 [106]
Benveneto, L.A. 152 [120]
Blakemore, C. 147 [82]
Bobrow, D.G. 6 [2], 60 [30]
Boullion, T.L. 40 [21]
Bower, C.H. 6, 9 [1]
Braitenberg, V. 149 [118]
Buneman, O.P. 148 [146], 159 [130]

Calvert, T.W. 94 [63]
Cavanagh, J.P. 130 [83]
Chopping, P.T. 130 [84]
Christian, C.N. 129 [99]
Clark, W. 158 [121]
Cline, R.E. 42 [22]
Colby, K.M. 6 [7]

Collier, R.J. 15 [9]
Collins, A. 6 [2]
Cooper, L.N. 159 [119,135]
Creutzfeldt, O.D. 152 [120,126]

Duda, R.O. 94, 96 [52]

Eccles, J.C. 129 [85,86], 139 [85], 140 [86]
Egyhazi, E. 129 [96]
Eistola, P. 76 [48]

Faddeev, D.K. 116 [72]
Faddeeva, V.N. 116 [72]
Farley, B. 158 [121]
Feldman, J.A. 5, 60 [3]
Foster, C.C. 66 [38]
Fu, K.S. 94 [53,54], 103 [66]
Fukushima, K. 159 [122]

Gabor, D. 130 [87]
Gardner, L.A. Jr. 104 [65]
Gilbert, P.C. 159 [123,124]
Goeppert-Mayer, M. 29 [26]
Golay, M.J.E. 89 [40]
Gold, B. 90 [41]
Gonzalez, R.C. 94 [60]

Gray, S.B. 88 [42]
Greville, T.N.E. 40 [20], 42 [20,23]
Griffith, J.S. 129 [88]
Grossberg, S. 159 [125]

Hale, J.K. 116 [73]
Hanlon, A.G. 12, 62 [10]
Hart, P.E. 94, 96 [52]
Hebb, D. 140, 141 [89]
Heerden, P.J. van 11 [11], 130 [90]
Hess, R. 152 [126]
Ho, Y.-C. 194 [55]
Hopgood, F.R.A. 52 [31]
Horn, G. 139 [91]
Hubel, D.H. 145, 147 [92,93,94]
Huttunen, M.O. 140 [95]
Hyden, H. 129 [96]
Hyvärinen, J. 147 [107]
Häll, L.-E. 76 [48]

Jansen, J.K.S. 137, 138 [113]
Johnson, L.R. 52, 57 [32]

Kanal, L. 94 [56]
Knight, G.R. 11 [13]

Kohonen, T. 19 [12], 33 [24], 42 [78], 73 [24], 76 [48], 79 [43,45], 110 [74], 118 [44], 144 [103], 149 [97], 159 [127, 128, 129]
Kuhnt, U. 152 [120]

Lashley, Y.S. 128 [98]
Lehtiö, P. 149, 159 [97]
Leiman, A.L. 129 [99]
Levine, M.D. 159 [46]
Lindsay, P.H. 6 [5]
Longuet-Higgins, H.C. 18 [18], 130 [100], 148 [146], 159 [130]
Love, H.H. Jr. 5 [6]

Malsburg, C.v.d. 159 [131, 147]
Mark, R. 129 [101]
Marr, D. 159 [132]
Mayer, J.E. 29 [26]
McCulloch, W.C. 135, 136 [102]
McIlroy, M.D. 52, 57 [33]
Mendel, J.M. 103 [66]
Minker, J. 62 [39]
Minsky, M. 7 [4]
Mitchell, D.E. 147 [82]
Morris, R. 52, 57 [34]
Mäkisara, K. 33, 73 [24]

Nagumo, J. 159 [133]
Nagy, G. 94 [57]
Nakano, K. 159 [133,134]
Nass, M.M. 159 [135]
Negishi, K. 152 [126]
Nemoto, T. 11 [15]
Newell, A. 5 [8]
Nilsson, N.J. 103 [67]

Nishida, N. 11 [15]
Norman, D.A. 6 [5]
Nygaard, K. 137, 138 [113]

Odell, P.L. 40 [21]
Oja, E. 110 [74,75], 111 [75], 118 [44], 121, 126 [75]

Palgen, J.J.O. 94 [58]
Parhami, B. 62 [14]
Patrick, E.A. 94 [59]
Penrose, R. 40 [27,28], 44 [27], 45 [28]
Peterson, W.W. 52, 57 [35]
Pitts, W.A. 135, 136 [102]
Poggio, T. 83 [47]
Pribram, K. 130. [105]
Pyle, L. 124 [80]

Rader, C.M. 90 [41]
Raphael, B. 60 [30]
Ratliff, F. 151 [136]
Reid, W.T. 116 [77]
Reuhkala, E. 33, 73 [24]
Riihimäki, E. 76 [48]
Riittinen, H. 85, 125 [49]
Ropponen, S. 90 [50]
Rose, S.P.R. 139 [91]
Rosenblatt, F. 158 [137,138]
Rosenzweig, M.R. 142 [106]
Rovamo, J. 147 [107], 149, 159 [97]
Rovner, P.D. 5, 60 [3]
Rumelhart, D.E. 6 [5]
Ruohonen, M. 79 [45], 110 [74]

Sakaguchi, M. 11 [15]
Savitt, D.A. 5 [6]
Schank, R.C. 6 [7]

Schay, G. 52, 57 [36]
Schmetterer, L. 104 [68]
Shepherd, G.M. 129, 144, 145 [108]
Silverstein, J.W. 159 [139]
Simmons, G.J. 159 [140]
Simon, H.A. 5 [8]
Spruth, W.G. 52, 57 [36]
Stent, G.S. 140, 141 [109]
Steinbuch, K. 148, 158 [16]
Stroke, G.W. 15 [17]
Szentagothai, J. 132, 145 [110]

Thompson, R.F. 128, 129, 139, 147 [111]
Tou, J.T. 94 [60]
Troop, R.E. 5 [6]
Tsypkin, Ya.Z. 104 [69, 70], 105 [70]
Tähti, E. 76 [48]

Uhr, L. 94 [61]
Ullmann, J.R. 94 [62]
Ungar, G. 129 [112]
Uttley, A.M. 159 [141]

Vainio, L. 33, 73 [24]

Walløe, L. 137, 138 [113]
Watanabe, S. 94 [64]
Westlake, P.R. 130 [114]
Widrow, B. 158 [142]
Wiesel, T.N. 145, 147 [92, 93, 94]
Wigström, H. 159 [143,144]
Williams, J.G. 52 [37]
Willshaw, D.J. 18 [18], 148 [146], 159 [130, 145,147]

Young, T.Y. 94 [63]

Subject Index

Abnormalities, enhancement   74-76
Adaptations, successive   117-118
Adaptive elements, capacitors   107-108
--, realizability   105-108
--, resistors   107
Adaptive feedback   102-103, 114-115
Adaptive filters in biological memory
   69, 129-130
-- for orthogonal projections   108-122
Adaptive formation of associations
   2, 71, 102-127, 129, 147-159
Adaptive linear systems   102-127
Adaptive linear unit, physical implementation   102-103
---, analysis by matrix products
   112-114
---, analysis by stochastic approximation   104-105
Address line   12-13, 64-65
Addressable memory, see local memory
Afferent axons, see afferent connections
- connections   132, 145
All-or-none principle   136
Amplitude spectrum   88
Analog associative memory   11-12,
   15-22, 69-159
Angle between vectors   25, 96-97
Anomalies, enhancement   74-76
Antagonistic encoding   154-157, 159
Apical dendrite   131-132
Arising reticular activation system   147

Array, matrix   34-36
Artificial intelligence   158
Association fibres   132, 145
Associations, adaptive formation   2,
   71, 102-127, 129, 147-159
-, identification with relations   5
Associative data structures   1-10,
   60-61
Associative encoding   11, 76-78, 80
Associative identification   76-78, 80
Associative information structures,
   see associative data structures
Associative mappings, adaptive
   formation   102-127
--, error-correction   69-70, 79
--, hash-coding   13-14, 51-59
--, optimal   69-94, 97-98, 102-127
--, optimal linear   78-83
--, optimal nonlinear   83-86
--, recursive computation   122-127
Associative memory, analog   11-12,
   15-22, 69-159
--, basic characteristics   10-12
--, definitions   2, 5, 7, 12, 61-62
--, distributed   11-12, 15-22,
   see associative memory, neural
   associative memory, optimal
--, holographic   15-17, 130
--, neural   147-158
-- in Novelty Filter   76
--, optimal   69-94, 97-98, 102-127

Associative memory, resistor network 18-20
--, reviews 62
-- for sequences 6-10
--, system models 2, 7-8, 70-71
--, temporal 6-10
Associative net 148
Associative network paradigm 148
Associative processing language 60-61
Associative recall from CAM 12-13, 61-69
-- by correlation matrix 17-22, 96-98, 148-154
--, definitions 2, 10-11
--, demonstrations 20-22, 72-78, 82-86, 97, 150-151, 153-154
--, holographic 16-17
-- by linear mappings 18-22, 69-83, 96-98, 148-154
-- of missing fragments 20-22, 72-76, 150-151, 153-154
-- by orthogonal projections 71-78
-- by partial match 62-67
-- of sequences 6-10
--, simulations 20-22, 72-78, 82-86, 97, 150-151, 153-154
--, standardizing property 72, 79
--, temporal 6-10
Associative search from data structures 5, 60-61, see associative recall
--, hash-coding 13-14, 51-61
Associative structure, see relational structure
Asymptotic properties of adaptive networks 71
Attention 146-147
Attribute 1, 3
Augmented pattern 77
Autoassociative encoding 76-78
Autoassociative memory, definition 10, see autoassociative recall
--, Novelty Filter 76

Autoassociative recall from CAM 13, 62-66
--, definition 10
-- by orthogonal projections 71-73
--, simulations 20-22, 73-78, 150-151, 153-154
Autoradiographic images 75-76
Axon 131-134, 145
Axon collaterals 132
Axon hillock 134

Background activity 138-139
Basal dendrite 131-132
Basilar dendrite, see basal dendrite
Basis, orthogonal 27-28
- vectors, definition 26
--, orthogonal 27-28
--, orthonormal 48
Bayesian probability 100
Bernoulli equation, asymptotic solutions 117-120
--, derivation 115
-- for neural network 158
--, solution 116
Best linear unbiased estimator, see estimator
Beta function 32
Biological memory 1, 2, 69, 76, 128-159
Bit cell, see memory cell of CAM
Bit match 63-64
Bit-serial comparison 66-67
Bit-storage 64
BLUE, see estimator
Brain stem 147

CAM, see content-addressable memory
CAM organization 65-67
Calculated address, see computed address
Capacitor memory 107-108
Cerebellum 132-133

Characteristic equation   37-38
Classification by comparison   96-97
Climbing fibre   132-133
Cluster   94
Collaterals of axons, see axon collaterals
Collateral branches, see axon collaterals
Collective effects in memory   11-12, 15-20, 69-70, 102-103, 128, 148-159
Collision   14, 52-59
Columns of matrix   34-35
Column vector   35
Combination search   58, 61
Comparand, see search argument
Compartments of cortex   149
Computed address   14, 52-54, 58-59
Conditional average loss   99-100
Conditional probability   99-101
Conditioned responses, implementation   102-108
Conflict situation, see collision, multiple match
Conformational changes   140
Conjunction theory of learning   140
Consolidation of receptors   144
Content-addressable memory, general description   11-13, 61-62
---, hardware implementation   64-65
---, logic description   62-63
---, reviews   62
Content-addressing   12-14, 51-69, see hash-coding
Context   2, 5-10
Convolution in preprocessing   81-83
Convolution function   18
Corrective process   103, 105, 122
Correlation function   18
Correlation matrix, theoretical   93-94
Correlation matrix memory   19-22, 98, 147-159

Cortex   131-132, 144-147, 151-152, see neocortex
Cost function   99-100
Covariance matrix   101
Cross-talk   20, 71, 150-151
Cytoplasm   131

Decomposition theorem   29
Deletion from memory   55-56
Dendrite   131
Depolarization   134
Derivative of matrix   48-50
Descriptor   52, 58-59, see key word, search argument
DFT, see discrete Fourier transform
Diagonal matrix, definition   35
--, pseudoinverse   42
Discrete Fourier transform   88
Discriminant function, general description   94-96
--, statistical definition   99-101
Distance, definition   24
-, Euclidean   24-25
-, Hamming   24
- in pattern classification   96
Distributed memory, biological   128, 130, 158-159
--, definition   11-12
--, holographic   15-17
--, information capacity   145-146
--, nonholographic   17-22
--, relation to associative mappings   70, see analog associative memory
Distribution functions   99-101
DNA   129
Document retrieval   57-59

Efficacy of synapse   134-135, 139-143, 146, 159
Eigenvalue   37-38
Eigenvector   37-38
Electroplating   18, 107

Elementary matrix, definition   38-39
--, limit theorem   110-112
ELINOR   6
Enhancement of abnormalities   74-76
Error-correction, definition   69-70
-- in optimal associative mapping   79
-- by orthogonal projections   72-73
--, simulations   73,
    see noise attenuation
Error criterion, quadratic   104
Estimator   93-94
Euclidean distance   24-25
- matrix norm   39
- vector   71
- vector norm   25
Excitatory synapse   135
Exclusive *or*   63

Fast Fourier transform   88
Feature analysis   84-89
Feature detection   147
Feature vector   84-85, 87-89
Feedback for sequential recall   7-8
Feedback matrix   115
Filling ratio   57, 59
Filter functions in neural realms   158-159
Forgetting during adaptation   120-122
Formal neuron   135-136
Fourier diffraction   17
Fourier expansion   48
Fourier transform   88
Frequency analysis   88
Frequency-to-frequency transfer function   136-139, 149
Frequency spectrum   88
Fresnel diffraction   15-17

Gain vector   122-123, 125-127
Gamma function   32-22
Gauss-Jordan elimination method   40, 126

Golay surroundings   89
Gradient, definition   49-50
-, difference approximation   81
Gradient method   104-105
Gradient projection method   123-125
Gram-Schmidt orthogonalization, definition   27-28
--- for gradient projection method   124
--- for Novelty Filter   75
--- and orthogonal projection operators   47
--- for orthogonal projections   71-72
--- for orthogonality test   82
Greville's theorem for projection operators   46-47
-- for pseudoinverse computation   42-43
-- for recursive processes   123-127
Grey substance   131-132
Grid function   81

Habituation   147,
    see Novelty Filter
Hadamard product   36
Hamming distance   24
Hash-addressing   52,
    see hash-coding
Hash-bit extraction   14, 53
Hash-coding, description   13-14, 51-61
-- in multiple-keyword search   57-59
Hash-index table   57-59
Hash table   57-59
Hashing algorithm   53-54
Hebb's hypothesis   140-143
Hermitian matrix   40
Heteroassociative recall, definition   11
Hologram   15-17
Holographic associative memory   15-17, 130

Hyperplane   25, 94-95, 101
Hypersphere, definition   29
-, mass projection   30-33
-, volume   29-30
Hypersurface, separating   94-96, 101

Idempotent matrix   38
Identification by angles   96-98
-, linear   76-78, 80
-, nonlinear   84-85
Inequality search   67-68
Information capacity, see memory capacity
Inhibition, lateral   149-155
Inhibitory synapse   135-136
Inner product, definition   24
-- in linear mixtures   20, 98, 150
Interneuron   131-132
Intracortical connections   132
Invariance in recognition   3, 86-92, 130-131
-, translational   88-91
Inverse of matrix   39-40
Iteration in adaptive process   105, 118-120
Iterative circuit   67-68

Key in associative recall   2-3, 7-10, 70
- pattern   71
- word   13-14, 58-59,
    see descriptor, search argument
Knowledge, representation   1, 3
- structure   6-9
Kronecker delta   28, 95
- symbol, see Kronecker delta

Laminated structures   131-133
Laplace's operator   81, 97, 153
Laplacian, see Laplace's operator
Lateral inhibition   149-155
LEAP language   60-61

Learning matrix   148
Left inverse   40
Lesion experiments   128, 139, 144
Linear classifier   95-96,
    see identification
- combination   25-26, 71, 74
- dependence   25-26, 89-91,
    see linear independence
- estimation   92-94
- independence   25, 79, 83, 146
- manifold   25-26
- mapping   18-22, 92-94,
    see associative mappings
- mixture   71, 150
- regression   71, 92-94
- transformation   18-22, 33-34, 70, 92-94,
    see associative mappings, linear mapping
- vector space   23
Linearization assumption   137-139
Linguistic expression   1, 3, 4, 6
Linked-list organization   55-57
Local Features   88-89
Local memory, definition   11
Logical and   63
- equivalence   63
- negation   63
- or   63
Long-term memory   144
Loss function   99-100

Machine learning   102
Macromolecules   129-130
Magnitude comparison   67-69
Manifold, linear   25-26
Mask word   13, 63
Masked search   63-64
Match   13, 63-64
- bit   66, 68-69
Matrices, array representation   34-36
-, characteristic equation   37-38

-, columns   34-35
-, derivatives   48-50
-, diagonal   35
-, differential calculus   48
-, eigenvalues   37-38
-, eigenvectors   37-38
-, elementary   38-39, 110-112
-, equations   39-45
-, Hadamard product   36
-, Hermitean   40
-, idempotent   38
-, indexing   33, 35-36
-, inverse   39-40, 126
-, left inverse   40
-, Moore-Penrose generalized inverse   40-43
-, nonsingular   37
-, norm   39
-, norm, Euclidean   39
-, notations   33-36
-, null space   36-37
-, partitioning   35-36
-, positive definite   38
-, powers, derivative   49
-, product   33-34
-, product of partitioned   36
-, pseudoinverse   40-43
-, range   36-37
-, rank   37
-, right inverse   40
-, rows   34-35
-, singular   37
-, spectral radius   38
-, sum   33
-, symmetric   35
-, trace   39
-, transpose   35-36
-, unit   35
Matrix Bernoulli equation   115, see Bernoulli equation
Matrix differential calculus   48
Matrix equations   39-45

Matrix equations, approximate solution   45
--, best approximate solution   45
--, minimum-norm approximate solution   45
--, minimum-norm solution   44
--, Penrose solution   44
--, solution   43-44
- inversion lemma   40
- operations   33-36
- operator   78-80
- product   33-34
- sum   33
Matrix-vector-product   34
Maximum search   68-69
Medium-term memory   144
Memory, addressable   11, 15
-, associative, see associative memory
-, biological   128-159
- capacity   144-147
-, chemical theories   129-130
-, correlation matrix   18-22, 98, 153, 159
-, distributed, see distributed memory
-, holographic   15-17, 130
-, local   11
- location   2, 11
-, neural theories   129-130
-, nonholographic distributed   17-22, 130
-, physiological foundations   128-147
- cell of CAM   64
- molecules   129-130
Metric   24
Minimum polynomial   116
- search   69
Mismatch   63
Missing fragments, recall, see autoassociative memory

Moore-Penrose generalized inverse 40, see pseudoinverse
Motoneuron 135
Multiple-keyword search, 57-59, 61
Multiple match 10, 13, 65-66, 68
-- resolver 65-66, 68
Multiplication, implementation 106-107
Multiplicative congruence 53

Nearest-above search 69
Nearest-below search 69
Neocortex, neural structures 131-132
-, organization 144-147
Neural cell, see neuron
- impulse 134
- networks, modelling 147-158
- signals 133-135
Neuron, functional description 135-144
-, physiological description 131-135
-, symbolic notation 139
Newton's rule 130
Noise attenuation in associative mappings 12, 30-33, 72-73, 79, 85-86
Noise-suppression, see error-correction, noise attenuation
Nonholographic distributed memory 17-22
Nonlinear transformations 83-84
Norm, Euclidean, of matrix 39
-, Euclidean, of vector 25
- of matrix 39
- of vector 24-25
Novelty 74, 82
Novelty Detector 108-112
Novelty Filter, adaptive generation 114-122, 154-158
--, definition 74-76

--, habituation 147
--, system model 114-115
Null space 36-37

Observation matrix 35-36, 78-79
Optimal associative mappings 78-86, 122-127
Optimal estimator 92-94
- linear identification 80
Ordered triple 3-5, see triple
Orthogonal complement of space 27
Orthogonal component, see orthogonal projections
Orthogonal projections for autoassociative recall 71-78
--, formation by adaptive filter 108-122
--, introduction 26-29
-- for Novelty Filter 74-76
Orthogonal projection operator, as asymptotic solution 118-120
---, computational formula 46-47
---, iterative formation 113
Orthogonal space 26
- vector basis 27, 28
Orthogonality, definition 25
- test 82
Orthogonalization process, Gram-Schmidt 27-28
Orthonormal basis vectors 48
Overflow area 56

Page 59
Paired-associate 70
Parallel fibres 132-133
Parametric classification 98-101
Partitioning of matrix 35-36
Pattern 22-23
- classification 94-101
--, parametric 98-101

Pattern classification, statistical 98-101
- recognition, linguistic approach 92
- vector 22-23, 70, 87
Penrose solution 44, 79, 93
Perceptron 103-104
Peripheral nerves, signal coding 136
Phasic information 147
Picard-Lindelöf method 116
Picture element 23
Plasticity coefficient of synapse 141, 143, 149, 155
Plating process, see electroplating
Pointer 52, 55-59
Polarity-reversal of membrane 142
Polynomial transform 83-84
Positive definite matrix 38
Positive semidefinite matrix 38
Postsynaptic potentials 138
Power spectrum 88
Preprocessing, biological 130-131
- in comparison method
- for correlation matrix memory 20, 22
-, extraction of local features 88-89
- by frequency analysis 88
- by lateral inhibition 153
-, nonlinear 84-86
- for optimal associative mapping 80-83
-, organization 87-88
Presynaptic coupling 140, 147
Priority logic 66
Probabilistic notations 99
Probability density 99-101
- function 99
Probing, comparison of methods 57
-, construction of pointers 55

-, definition 54
-, linear 54, 57
-, random 54-55, 57
Projection density 31
Projection matrix 46, 110-111, see orthogonal projection operator
Projection operator 38, 45-48
Projection theorem 27
Projections of neurons 145
Projections, orthogonal 26-29
Pseudo-random numbers 54-55
Pseudoinverse, definition 40, 42
-, formulas 41, 43
-, identities 43
-, notation 41-42
- in vector equation 41
Pulse-frequency modulation 106, 136
Purkinje cell 132-133
Pyle's method 124
Pyramidal cell 131-132
Pythagoran formula, generalized 31

Quadratic form 38, 50

Range of matrix 36-37
Rank of matrix 37
-, full 37
Recall, associative, see associative recall, autoassociative recall
-, temporal 7-10
Receptive fields 145
Receptors, chemical 134, 139, 141-144
Recognition system, organization 87-88
Recursive computation of associative mapping 122-127
Redistribution of receptors 141-143
Reference vector 30
Reference pattern 71

Regression   84
- solution   104-105, 124-125
Relation   1, 3-10, 60-61
Relational structure   1, 3-10, 60-61
Representation of knowledge   1, 3-10
- of negative weights   19, 106
- vector   22-23
Reserve address, see reserve location
- location   14, 52-56, 59
Resistor network   18-20
Reticular activation system   147
Riccati equation   116
Right inverse   40
RNA   129
Row of matrix   34, 35
- vector   35

Saccadic movements   131
Safety margin   78, 83, 86
Scalar   22
Scalar product   24
Scatter addressing   52,
   see hash-coding
Search argument   52-54, 65, 70,
   see descriptor, key word
Self-organizing system   158
Semantic structure   3, 6, 60-61
Separating surface   94-96, 101
Sequence, structured   6-10
Sequential machine   7
- recall   7-10, 159
- system   7-9
Singular matrix   37
Soma of neural cell   131
Spanning of a space   26
Spare location, see reserve location
Spatial differentation   22, 80-83,
   97, 153
- frequency   88-91
- summation   135
Spectral radius   38

Spine   134, 142, 144
Spontaneous activity   138
Sprouting of axon collaterals   139
Stack   59
Standardizing property·   72
Steepest descent   104
Stent's hypothesis   141-143
Stimulus   9
Stimulus equivalence   3, 86-87,
   130-131
Stochastic approximation   104-105
Subcortical connections   132
Subspace   25-29, 71
Synapse, description   134-135
-, efficacy   134-135, 139, 143, 146,
   159
-, excitatory   135
-, inhibitory   135-136
Synaptic connection, see Synapse
- delay   136
- modifiability, see synaptic
   plasticity
- plasticity, description   139-144
--, kinetic model   142-144
--, physiological theory   141-142
- terminal   134

Tag   11, 52-53, 59, 76, 80
Temporal differentiation   146-147
- recall   7-10, 159
- summation   135
Theorem of Greville   42-43
Threshold-logic unit   103
Threshold, triggering   134-137
Threshold triggering device   158
TLU, see threshold-logic unit
Trace of matrix   39
Transfer function of neuron   135-139
Translational invariance   130-131
Transmission, synaptic   134-136
Transmitter substance   134

Transpose of matrix   35-36
Triggering threshold   134-137
Triple   3-5, 60-61

Unit cost   99
- matrix   35
- vector   76-78
Univariate process   101

Value of relation   3-4, 60
Vector, basis   26-28, 48
-, column   35
-, magnitude   24-25
-, norm   24-25
-, reference   30
-, representation   22-23

-, row   35
Vector basis, *see* basis
Vector equations   41
Vector formalism   22-23
Vector space, definition   22-23
-, distance   24
-, linear   23
-, metric   24
Virtual image   16, 154
- storage   59
Visual cortex   145
Voice identification   87

Weight vector   95
White substance   132
Wired *or*   64

H. Haken

Synergetics

An Introduction

Nonequilibrium Phase Transitions and Self-Organization in Physics, Chemistry and Biology

2nd enlarged edition. 1978. 153 figures. Approx. 360 pages.
ISBN 3-540-08866-0

Synergetics deals with profound and striking analogies recently discovered between the self-organized behavior of seemingly quite differnt systems in physics, chemistry, biology, sociology and other fields. The cooperation of many subsystems such as atoms, molecules, cells, animals, or humans may produce spatial, temporal or functional structures. Their spontaneous formation out of chaos is often strongly reminiscent of phase transitions.

This book, written by the founder of synergetics, provides an elementary introduction into the basic concepts and mathematical tools. Numerous exercises, figures and simple examples greatly facilitate the understanding. The basic analogies are demonstrated by various realistic examples from fluid dynamics, lasers, mechanical engineering, chemical and biochemical systems, ecology, sociology and theories of evolution and morphogenesis.

The second edition differs from the first by an additional chapter on chaotic motion, a rapidly growing field, and by new sections on laser pulses and on morphogenesis.

J. Schnakenberg

Thermodynamic Network Analysis of Biological Systems

Universitext

1977. 13 figures. VIII, 143 pages
ISBN 3-540-08122-4

This book is devoted to the question: what can physics contribute to the anlalysis of complex systems like those in biology and ecology? It addresses itself not only to physicists but also to biologists, physiologists and engineering scientists. An introduction into thermodynamics particularly of non-equlibrium situations is given in order to provide a suitable basis for a model description of biological and ecological systems. As a comprehensive and elucidating model language bondgraph networks are introduced and applied to quite a lot of examples including membrane transport phenomena, membrane excitation, autocatalytic reaction systems and population interactions. Particular attention is focussed upon stability criteria by which models are categorized with respect to their principle qualitative behavior. The book intends to serve as a guide for understanding and developing physical models in biology.

Springer-Verlag
Berlin
Heidelberg
New York

Digital Pattern Recognition

Editor: K. S. Fu
1976. 54 figures, 4 tables. XI, 206 pages
(Communications and Cybernetics,
Volume 10)
ISBN 3-540-07511-9

Contents:
K. S. Fu: Introduction. T. M. Cover,
T. J. Wagner: Topics in Statistical Pattern
Recognition. E. Diday, J. C. Simon: Clustering
Analysis. K. S. Fu: Syntactic (Linguistic)
Pattern Recognition. A. Rosenfeld,
J. S. Weszka: Picture Recognition. J. J. Wolf:
Speech Recognition and Understanding.

Digital Picture Analysis

Editor: A. Rosenfeld
1976. 114 figures, 47 tables. XIII, 351 pages
(Topics in Applied Physics, Volume 11)
ISBN 3-540-07579-8

Contents:
A. Rosenfeld: Introduction. R. M. Haralick:
Automatic Remote Sensor Image Processing.
C. A. Harlow, S. J. Dwyer, G. Lodwick: On
Radiographic Image Analaysis. R. L. McIlwain:
Image Processing in High Energy Physics.
K. Preston: Digital Picture Analysis in Cytology
J. R. Ullmann: Picture Analysis in Character
Recognition.

Picture Processing and Digital Filtering

Editor: T. S. Huang
1975. 113 figures. XIII, 289 pages
(Topics in Applied Physics, Volume 6)
ISBN 3-540-07202-0

Contents:
T. S. Huang: Introduction. –
H. C. Andrews: Two-Dimensional Trans-
forms. – J. C. Fiasconaro: Two-Dimensional
Nonrecursive Filters. – R. R. Read, J. L. Shanks,
S. Treitel: Two-Dimensional Recursive Filter-
ing. – B. R. Frieden: Image Enhancement and
Restoration. – F. S. Billingsley: Noise Consid-
erations in Digital Image Processing Hardware.

T. Pavlidis
Structural Pattern Recognition

1977. 173 figures, 13 tables. XII, 302 pages
(Springer Series in Electrophysics, Volume 1)
ISBN 3-540-08463-0

Contents:
Mathematical Techniques for Curve Fitting.
Graphs and Grids. Fundamentals of Picture
Segmentation. Advanced Segmentation
Techniques. Scene Analysis. Analytical
Description of Region Boundaries. Syntactic
Analysis of Region Boundaries and Other
Curves. Shape Description by Region Analysis.
Classification, Description and Syntactic
Analysis.

Syntactic Pattern Recognition, Applications

Editor: K. S. Fu
1977. 135 figures, 19 tables. XI, 270 pages
(Communication and Cybernetics,
Volume 14)
ISBN 3-540-07841-X

Contents:
K. S. Fu: Intruduction to Syntactic Pattern
Recognition. S. L. Horowitz: Peak Recognition
in Waveforms. J. E. Albus: Electrocardiogram
Interpretation Using a Stochastic Finite State
Model. R. DeMori: Syntactic Recognition of
Speech Patterns. W. W. Stallings: Chinese
Character Recognition. Th. Pavlidis,
H.-Y. F. Feng: Shape Discrimination.
R. H. Anderson: Two-Dimensional Mathe-
matical Notation. B. Moayer, K. S. Fu: Finger-
print Classification. J. M. Brayer, P. H. Swain,
K. S. Fu: Modeling of Earth Resources Satellite
Data. T. Vámos: Industrial Objects and
Machine Parts Recognition.

Springer-Verlag
Berlin
Heidelberg
New York